Traumatic Experience in the Unconscious Life of Groups

The International Library of Group Analysis

Edited by Malcolm Pines, Institute of Group Analysis, London

The aim of this series is to represent innovative work in group psychotherapy, particularly but not exclusively group analysis. Group analysis, taught and practised widely in Europe, derives from the work of SH Foulkes.

Other titles in the series

The Social Unconscious
Selected Papers
Earl Hopper
ISBN 1 84310 088 6
International Library of Group Analysis 22

Building on Bion: Roots
Origins and Context of Bion's Contributions to Theory and Practice
Edited by Robert M. Lipgar and Malcolm Pines
ISBN 1 84310 710 4
International Library of Group Analysis 20

Building on Bion: Branches
Contemporary Developments and Applications of Bion's Contributions to Theory and Practice
Edited by Robert M. Lipgar and Malcolm Pines
ISBN 1 84310 711 2
International Library of Group Analysis 21
Two volume set ISBN 1 84310 731 7

Relational Group Psychotherapy
From Basic Assumptions to Passion
Richard M. Billow
ISBN 1 84310 739 2 pb
ISBN 1 84310 738 4 hb
International Library of Group Analysis 26

Dreams in Group Psychotherapy
Theory and Technique
Claudio Neri, Malcolm Pines and Robi Friedman
ISBN 1 85302 923 8
International Library of Group Analysis 18

Group
Claudio Neri
ISBN 1 85302 416 3
International Library of Group Analysis 8

Rediscovering Groups
A Psychoanalyst's Journey Beyond Individual Psychology
Marshall Edelson and David N. Berg
ISBN 1 85302 726 X pb
ISBN 1 85302 725 1 hb
International Library of Group Analysis 9

Self Experiences in Group
Intersubjective and Self-Psychological Pathways to Human Understanding
Edited by Irene N.H. Harwood and Malcolm Pines
ISBN 1 85302 587 6 pb
ISBN 1 85302 596 8 hb
International Library of Group Analysis 4

INTERNATIONAL LIBRARY OF GROUP ANALYSIS 23

Traumatic Experience in the Unconscious Life of Groups

The Fourth Basic Assumption: Incohesion: Aggregation/Massification or (ba) I:A/M

Earl Hopper

Foreword by Malcolm Pines

Jessica Kingsley Publishers
London and Philadelphia

For permission to reprint the text contained in this book Earl Hopper would like to thank the following publishers: 1. 'Difficult patients in group analysis: The personification of (ba) I:A/M', published originally in 2001 in *Group 25*, 3, 139–172. Reprinted by permission of Kluwer Academic/Human Sciences Press. 2. 'Traumatic experience in the unconscious life of groups: A fourth basic asssumption', published originally in 1997 in *Group Analysis 30*, 4, 439–470. Reprinted by permission of Sage Publications Ltd. from Author, Title, Copyright (c) Group Analytic Society. 3. 'Encapsulation as a defence against the fear of annihilation' published originally in 1991 in *The International Journal of Psychoanalysis 72*, 4, 607–624. Excerpts reprinted by permission of *The International Journal of Psychoanalysis*.

Earl Hopper would also like to thank: 1. Creators Syndicate International for the permission to reprint The Far Side ® cartoon by Gary Larson © 1994 Far Works, Inc. All Rights Reserved. 2. Art Wolfe, Inc. for photo-use permissions: Copyright Art Wolfe/www.ArtWolfe.com 3. McCelland & Stewart Ltd. for the permission to use the quote from *Fugitive Pieces* by Anne Michaels.

First published in the United Kingdom in 2003
by Jessica Kingsley Publishers
116 Pentonville Road
London N1 9JB, UK
and
400 Market Street, Suite 400
Philadelphia, PA 19106, USA
www.jkp.com

Printed digitally since 2005

Library of Congress Cataloging in Publication Data

Hopper, Earl.
Traumatic experience in the unconscious life of groups: the fourth basic assumption: incohesion: aggregation/massification or (ba) I:A/M / Earl Hopper; foreword by Malcolm Pines.
p.cm. – (International library of group analysis; 23)
Includes bibliographical references and index.
ISBN 1-84310-087-8 (pb. : alk. paper)
1. Group psychotherapy. 2. Group psychoanalysis. 3. Psychic trauma. 4. Social groups. 5. Subconsciousness. I. Title. II. Series.

RC488.H586 2003
616.89'152--dc21 2002043372

British Library Cataloguing in Publication Data
A CIP catalogue record for this book is available from the British Library

ISBN-13: 978 1 84310 087 4
ISBN-10: 1 84310 087 8

Contents

List of Tables and Figures

...can anyone tell with absolute certainty the difference between the sounds of those who are in despair and the sounds of those who want desperately to believe?

from Fugitive Pieces
by Anne Michaels

For my daughter
Rachel Sarah
a constant source of inspiration

Foreword

For more than forty years – from the war in Vietnam to the war in Iraq – Earl Hopper has steadily evolved his theory of social, cultural and political cohesion and incohesion. He has also applied his ideas to clinical practice with traumatised persons, including drug addicts, criminals, and sexual deviants, as well as survivors of massive social trauma. He has worked with traumatised organisations of various kinds, and has been an advisor to film directors and studios about the psychological and social dynamics of scripts and their production. In this monograph Hopper shares his rich clinical and consultancy experience, and demonstrates the vital importance of working within the transference and countertransference relationship.

In his Acknowledgements, Hopper writes about a broken vase in his childhood home. He loved this mysterious, beautiful object, wondering how it held together, and who it carried across the sea. Hopper, too, has crossed the sea. In the United Kingdom, he has dedicated himself to the study of integration, solidarity and coherence, and to helping broken persons to become whole again. Eugene O'Neill (1926) has written that although Man is born broken, he lives by mending, and the grace of God is glue. Indeed, this may be why psychoanalysts and group analysts know that their work always has both religious and political dimensions.

Group analysis is a broad church. Earl Hopper's style of work, as that of all mature workers, is an expression – a 'personification' – of his own integration of his different educations and trainings in sociology, group analysis and psychoanalysis, matrices of family and cultures, debates with colleagues and a deep, extensive knowledge of the literature of our discipline. Traumatic Experience in the Unconscious Life of Groups is one of the products of his labour. Yet another is his (2003) selection of papers The Social Unconscious. I am proud to include these important new books in this series, which has encouraged many significant contributions to group analysis.

Malcolm Pines, Institute of Group Analysis, London

References

Hopper, E. (2003) *The Social Unconscious: Selected Papers.* London: Jessica Kingsley Publishers.

O'Neill, E. (1926) *The Great God Brown.* In *Desire Under the Elms and The Great God Brown.* London: Nick Hern Books, 1995.

Acknowledgements

I first began to think systemically about the cohesion of social systems within the context of traumatogenic processes during the early 1960s. Those were the days of assassinations and Vietnam, drugs and revolution, not to mention rock and roll. Clearly, it has taken me a very long time to write this book.

One reason for the lengthy gestation is that the topic of cohesion is very complex. It has been necessary to study an abundant literature from several disciplines, and to acquire sufficient clinical and consultancy experience to illustrate – if not to test – the theory of social cohesion that ultimately I have developed. Another reason for the lengthy delay is that it was difficult to find colleagues who shared my interests, and with whom I could discuss my work. American sociologists were unfamiliar with the work of the European Fathers of Sociology, namely, Marx, Weber and Durkheim, and with the great debates concerning conflict and consensus paradigms for the study of social systems. Indeed, 'social system' precluded the study of social change. However, British sociologists regarded applied psychoanalysis as useless, and were not familiar with the fields of group dynamics, group relations and group analysis, and with the work of Bion and Foulkes. Similarly, psychoanalysts and group analysts barely acknowledged one another as members of reputable professions, and hardly credited sociologists as having a legitimate field of study.

It is, therefore, a pleasure to acknowledge the encouragement that I received to pursue my particular intellectual quest by the sociologist Norbert Elias and by the psychoanalysts and group analysts S.H. Foulkes, the Father of Group Analysis, and Robert Gosling, who at the time was the Chairman of the Tavistock Clinic.

I also received enormous help and support from several organisations, colleagues and friends. In 1968, the Group Analytic Society and The Institute of Group Analysis (London) offered me an opportunity to study group dynamics from the points of view of sociology, psychoanalysis and group analysis as a student on Introduction to Group Analysis (London). Not only did I participate in a weekly 'experiential' group for thirty weeks, but also in a so-called 'large group' for ten weeks, and had the chance to read the work of both Bion and Foulkes and their early collaborators. This course was, and perhaps still is, unique. Later, I was on the staff of the course, and it is hardly fortuitous that I now co-convene this course with Roberta Green. Our staff team consists of Geraldine Festenstein, Sonia Ingram, Patrick Mandikate, Percival Mars, Carmen O'Leary and Christopher Scanlon, with whom I have had many stimulating discussions about the dynamics of social cohesion. In fact, I first presented my ideas about social cohesion in terms of a fourth basic assumption in the unconscious life of groups and group-like social systems in 1986 in one of my lectures for the course, entitled 'A Deeper View of Groups'. (The other lecture was called 'A Wider View of Groups', and was the central theme of *The Social Unconscious: Selected Papers* [Hopper 2003], the companion to the present book.)

Subsequently, I have presented versions of my theory and various clinical illustrations of it to colleagues and students throughout the world. My work has benefited from their critical comments and difficult questions, and I hope that they recognise their influence. I very much appreciate the hospitality that I have been given by colleagues who I have met through our work and play at various conferences, in committees and on the Boards of the Group Analytic Society (Europe), the International Association of Group Psychotherapy and the International Psychoanalytical Association.

In 1989, I committed to writing a very early version of my theory of the fourth basic assumption in 'Notes on Psychotic Anxieties and Society: Fission (Fragmentation)/Fusion and Aggregation/Massification' for a Plenary Lecture for a meeting in Cambridge of the Psychotherapy Section of the Royal College of Psychiatry. Although these 'Notes' were rough, or perhaps because they were rough, I received many helpful comments and questions from psychiatrists and other members of the mental health profession who were not psychoanalysts and group analysts, but who were generally interested in my attempt to conceptualise what so many of them experienced daily in their work with difficult, traumatised patients within organisations that were chronically under-funded and under constant administrative and political pressure.

In 1996, I presented a more developed version of this work as the Ilse Seglow Memorial Lecture for the London Centre for Psychotherapy. My lecture 'Incohesion (Aggregation/Massification): A Fourth Basic Assumption of Unconscious Life in Social Systems' (Hopper 1996a) was reported by Sally Baldwin in *Reflections*, the journal of the London Centre for Psychotherapy. Her report made me realise how many links I had omitted from my argument.

In 1997, I presented the 21st Annual S.H. Foulkes Lecture 'Traumatic Experience in the Unconscious Life of Groups: A Fourth Basic Assumption'.

The Group Analytic Society Committee reminded me that 1997 was the centenary of the birth of Norbert Elias. They hoped that as Norbert's colleague I might be able to present ideas that reflected his influence on my thinking and on group analysis in general. It is not generally recognised that in my lecture I tried to do precisely this through my emphasis on helplessness in the traumatogenic process, as opposed to innate, malign envy. However, in retrospect, I can see that in the context of the ambiguities of my argument I did not give sufficient emphasis to the importance of Norbert's ideas concerning the relationship between the individual and the group in terms of what he might have termed a 'recursive figuration'. I have tried here to put the record straight.

Lionel Kreeger (1997) was the Respondent to my lecture. He said that my argument constituted a kind of 're-punctuation' of Turquet's (1975) 'Threats to Identity in the Large Group', which Lionel included in (Kreeger 1975) *The Large Group: Dynamics and Therapy,* and that through this I had changed the meaning of what Turquet had written. To illustrate his point, he told an especially apposite joke:

> During the celebratory parade in Red Square following Leon Trotsky's exile, a cablegram is handed to Joseph Stalin who is standing proudly on Lenin's great tomb. He raises his hand to still the proceedings and declaims, 'Comrades! A most historic event! Trotsky sends me congratulations!'
>
> The masses cheer and Stalin reads the historic cable aloud: 'Joseph Stalin, Kremlin, Moscow. You were right and I was wrong. You are the true heir of Lenin. I should apologise. Trotsky'.
>
> You can imagine the roar of astonishment and triumph that greeted this communication, but in the front row below the podium a little tailor calls out, 'Comrade Stalin, such a message, but you read it without the right feeling'. Stalin again raises his hand to quieten the crowd and says, 'Comrades! This simple and loyal worker, a good Communist, tells me that I have not read the message from Trotsky with enough feeling. Come up here, comrade worker, and you read it to us correctly!'
>
> The tailor mounts the reviewing stand, takes the cablegram, clears his throat and reads: 'Joseph Stalin, Kremlin, Moscow. *You* were right and *I* was wrong? *You* are the true heir of Lenin?? *I* should apologise???!! ... Trotsky'.

I later learned from Lionel that the original manuscript for Turquet's chapter was submitted at the last moment in the form of lecture notes, and that the manuscript that was eventually published reflected his extensive and creative editorial work. At the time I was in supervision with Lionel, and was writing my own chapter for his book (Hopper 1975). I also had several conversations with Turquet about his theory of Oneness, in particular about why he had stopped referring to it as a fourth basic assumption. I was familiar with both the ambiguities in his argument and on how much it was based on the Kleinian theory of envy. I am pleased that I may have succeeded in re-punctuating Turquet's theory in order to emphasise a slightly different set of assumptions and core hypotheses, but I can see that this may have been an attempt to maintain a dialogue with Lionel and Pierre. It has taken me two decades to appreciate the brilliance and richness of their contribution.

I would also like to acknowledge several helpful comments and questions from the participants in the ListServe moderated by Haim Weinberg, who in 1999 published an early draft of *Difficult Patients in Group Analysis*, which contained a statement of parts of my theory and one clinical illustration of it. I am very impressed with this mode of communication in which readers become part of the process of writing and of publication and, in effect, partners in creativity. A highly condensed statement of my theory of Incohesion was published as 'Incohesion: Aggregation/Massification: The Fourth Basic Assumption in the Unconscious Life of Groups and Group-Like Social Systems' in *Building on Bion: Roots* edited by Lipgar and Pines (2003), who turned up the editorial heat so high that the chapter consists of only the barest bones of my argument. However, my monograph has benefited from my having been forced to 'parse' my argument. It has also benefited from critiques by my friends and colleagues Hans Reijzer from Amsterdam and Gerhard Wilke from London, who brought a special sensitivity to their reading of my manuscript, not only because they are steeped in the social sciences, and have lived and worked in countries other than the ones in which they were born. Priscilla Kauff and Bennett Roth also read and commented on a previous draft.

As usual, I am grateful to my patients who have taught me much of what I know about the cohesion of groups and group-like social systems. They have trusted me to hold them and to contain their projected mental life while they experienced and re-experienced both terror and horror. Although it may not have been apparent to them, they have sometimes done the same for me. My wife Cicely and our daughters, Catherine Isabel and Rachel Sarah, realised how important this book is to me, and again gave me the time and space to think and to write. My personal assistant, Céline Stakol, has prepared this manuscript for publication, as she did the various lectures and articles from which it was developed. I am very grateful for her loyalty and commitment.

I will conclude by referring to an inanimate object that was for me a transitional- (Winnicott 1953), linking- (Volcan 1972), evocative- (Bollas 1989), and self- (Kohut 1976) object. I was able to finish this manuscript only when I 'remembered' it. Locked behind the glass doors of an old mahogany 'break front', my mother kept a vase that was about eight or nine inches high, and tapered from a base of about four inches wide to an opening of about six inches. Made in Poland of transparent pale blue crackled glass, an old-fashioned galleon with a red hull and many billowing white sails was painted on it. I always knew that this vase had been brought to the United States by her mother, my grandmother. As a child I used to contemplate this mysterious, beautiful object, wondering how it held together, and who it carried across the sea. Around the time that I started writing about the cohesion of social systems within the context of the traumatogenic process, I asked my mother the whereabouts of this vase. She found it, but it was broken. The pieces were collected inside what remained of the whole. I told her a little about why the vase was important to me. She was immediately filled with remorse, but rather than talk about it, she rushed to the kitchen and threw the remains into a rubbish bin. It seems unnecessary to analyse here the many meanings that this object has for me. Naturally, I try continuously to integrate them in a creative way.

Introduction

The topic of this monograph is the social cohesion and incohesion of groups and group-like social systems within the context of the traumatogenic process, in terms of a theory of the fourth basic assumption, which I call 'Incohesion: Aggregation/Massification' or (ba) 'I:A/M'. The theory is illustrated with brief examples from traumatised societies and organisations of various kinds, and with clinical data from group analysis.

This work is based on my view that the relationship between the individual and the group is systemic, recursive and kaleidoscopic (Hopper 1982a). A deeper view of persons and groups is not inconsistent with a wider view: it is necessary to think in terms of 'horizontal depth'. In other words, the fourth basic assumption in the unconscious life of social systems must always be contextualised in time and space (Hopper 2003).

In the context of psychoanalysis, group analysis and the social sciences, it is important to remember that societies and their geographical parts, like cities, towns and villages, and organisations and families, are not actually groups. These various social formations have their own structures and dynamics. Size is not the sole criterion for distinguishing among various kinds of social system. Although inferences from the study of groups to more complex social systems, and vice versa, may illuminate certain properties and processes, the value of this information depends on the degree to which social systems are isomorphic in structure and kind. Indiscriminate comparison hides a variety of assumptions about human nature that consciously and unconsciously influence the kinds of data that are used and the kinds of conclusions that are drawn. However, under certain conditions inferences can be made, and may be especially relevant to the study of social cohesion. For example, when a social system is traumatised, it is likely to evince processes that may be described in terms of regression from the complex to the simple: integration is weakened and may even fail entirely; overall cohesion is based on solidarity, communication becomes more concrete and culture becomes more open to the intrapsychic and intersubjective lives of people.[1] In other words, traumatised societies become like groups, and traumatised groups become like people, and our knowledge of one becomes applicable to the others. Various metaphors, such as 'the sane society', 'constipated communication', or 'ossified decision making', all become both relevant and virtually explanatory. Thus, only when they are traumatised is it apposite to use 'group' to refer to more complex social systems (Hopper 1975).

In the study of social cohesion the same words are often used to refer to different phenomena, and different words to the same phenomena. The plethora of theories and concepts and clinical, empirical and even anecdotal illustrations of them are confused, inconsistent, partial and contradictory. This stems partly from the fact that the topic has been studied from various points of view in various disciplines which are based on competing axioms, meta-theories and ideologies. It is hardly surprising that the topic continues to generate passion and bias. For example, usually patterns of integration have been of more interest than patterns of disintegration, except when students have taken a greater interest in social change than in permanence, and thus, in instability rather than stability, or in other words, when their work has reflected a 'left-wing' rather than a 'right-wing' point of view.

It is easy to identify with the predicament of the characters in one of Larson's cartoons as illustrated in Figure 0.1.

The central characters of this cartoon are bees or wasps. Fred and his friend are lost on a surface of infinite regularity. Ordinarily, their activities would be governed almost entirely by instinct. However, their predicament is highly unusual, which suggests that a catastrophe has occurred. Instinct alone has proved to be an inadequate guide. How exciting for them. Equally, how traumatic. Of course, these stinging creatures are highly condensed icons for our deepest anxieties and protections against them.

In due course, I will discuss some of the implications of this cartoon. For example, why wasps? Meanwhile, I am reminded of the joke about the stranger who stops a local resident to ask directions from, say, the University of London in Bloomsbury to, say, The Institute of Group Analysis in Hampstead, only to receive the advice that if he were going to Hampstead, he would not start from Bloomsbury. Usually this joke has an ethnic coloration in that the stranger is on the way from Dublin to Belfast, or from Minsk to Pinsk, and so on. In fact, it is of more than passing interest that Kreeger (1975) and Lawrence (2000), two of the leading students of large groups, each use this

THE FAR SIDE® By GARY LARSON

"Face it Fred- you're lost!"

story in order to illustrate the usual predicament of the experienced consultant to them. He is lost but knows it, and is aware of his marginality. In other words, it is best for someone who is helpless to be able to acknowledge it, because this is a pre-condition for being able to think about both one's own state of mind and that of others, and one's own situation and that of the group and its participants.

Another moral of the cartoon and the joke is that in order to achieve a better understanding of social cohesion, we must start from the intellectual position in which we find ourselves. Thus, I have summarised in Appendix I some important conceptual distinctions from the sociology and social psychology of social formations that inform my discourse.

I will now review a selection of contributions from various disciplines to the study of social cohesion of groups and group-like social systems. This review is ordered according to my own personal introduction to them.

General systems theory (Von Bertalanffy 1966)

Disintegration and integration and the tensions between them are always properties of a system, whether mechanical or organic, whether physiological, psychological or social, and whether at the level of micro-systems, such as motherboards, brains, minds or educational institutions, or macro-systems, such as computers, organisms, persons or societies, respectively. General systems theory (GST) enables the discussion of structure and process and apparent stability and apparent change in all kinds of systems. However, it ignores their detail, variety and idiosyncrasies, especially when applied to the study of human social systems.

Many questions may be asked about disintegration and integration of human social systems. For example, in the longer term, how and why do they hold together for the benefit of the whole, when in the shorter term specific parts may benefit more from competition for scarce resources? How and why do some members of such systems benefit from the pursuit of vested interests, rather than from co-operation, loyalty and sacrifice? Put the other way round, and more specifically, in the shorter term why do people, groups and organisations behave so destructively and self-destructively when in the longer term they can gain so much from maintaining and developing the integrity of their social systems? These questions might also be asked with respect to societies, regions and to the world as a whole.

Answers to such questions require a unified theory of both disintegration and integration, or more generally of incohesion and cohesion. The functionalist project to the effect that all questions must be framed in terms of the contribution to the long-term survival of the system within specific contextual parameters is not very interesting, although it has always offered a starting point for further study.

Social biology (E.O. Wilson 1975)

From the point of view of social biology, the key question about the tension between disintegration and integration is how to explain altruism and enlightened self-interest. The answer to this question always emphasises the survival of the higher level components of the system. However, it is generally assumed by social scientists that the explanation of any property of a social system must be explained in terms of other properties of the same system, of an interdependent system or of a larger and more complex system, but not in terms of lower level component parts of these systems. In other words, a reductionist explanation is not acceptable, because it ignores the variability and idiosyncrasies of higher order systems. It also ignores questions about hierarchies of power and their particular histories

Classical psychoanalysis

From the point of view of classical Freudian psychoanalysis, the integration of a social system is based on the mutual sharing of common objects, imitation, identification, empathy, relatedness, sympathy and common purpose, because the members of the system have projected their ego-ideals into the same person, who is, by definition, their 'leader', and similarly the 'system' or 'group' is that collection of people who have projected their ego-ideals into the same person (Freud 1921). Disintegration is explained in terms of the dilution of mutual identifications, and the eruption of self-destruction associated with the so-called 'death instinct', associated with the trans-generational Oedipal struggle (Freud 1920). The attack on, and the loss of, the leader are followed by panic which lasts until a new leader takes the place of the one who was deposed.

In this perspective the social context is taken for granted. The structure of authority is not taken as problematic. Also, the assumption of the universality of the Oedipus complex is based on a Lamarckian notion of the repetition of historical, if not mythical, situations that are said to have been genetically encoded into the biological unconscious. The explanatory thrust is from the species and the organism to the social system and the person.

Psychoanalytical models neglect the constraints of the social unconscious and the diversity and variety of social systems. What is true for a horde is hardly true for a group, whether large or small, not to mention more complex social formations, such as a bureaucratic organisation or a society. Most importantly, however, is that in the classical psychoanalytical theory the question of the formation and the maintenance of a 'group' is confused with the question of the cohesion of it, which, in turn, is defined in terms of social glue or stickiness, which may be crucial for a crowd or mass, but is too general for other kinds of social system, and may not even be correct for many kinds of social system, such as committees. Nonetheless, a careful reading of *Group Psychology and the Analysis of the Ego* (Freud 1921) suggests that Freud indicated many of the ingredients that are essential for a more comprehensive theory of incohesion.

Sociology

The nature of social disintegration is the core problem in the social sciences and especially in sociology (Elster 1989). Since its inception, sociology has been characterised by competing schools of thought about this problem, and by attempts to synthesise what are generally known as either Durkheimian or Marxist solutions to it. Following developments in social philosophy in the work of Locke, Hobbes, Rousseau and others, on the one hand, and in the work of Hegel and Feurbach, on the other, the study of order reached its zenith in the views of Durkheim. He argued that society was an overarching moral and religious entity, maintained through relationships of various kinds. The study of disorder reached its zenith in the views of Marx, who argued that the cultural super-structure of a society was based on its economic sub-structure, including both the technical and social relations of the means of production. Although these two basic perspectives were developed by many, and over simplified by many, both remain true, yet incomplete, only partly because the means of production have become de-materialised.

There have been three major contributions to our understanding of the problem of disorder and order from the fields of sociology and social psychology:

1. The work of Durkheim and Marx helped us to realise what in retrospect seems to be a simple or even banal truth, namely, that the study of disintegration and integration is about both degree and kind. Durkheim understood that whereas complex and simple societies may be equally well integrated, they have different modes of integration. Complex societies are characterised by the degree to which their interaction systems, based mainly on work and the economy, are integrated, that is, the degree to which people are interdependent for goods and services (so-called 'organic solidarity'). In contrast, simple societies are characterised by the degree to which their normative systems are characterised by solidarity, that is, people possess similitude, or share similar beliefs, norms and values (so-called 'mechanical solidarity'). Marx understood these distinctions in terms of the mode of production that typified a particular kind of society, for example, agrarian or capitalist. For our purposes, we can leave to

one side that Durkheim and Marx were old-fashioned evolutionists: for Durkheim, simple societies had developed, and more or less inevitably would continue to develop, into more complex ones; and for Marx, pre-capitalist societies had developed into capitalist ones, which would, in turn, more or less inevitably, continue to develop into socialist and communist societies. Of course, 'develop' did not mean 'grow' like an organism or a person; political processes were always necessary and always would be necessary, and such processes were often violent, and would often be violent, until the ultimate Utopian stage of development would be realised. In a way, these arguments are similar to the widely held view that primitive people were like children, and Western industrial societies were like adults. Clearly, Marx, Durkheim and Freud were all the children of Queen Victoria and Charles Darwin.

2. In his struggle to integrate Marxist and Durkeimian sociologies, Lockwood (1964, 1992) introduced the distinction between 'system integration' and 'social integration'. The meaning of these phrases is not self-evident, but he intended to show that without the supplementary and complementary analysis of the relations among categories of people and groups of people, the analysis of social systems in terms of their institutional arrangements is incomplete. However, Lockwood realised that he treated 'social integration' as a residual category, which needed to be developed by others. Although he eschewed the study of social psychology, he referred to the work of Malinowski and, therefore, by implication to the work of Freud, and that the study of social integration required the theories and concepts of social psychology, if not psychoanalysis or other forms of 'depth psychology'. For example, although my (Hopper 1981) own study of feelings of relative deprivation and various forms of insatiability was a study primarily of social integration, I suggested in it that social integration was connected to system integration through forms of instrumental adjustment to feelings of relative deprivation that had themselves been caused by social factors, or in other words, that both modes of integration were recursive.

3. The development of role theory and the concept of the actor as a person who interprets the requirements of a role both consciously and unconsciously, and both as a result of external and internal coercion, constituted an important step towards thinking in terms of both

> system and social integration. In other words, psychic life is characterised not only by internalised objects, but also by internalised social systems. Moreover, social life is characterised not only by the structures of society and culture, but also by their enactment by actors who interpret the constraints of such structures in terms of personal idiosyncrasies. In fact, new sociologies were developed in order to draw special attention to the importance of the individual person, as opposed to the constraints of their social systems. Many years ago this was discussed in terms of the so-called 'over-socialised', as opposed to the 'under-socialised', conception of man (Wrong 1961), which was based on similar discussions of the so-called 'consensus' perspective as opposed to the 'conflict' perspective in the social sciences (Hopper 1981).

Despite these three major developments (that is, the relationship of types of society to the type of integration, the distinction between system integration and social integration, and the development of role theory and the notion of the actor), serious problems remain in the sociological perspective to the study of social integration and disintegration. For example, the scope for personal interpretation of roles depends on the degree to which they are institutionalised, and on how central they are to the core institutions of the society: whereas groups offer enormous scope for the interpretation of their exceedingly limited number of diffuse roles, government bureaucracies offer very little scope for the interpretation of their many highly specific roles. More importantly, sociology and social psychology have never come to terms with the 'unconscious mind' of psychoanalysis, in which emphasis is given, for example, to fantasy, to introjected objects which are highly modified versions of the objects introjected, and the propensity of people to think, feel and act in terms of 'transferences' of the infant, child, adolescent and younger adult who continue to reside within the continuously developing and ageing person. In other words, the study of disintegration and integration in all social systems, but especially in groups, must draw on the study of what appears to be 'irrational'. Of course, the irrational, like the 'primitive', is usually only that which is not or cannot be understood in terms of a particular perspective (Hopper 1977). Actually, sociologists and social psychologists believe that the constraints of social and cultural facts on the psychic life of persons and their actions are the basis of the concept of the social unconscious (Hopper 1996b).

Group dynamics or group relations, group psychotherapy and group analysis

The field of 'group dynamics' or 'group relations' has emerged from attempts to integrate the complementary and alternative perspectives concerning the study of groups in each of the fields considered above. 'Group psychotherapy' involves the application of the study of group dynamics to clinical work, and 'group analysis' emphasises the contributions of psychoanalytical thinking to this. In practice, it is impossible to distinguish these perspectives, because they share many of the same preoccupations, concepts and even data.

The relevant literature on cohesion in groups was studied in depth in *Group Cohesion* edited by Kellermann (1981). However, Marziali, Munroe-Blum and McCleary (1997) who have recently referred to cohesion as '...the most frequently studied group-process dimension...', write:

> Cohesion has been the focus of considerable theoretical debate (Bednar and Kaul 1994; Bloch and Crouch 1985; Braaten 1991; Drescher, Burlingame and Fuhriman 1985; Mudrack 1989; Piper *et al.* 1983; Yalom 1975). It appears to be multifactorial and includes the dimensions of a basic bond or uniting force (Piper *et al.* 1983); connectedness of the group demonstrated by working together toward a common therapeutic goal (Budman *et al.* 1987); acceptance, support and identification with the group (Bloch and Crouch 1985); affiliation, acceptance and attractiveness of the group (Yalom 1975); and engagement (functioning of group as a whole) (MacKenzie and Tschuschke 1993). (p.476)

They conclude, however, that 'despite these developments, Bednar and Kaul (1994) believe that the construct of cohesion continues to defy definition. There is little consensus about the dimensions that best describe the complex phenomena that comprise group cohesiveness' (p.476).

Among the many findings that have emerged from the study of group cohesion are that cohesive groups are more productive, and their members take more pleasure in their work. An optimal degree of cohesion exists for various phases of group development and for various kinds of social system. For example, too much cohesion is likely to be associated with the loss of individual identity, as is sometimes seen in cults, crowds and audiences. Groups that are too cohesive may inhibit the idiosyncratic creativity of their individual members, and their ability and willingness to exercise their own super-ego controls. Such groups may make it difficult for members to accept new people from the environment, or to release those who wish to leave, or in general for members to be open to new ideas that are vital for survival. Groups can evince pathological kinds of cohesion, in that certain phenotypes of cohesion can cover certain genotypes of incohesion. For example, some groups may be able to maintain the total allegiance of their members, while at the same time not be able to work effectively and to meet challenges posed by their environment.[2]

In his implicit modifications to Freud's theory of social cohesion, Battegay (1973) states that under certain circumstances groups may become 'mobs on a small scale'; he refers to such regression as 'defective development(s)' characterised by too much 'we-ness'. He describes one kind of 'fusion group' in terms of an hallucinated merger with a shared imago of a suffocating mother, and the other kind in terms of total submission to a shared imago of a dictatorial father. In an attempt to deconstruct the phenomenon of fusion, Hartman (1981) suggests that although adhesive attachments may be very binding, they do not involve much integration and, therefore, that an 'adhesive' group is less cohesive than a 'cohesive' one. Drawing on the psychoanalysis of borderline states, separation anxieties and the psychic representation of skin, Ben Yakar (1987) suggests that in group development adhesion precedes authentic cohesion.

Studies of leadership and the political systems of groups have been a central focus in the field of group dynamics, especially during the decade after World War II. It has often been discovered that the behaviour of the leader is an important determinant of the degree of cohesion, and of the likelihood that a group will evince optimal cohesion (e.g. Battegay 1987; Behr 1979; Yalom 1975). For example, does the leader induce scapegoating within the group? Does he/she seek other groups as targets for aggression? Does he/she encourage the idealisation of his/her own group and the denigration of others? Of course, many have stressed that both the members of groups and their leaders tend to be unconscious of these dynamics.

Within the context of studies of unconscious processes in groups, Liff (1981) acknowledged the influence of Bion's distinction between the experiential or basic assumption group and the work group, and advised that the leader of a therapy group might have to 'discourage' cohesion based on massive and deep regression within the experiential group, and 'promote' an optimal degree of cohesion in the work group. Optimal cohesion and a collaborative therapeutic alliance are positively correlated, and are important to the favourable outcomes of group therapy for borderline patients (Marziali, Munroe-Blum and McCleary 1997). It is generally recognised that the skills of a therapist in fostering and maintaining an optimal degree of group cohesion are especially important in the treatment of borderline and schizophrenic patients (e.g. Battegay 1994; Pines 1986; Wexler *et al.* 1984).

A small number of psychoanalysts who have taken a special interest in the study of groups, such as Anzieu, Bion, Chasseguet-Smirgel, Kernberg and Turquet, have focused on the effects on cohesion of pre-Oedipal phenomena. For example, Kernberg (1994a) writes: 'mass psychology pre-dates the crystallisation of the identification with the leader' (p.44). It is sometimes assumed that in emphasising the importance of pre-Oedipal phenomena, these psychoanalysts are 'post-Freudian'. However, Freud himself argued that group formation is based on the collective investment of ego-ideals, which is, by definition, pre-Oedipal. It should also be noted that although these psychoanalysts occasionally cite the work of sociologists, philosophers, historians and political scientists, their arguments are not really informed by it.

Another small number of psychoanalysts and psychoanalytical psychotherapists have studied cohesion from the alternative but overlapping point of view of 'Group Analysis', based on the work of S.H. Foulkes and his collaborators, such as Anthony, Brown, de Maré, Hume, Kreeger, Main, Pines, Skynner and others. These 'group-analysts' have drawn explicitly on the work of sociologists, general systems theorists, Jungian Analytical Psychologists, and especially psychoanalysts associated with the Group of Independent Psychoanalysts of The British Psychoanalytical Society, such as Rickman, Fairbairn, Winnicott, Balint, Bowlby and King, and others. Their concepts and theories of the group matrix, the sociality of human nature, the social unconscious, and of groups as open systems are essential to the group analytical study of cohesion (Hopper 2003).

In Chapter 1, I will outline and discuss the theory of group cohesion proposed by Bion and Turquet and developed by Kernberg and others. In the subsequent two chapters I will present my own theory, which draws mainly from the work of the group analysts and independent psychoanalysts, and which is addressed to the explanation of *incohesion* rather than cohesion. I will then illustrate the basic hypotheses in this theory of incohesion with clinical data from group analysis. In the last chapter I will summarise my argument and present invited critical commentaries from several group analysts and psychoanalysts, and suggest several lines of enquiry for further research and application.

Notes

1 With reference to groups, Scheidlinger (1968) provided a comprehensive summary of the concept of regression. With reference to complex social systems, and using an object relations psychoanalytical frame of reference, regression was delineated by King (1969), who drew on the work of Emery and Trist (1960), Cohn (1957, 1967), Fairbairn (1952) and Rickman (1938). Dunning and Hopper (1966) have stressed that processes of civilisation (Elias 1938) are not inevitable and continuous, and that processes of social regression may occur. Some sociologists refer to processes of social regression as processes of 'de-civilisation' (de Swaan 1999).

2 Durkheim's distinction between degrees and kinds of social cohesion has been discovered repeatedly. For example, it is especially apposite that he connected 'normal' and 'abnormal' forms of social cohesion, based on variations in the social and cultural structures associated with the kinds and degrees of the division of labour, with 'egoistic' and 'anomic' forms of suicide, on the one hand, and 'altruistic' and 'fatalistic' forms of suicide, on the other (Hopper 1975, 1981). Durkheim argued that altruistic suicides were likely to occur in association with a high degree of normal cohesion, and egoistic suicides, with a low degree; and that, in contrast, fatalistic suicides were likely to occur in association with a high degree of abnormal cohesion, and anomic suicides, in association with a low degree. However, his argument did not quite work, mainly because altruistic and fatalistic suicides were more likely to occur in simple than in complex societies, and egoistic and anomic suicides were more likely to occur in complex societies than in simple societies, in the context of forms of cohesion that were normal for them, i.e. social integration in complex societies, and cultural solidarity in simple societies. This was crucial for all subsequent studies of these phenomena.

CHAPTER 1

The Theory of Cohesion Proposed by Bion and Turquet, and Modified by Others

Experiences in Groups (Bion 1961), which includes all Bion's papers on group dynamics, constitutes a time marker in the psychoanalytical study of groups that should be known as 'zero', all previous studies to be dated 'BB' and all subsequent ones 'AB'. Acknowledging the influence of Freud, Klein and Rickman, Bion provided the first coherent psychoanalytical theory of three ubiquitous group processes called 'basic assumptions'. Although he did not regard his theory of 'basic assumptions' in the unconscious life of groups as a theory of social cohesion, it can be understood in this way, because groups who are under the sway of basic assumptions are likely to be incohesive. Actually, Bion's theory of basic assumptions is a theory of incohesion.

1. I will now outline the main hypotheses that comprise Bion's theory, and indicate a few of the problems that I have with it. However, I cannot improve on the summaries provided by others, and I will, therefore, quote from them at length:

    (a) Lawrence, Bain and Gould (1996) write:

    > When any group of people meet to do something, i.e. a task, there are in actuality two groups, or two configurations of mental activity...the sophisticated work group (referred to as the W group)...[and]...the basic assumption groups (referred to as the ba groups)...

What is the experience of being in a W group? ... All the participants are engaged with the primary task because they have taken full cognisance of its purpose. They co-operate because it is their will. They search for knowledge through using their experiences. They probe out realities in a scientific way by hypothesis testing and are aware of the processes that will further learning and development. Essentially, the W group mobilises sophisticated mental activity on the part of its members which they demonstrate through their maturity. They manage the psychic boundary between their inner and outer worlds. They strive to manage themselves in their roles as members of the W group. Furthermore, the participants can hold in the mind an idea of wholeness and interconnectedness with other systems. The participants use their skills to understand the inner world of the group, as a system, in relation to the external reality of the environment. In a W group the participants can comprehend the psychic, political, and spiritual relatedness in which they are participating and are co-creating. The W group can be seen as an open-system. The major inputs are people with minds who can transform experiences into insight and understanding.

Groups which act in this consistently rational manner are rare, however, and, perhaps, are merely an idealised construct. In actuality...people in groups behave at times collectively in a psychotic fashion or, rather, the group mentality drives the process in a manner akin to temporary psychosis.

The term 'psychotic' is being used in this context to mean a 'diminution of effective contact with reality' ... (Menzies-Lyth 1981, p.663). This is a group mentality that has such a culture that the individual, despite his or her sophisticated and mature skills, can be caused to regress to and be temporarily caught up in primitive splitting and projective identification, depersonalization, and infantile regression. (p.94)

(b) Psychotic group mentality can be described and analysed in terms of three 'basic assumptions': 'Dependency', 'Fight/Flight', and 'Pairing'. According to Kernberg (1998):

In the 'Dependency' group, ...(m)embers perceive the leader as omnipotent and omniscient and themselves as inadequate, immature and incompetent. They match their idealization of the leader with efforts to extract knowledge, power and goodness from him. The group members are thus both forever greedy and forever dissatisfied.

When the leader fails to live up to their ideal, they react first with denial and then by rapidly and completely devaluing the leader and searching for a substitute. Thus, primitive idealization, projected omnipotence, denial, envy and greed, together with their accompanying defenses, characterize the basic Dependency group.

In the Fight/Flight group, ...(m)embers are united against what they vaguely perceive to be external enemies. This group expects the leader to direct the fight against such enemies and also to protect the group from infighting. Because the members cannot tolerate opposition to their shared ideology, they easily split into subgroups, which fight with one another. Frequently, one subgroup becomes subservient to the idealized leader, while another either attacks the subservient group or flees from it. Prevalent features include the group's tendencies to try to control the leader or to experience itself as being controlled by the leader, to experience closeness through shared denial of intragroup hostility, and to project aggression onto an out-group. In short, splitting, projection of aggression, and projective identification prevail. In the Fight/Flight group, the search for nurture and dependency that characterizes the Dependency group is replaced by conflicts over aggressive control, suspiciousness, fighting, and dread of annihilation.

In the 'Pairing' group, ...(m)embers operate under a 'pairing' assumption. Members tend to focus on a couple within the group, one that is usually but not necessarily heterosexual. The focal couple symbolizes the group's positive expectation that it will, in effect, reproduce itself and thus preserve the group's threatened identity and ensure its survival. The Pairing group experiences general intimacy and sexual developments as potential protections against the dangerous conflicts over dependency and aggression that characterize the Dependency and Fight/Flight groups. Although the latter two groups have a pregenital character, the Pairing group has a genital character. (p.4)

2. Bion's work is complex, and his style, cryptic. I will, therefore, emphasise a few of the points made by Lawrence, Bain, Gould, Menzies-Lyth, Kernberg and others, and add some of my own, which offer a slightly different way of understanding the original theory of basic assumptions:

   (a) The three basic assumptions have been understood from many points of view, for example, in terms of: phallic/Oedipal, anal and oral levels of psychosexual development; instincts concerned with the perpetuation of the species, the control of territory and the food and sexual partners within it; and seeking dependable 'attachments'. However, Bion's work developed from the perspectives expressed in his earlier papers into those expressed in *Experiences in Groups.* His psychoanalytical views became more and more Kleinian (although subsequently they evolved into what is now called 'post-Kleinian'). Bion argues that when people are in group situations, they regress to levels of psychic life of an infant at the mother's body and breast, to be understood in terms of very early Oedipal phenomena, or to what some would call pre-Oedipal or triangularisation phenomena, involving relationships among the mouth, breast and nipple or the mouth, eye and hand or the mouth, ear and anus, etc. rather than in terms of relationships among the person, mother and father. In groups these relationships are experienced in terms of the vicissitudes of the primal scene, in terms of the prevailing anxieties and defences against them. Curiosity and the desire to know become especially important. As Bion puts it, the story of the Sphinx rather than that of Oedipus.

(b) Bion emphasised that the three basic assumptions are best understood in terms of the 'interplay' between the paranoid/schizoid and depressive positions. Although he was not clear about this, he implied that, based on the death instinct, innate pathological envy is the source of irrational and destructive rage, and that primal processes of splitting, denial and projection facilitate processes of idealisation and denigration in order to help the ego rid itself of painful rage and to protect its most important objects. Dependency develops from idealisation associated with the schizoid component of the paranoid/schizoid position, and Fight/Flight develops from denigration associated with the paranoid component. The basic assumption of Dependency protects people from the experience of helplessness and fear that they will be unable to fulfil the requirements of those tasks the completion of which is essential to life, such as, in infancy, obtaining food. Feelings of unsafety, uncertainty, being lost, of not knowing what to expect and what is expected, etc. are also involved. Pairing is based on sexualisation or erotisation as a manic defence against anxieties associated with the depressive position, involving the conviction that goodness and perfection exist nowhere, not within and not without. In other words, Pairing is not really a matter of genital sexuality.

(c) All basic assumptions are containers for psychotic anxieties. Although basic assumption processes can become grotesque and distorted, and interfere with the activities of the work group, they can also be used in the service of the activities of the work group. They can be used to mobilise and support particular patterns of action and sentiment that are essential to the survival of the group. For example, warfare requires a Fight/Flight mentality, but is undermined by a Pairing mentality. This is analogous to the way that neuroses and possibly psychoses in adults are grotesque versions of the mental life of normal children and infants. However, the existence of basic assumption processes in parallel with work group processes is also analogous to the existence of unconscious mental and emotional life characterised by primary process in parallel with the unconscious, rational, secondary processes of the ego.

(d) Basic assumption processes can be delineated in terms of patterns of interaction, normation and communication as properties of social systems. The following examples stress how each pattern is seen in any basic assumption: with respect to Pairing, a typical interaction would be a flirtation between a male and a female, encouraged by the rest of the group; a typical pattern of normation would be the expression of values that favour personal sacrifice for collective goals; and a typical pattern of communication would be an enthusiastic, hopeful and perhaps unrealistic discussion of future projects and plans. With respect to Fight/Flight: an apparently unsolvable argument between two members on behalf of factions that have arisen virtually from 'out of the blue'; the expression of values that favour debate and the importance of being true to principles; and discussion of the possibilities of forming two groups and of the various 'major' differences among the people within the group. And with respect to Dependency: very little interaction among the members of the group combined with hesitant participation; the expression of values that favour humility, risk aversion, conservatism on behalf of all rather than on behalf of individuality, and respect for authority; and discussion about 'being stuck' yet confident that the leader will soon help 'get us going', punctuated by long periods of silence.

(e) In any group, all three basic assumptions and combinations of them emerge kaleidoscopically, as do the correlates of the paranoid/schizoid and depressive positions on which they are based. For example, when the basic assumption of Pairing fails as a defence against depressive anxieties, certain kinds of paranoid/schizoid anxieties are likely to emerge, associated with denigration, which, in turn, generates the basic assumption of Fight/Flight. However, when other kinds of paranoid/schizoid anxieties emerge, associated with idealisation, the basic assumption of Dependency is likely to follow. The converse of these processes may also occur. For example, when Dependency fails as a defence against feelings of helplessness, envy is likely to occur and, in turn, either denigration develops and leads to Fight/Flight, or further idealisation develops and leads to an amplification of Dependency. In essence, the dynamics of the three basic assumptions are those of a closed system.

(f) These points, which will be discussed further below, are summarised in Table 1.1 and Figure 1.1.

Table 1.1 Alternative explanations offered for three basic assumption processes

Authors	Sources	Basic assumptions
1.	Sexuality	Pairing
Bion, W. (1940s and	Aggression (possibly the defence of territory)	Fight/Flight
1950s)	Prolonged dependence (possibly attachment in the sense of the term as used by Bowlby)	Dependency
2.	Regression to:	
Many authors of a 'Freudian' persuasion	Phallic/genital phase of development	Pairing
	Anal phase of development	Fight/Flight
	Oral phase of development	Dependency
3.	Psychotic anxieties and defences, defined in terms of Kleinian metapsychology:	
Bion, W. (1961) as understood by Hopper, E. (1980 and subsequently)	Sexuality and erotisation as a manic defence against anxieties associated with the depressive position	Pairing
	Denigration as a consequence of split-off and projected hatred arising from the anxiety inherent in the paranoid-schizoid position based on innate malign envy arising from the putative death instinct	Fight/Flight
	Idealisation as a consequence of split-off needs to bond with the mother and her body, and to ensure reciprocal responses, as a way of protecting oneself and one's internal objects from retaliation from external objects into whom envy has been projected	Dependency
4.	Birth and separation anxiety	Fusion (?)
Bion, W. (late 1960s)		

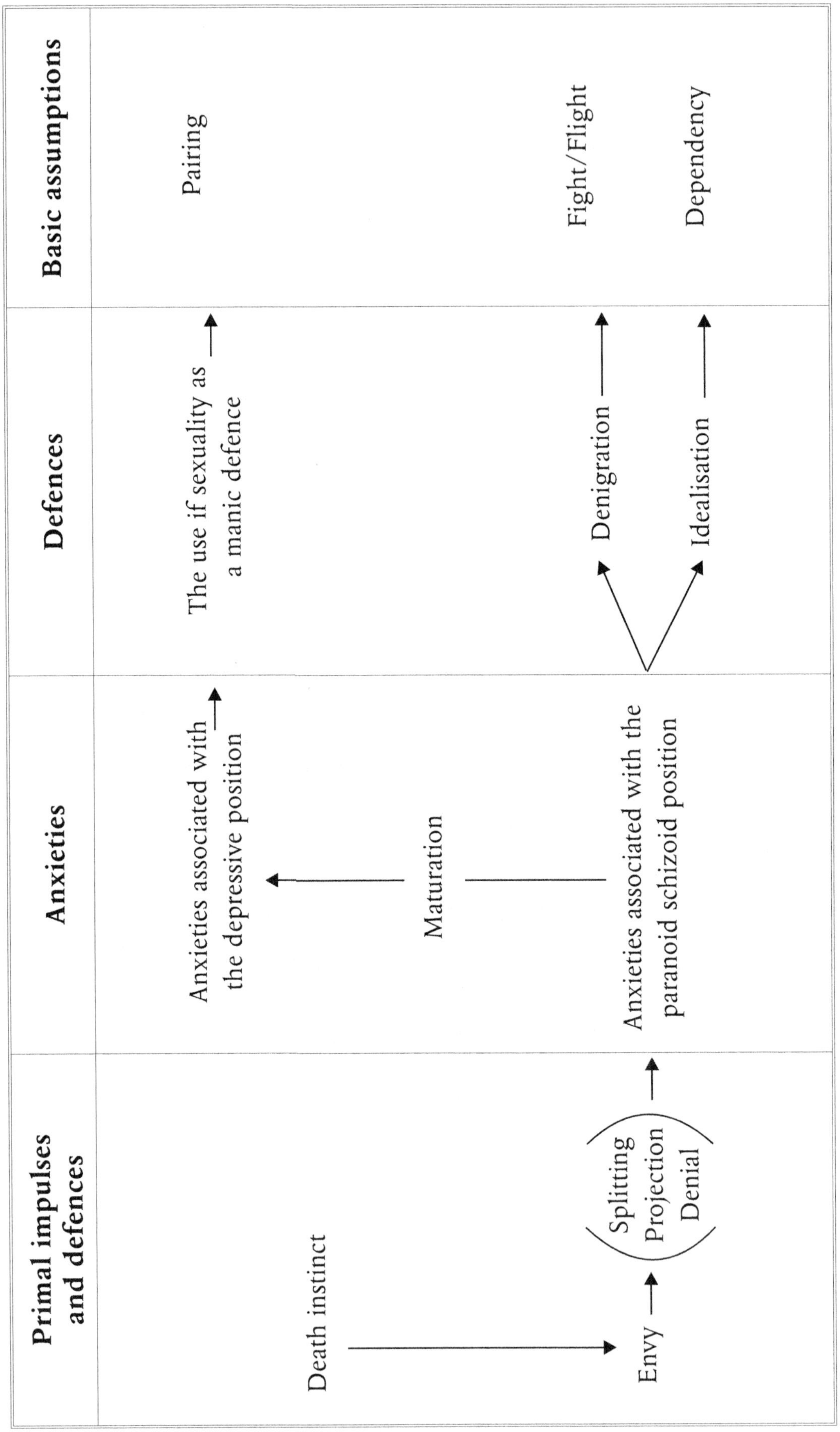

Figure 1.1 An explanation of basic assumption processes

(g) Bion also discussed the leadership of a group. He referred ambiguously to the leadership of the work group as well as of the basic assumption group. Bion argued that as a consequence of ubiquitous processes of projective identification, patterns of 'valence' arise through which particular people are attracted to the roles associated with particular basic assumptions. Valence for the roles of a particular basic assumption is not necessarily an indication of pathology as much as it is of a type of personality and character. The so-called 'leader' of a basic assumption group is someone with a valence for the roles and processes associated with a particular basic assumption. However, Bion implied that a 'real' leader is the leader of the work group, who is able to use basic assumption processes in the service of work, depending on the nature of the task at the time. In other words, the work group is like a cork floating on the sea of basic assumptions, and the leader of the work group is in chronic danger of being capsized, and likely to be replaced by a 'leader' of a basic assumption group. Leaders of a work group and leaders of basic assumption groups may exist and function simultaneously. Usually the situation is transitory and in flux.

3. An assessment of the strengths and weaknesses of the theory of basic assumptions has been provided elsewhere, for example, by group analysts such as Brown (1985), group psychotherapists such as Yalom (1975) and students of group dynamics such as Whitaker (1985). However, I would emphasise that the theory has stood the test of time: we are still talking about it, and although we play with the phrase 'beyond Bion', few of us have been able to get there. Rarely have we been able to identify and to explain so many diverse phenomena on the basis of so few concepts and propositions. Rarely have so few pages produced so much research and theory building, and so many diverse applications. Nonetheless, the theory is not without its problems, for example:

(a) Bion nominalised groups and group processes, and denied the reality of social facts. It is not generally remembered that although Bion studied groups as 'wholes', and stressed that people were social animals, he also expressed the view that groups do not really exist as such. He wrote that a 'group' is a fantasy that is shared by people who are in similar states of regression. In other words, Bion's work is characterised by a logical and substantive contradiction. He did not actually accept the reality of social facts.

(b) Bion ignored introjective processes by which people and groups internalise institutional and societal arrangements.[1] Instead, he emphasised the exclusive importance of projective processes. For example, Bion argued that certain institutions represent the three basic assumptions (for example, the Church represents Dependency, the Army, Fight/Flight, and the Aristocracy, Pairing). Apart from the fact that it is extremely misleading to infer from a group to a society and its diverse organisations without taking into account the degree to which they are isomorphic, this emphasis on projective processes leads to a very one-sided analysis of social systems that are more complex than groups. Actually, it also leads to a limited understanding of groups as such. For example, Bion did not consider the constraints of the social unconscious and the phenomenon of social equivalence (Hopper 1996b), that is, the recreation by groups of their contexts.

(c) Bion confined his discussion of aggression within the context of basic assumption groups to the basic assumption of Fight/Flight, as though particular patterns of aggression did not occur within the basic assumptions of Pairing and Dependency. For example, he did not consider the phenomena of perverse pairing and clinging, parasitical dependency, which constitute attacks on the work group and the possibility for the development of optimal cohesion and hopeful morale.

(d) Bion neglected the 'work group'. He was more interested in the basic assumption group, and how basic assumption processes might disrupt the work group. Similarly, he neglected the phenomenon of leadership, especially of the work group.

(e) Bion assumed that the basic assumptions were both ubiquitous and inevitable, because they were derived from envy and the anxieties associated with the paranoid/schizoid and depressive positions, and that people in groups regressed in such a way that their experience was dominated by the anxieties and defences associated with these universal features of human development. However, although basic assumptions are ubiquitous, they are not inevitable. They are not typical of all groups. They are a variable phenomenon. In part, basic assumptions depend on the style of a conductor or a leader. It is easy to conduct a group of, for example, inexperienced students in such a way that they are provoked into a state of fear and bewilderment. It is more difficult to facilitate the development of a work group who share a sense of community, characterised by optimal cohesion. Of course, if one waits long enough it will always be possible to find a basic assumption, but this is hardly the point.

(f) Within the context of the Klein/Bion model, it is impossible to conceptualise anxieties that are more primitive than schizoid anxieties, and, therefore, to imagine basic assumptions that are more primitive than Fight/Flight and Dependency, because it is assumed that whereas innate malign envy, which reflects the work of the so-called 'death instinct' on the mind leads, on the one hand, to denigration and Fight/Flight and, on the other, to idealisation and Dependency. Yet, empirical data and clinical experience suggest that there are additional psychotic anxieties and, therefore, that there are additional basic assumptions. Bion became aware of this problem, but he could not solve it because, I suspect, he could not bring himself to modify the Kleinian model of the mind from which the theory of basic assumptions was derived.[2] He would have had to ask the question that many years later Khaleelee and Miller (1985) and I (Hopper 1985), working independently, were led to ask: what happens when Dependency fails? The answer to this question is not that the members of the group experience the envy against which Dependency was a defence, but that in addition to envy, people experience feelings of profound helplessness and the fear of annihilation. In other words, it is possible that envy is not caused directly by the so-called 'death instinct' but that it arises as a defence against the fear of annihilation, and the phenomenology of the fear of annihilation gives rise to a fourth basic assumption, an idea which I will develop subsequently.

4. Although the theory of basic assumptions is in essence a theory of incohesion in general, this possible fourth basic assumption concerns incohesion specifically. Bion mentioned the possibility of a fourth basic assumption: once, as a manifestation of illusions of fusion and oneness based on an infant's need to protect against the anxieties associated with birth (Bion 1970); and later, more precisely, against the anxieties associated with the transformation from being a unique object of mother and foetus combined with the body of the mother, to being a separate object outside the mother (Bion 1965). However, Pierre Turquet, a Kleinian member of The British Psychoanalytical Society and one of the founders of the psychoanalytical study of the group relations movement, developed Bion's cryptic comments in two seminal papers: one, in 1967, to the Paris Society of Psychosomatic Medicine, which gave rise to the publication in 1974 of 'Leadership: The Individual in the group'; and the other, in 1969, as one of the winter lectures for the general public sponsored by The British Psychoanalytical Society, which was the basis of the publication in 1975 of 'Threats to identity in the large group'.[3] Focusing entirely on large groups within group relations conferences, Turquet argued:

   (a) There exists a fourth basic assumption, and it should be called 'Oneness' (BaO). Under the sway of this basic assumption members of a large group '...seek to join in a powerful union with an omnipotent force unobtainably high, to surrender self for passive participation, and thereby (to) feel existence, well-being, and wholeness' (1974, p.357). 'The group member is there to be lost in oceanic feelings of unity... If the oneness is personified...(the group member is there)...to be a part of a salvationist inclusion' (p.360).

   This basic assumption of Oneness results from a transformation or 'conversion' that people experience as a result of threats to their identity that occur when they attempt to participate in a large group, which is always characterised by 'multiple stimuli' and 'response bombardment'. A person begins in what is called a 'singleton' state, but in order to protect against the fear of annihilation and loss of identity that follow from unbridled envy associated with uncontrolled regression, a 'Singleton (S)' becomes either a 'Membership Individual (MI)' or an 'Isolate (I)', rather than an 'Individual Member (IM)'. Membership Individuals unconsciously create a state of social and cultural 'homogeneity', characterised by absolute equality, absolute sameness of belief, no role differentiation, no use of personal authority as the basis of the interpretation of the role, the use of language in order to convey their identity rather than the content of their ideas, and the use of 'speaking-in-tongues' in order magically to be at-one with the unified group as a whole. 'Homogenisation' is the process through which the basic assumption of Oneness is realised. It is implied that homogenisation is a manifestation of the desire for fusion as a defence against envy.

(b) There exists an alternative defensive process through which alienated Isolates create unconsciously a state of chaos and multiple splittings, characterised by 'errancy' and 'polarities'. It should be called 'dissaroy', which connotes that the king-father has been dispossessed of his power and authority. In itself, dissaroy is not a basic assumption, and is not connected to Oneness, at least not explicitly.

I would suggest that a metaphor for dissaroy as a state of social and cultural nothingness might be the exploding fragments of an atomic nucleus in a cyclotron, the boundaries of which are set only by the shape of the mechanical container. This metaphor is also apposite for the states of mind of Isolates and Membership Individuals. In other words, the so-called 'dissaroy' of the group and the states of mind of the individuals who comprise it can be understood as a collection of what Bion (1956) later called 'bizarre objects'.

(c) A good work group is characterised by 'heterogeneity'. It is implied that in order for a group to develop a work group characterised by heterogeneity, the majority of participants must have become 'Individual Members'. However, as for Bion, the 'work group' was primarily a foil for the analysis of the destructive processes of unconscious basic assumption groups and, thus, Turquet did not describe heterogeneity. In any case, it is implied that under conditions of Oneness the work group would only be momentary and transitory, and under conditions of dissaroy, the work group would cease to exist as, shortly thereafter, would the group itself.

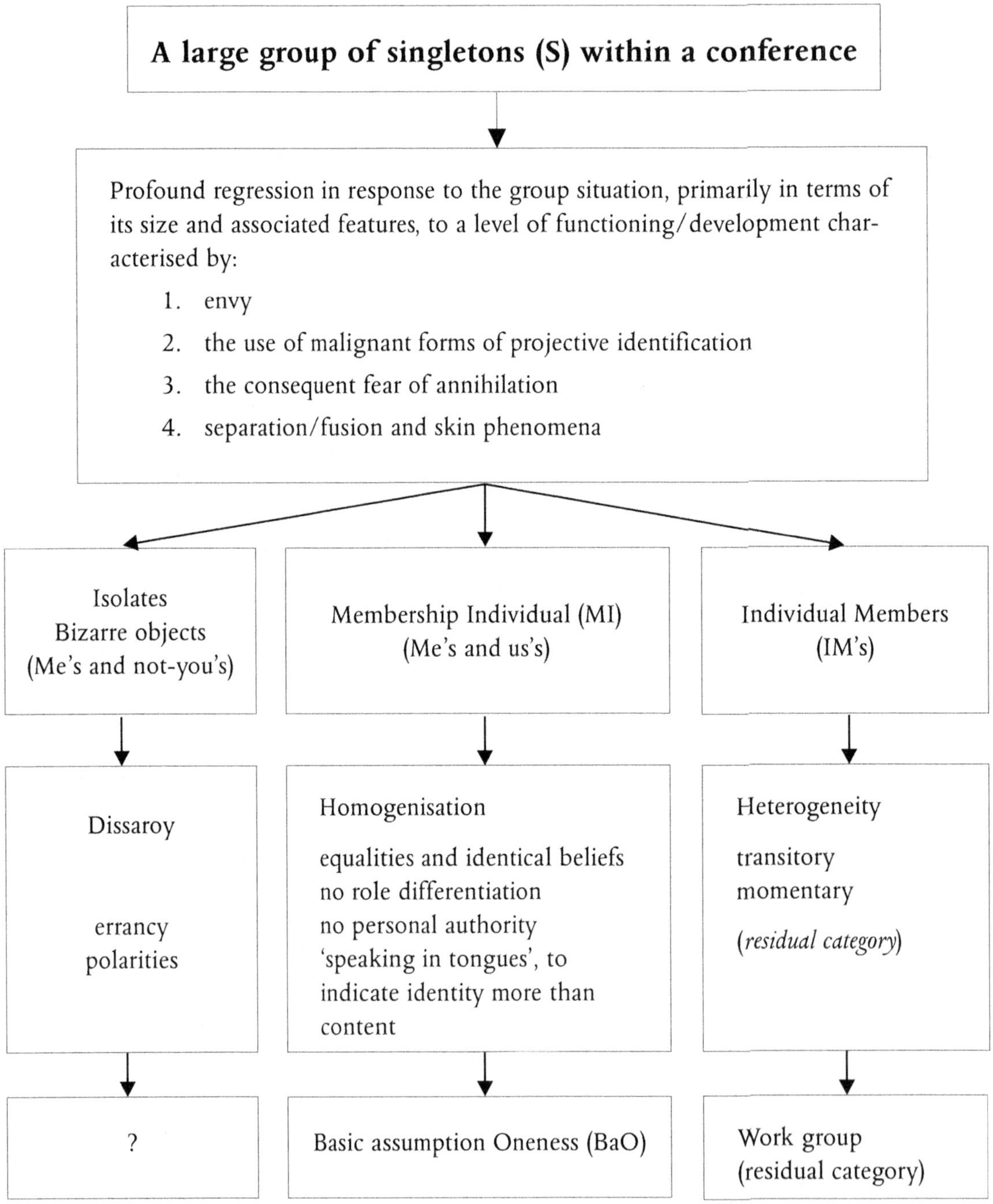

Figure 1.2 An explication of my version of Turquet's theory of Basic assumption Oneness or (BaO)

(d) My version of Turquet's theory is explicated in Figure 1.2.

(e) Having suggested that homogenisation is typical of charismatic movements in which people wish to be at-one with God, Turquet said that a leader of the basic assumption of Oneness is likely to be 'charismatic'. The charismatic leadership of Oneness groups differs from Bion's depiction of a god of Dependency groups or a Christ of Pairing groups, and certainly from a general of Fight/Flight groups.[4]

5. Turquet's brilliant and deceptively simple theory of Oneness is not without difficulties. Consistent with my reservations about the theory of basic assumptions in general, I would stress that:

(a) Although it is understandable that Turquet argued that Oneness is both ubiquitous and inevitable, because he accepted that envy, derived from the death instinct, is both ubiquitous and inevitable, the actual data from the study of large groups suggests that Oneness is not both ubiquitous and inevitable. In fact, envy, dissaroy, homogenisation and Oneness in large groups in training conferences, which were the only source of Turquet's observations, are based on failed Dependency, often in connection with inappropriate and plunging interpretations (Foulkes 1968) and confusion in the management and administration of such events that have insulted the integrity of the group. Moreover, in training conferences participation in large groups tends to be experienced by people who are used to small groups, as an attack upon them by the staff who have required them to participate in such unpleasant situations, rather than as a developmental challenge that might be related, for example, to a shift from the family to the school, or to the integration of multiple facets of the internal world. However, what may often be true of large groups in training conferences is not true of large groups in other settings (Brown 2002).

(b) Although Turquet mentioned that members of large groups introject both projected anxieties and defences against them, like Bion he took projective processes to be primary. He concentrated almost entirely on the ways in which persons who are extremely regressed and frightened about their loss of identity project these emotions into others, who are similarly frightened, and who become ever more frightened and who, in turn, project their fears into those around them. Thus, for Turquet, as for Klein and Bion, the fear of annihilation is based on the fear of retaliation from objects into whom envious impulses to annihilate have been projected. In other words, for Turquet the state of dissaroy is created from projections. He neglects the effects of the situation on the feelings and fantasies of those who are participants in it. In fact, 'dissaroy' and 'Oneness' imply an aetiology: 'dissaroy', that the paternal order has ceased to be recognised and that rebellion has occurred; and 'Oneness', that false reparation with the mind and body of the mother has occurred. Therefore, although the theory of oneness is addressed to pre-Oedipal mass psychology, the polarity of dissaroy/Oneness actually suggests that the Oedipal father has failed and the people have been caught up in the illusionary embrace of the pre-Oedipal mother. However, the dynamics of the fourth basic assumption may be traced to failures of pre-Oedipal maternal dependencies just as much as the vicissitudes of struggle with the Oedipal father.

(c) Turquet implied that aggression was non-existent within the context of Oneness, because Oneness is based on homogenisation as a defence against the dissaroy that follows rampant envy. However, Oneness is never perfect, and any threat to it precipitates aggression towards the people and sub-groups who are seen to be associated with the threat. This is not so much a matter of envy as it is of attacks on perceived obstacles to merger. In other words, helplessness and frustration lead to aggressive feelings, which may or may not be expressed in aggression (Hopper 1965).

(d) Although Turquet suggested that the leaders of Oneness groups were likely to be 'charismatic', he did not develop this idea, or examine the notion of charismatic leadership.

It must be acknowledged that as hard as they have tried, students of the theory of basic assumptions have been unable to integrate Turquet's theory of Oneness as a fourth basic assumption specifically with Bion's theory of three basic assumptions in general.[5] The main problem is that Turquet argues that innate malign envy leads to the fear of annihilation and, therefore, to the basic assumption of Oneness. However, if envy leads to Fight/Flight and Dependency, how can it also lead to Oneness? Can envy be used to explain all basic assumptions? Clearly, the answer is no. Either Turquet's theory of Oneness contradicts Bion's theory of basic assumptions or it is inconsistent with it.

The way out of this conundrum lies in a reconsideration of Bion's cryptic aside about the anxieties inherent in the trauma of birth: actually, the hypothesis that birth is always traumatic is both more parsimonious and more consistent with empirical data than the hypothesis that life begins with the experience of envy as a consequence of the death instinct. It is necessary to give more importance to the role of traumatic experience as a consequence of failed dependency in the aetiology of psychotic anxieties, and to the development of basic assumptions as a defence against them.

6. Otto Kernberg is one of the few psychoanalysts who has taken a serious and deep interest in group dynamics, primarily in complex organisations, particularly hospitals and institutes of psychoanalysis. In a series of papers (a collection of which were published in 1998 as *Ideology, Conflict, and Leadership in Groups and Organizations*) he introduced the theory of basic assumptions to psychoanalysts, whose understanding of group dynamics was based almost entirely on Freud's *Totem and Taboo* (1913) and *Group Psychology and the Analysis of the Ego* (1921). He also clarified Bion's argument and made slight but significant modifications to it. With a degree of editorial licence, I will summarise Kernberg's contribution to our understanding of what he would call the dynamics of 'mass psychology', which in essence develops as a defence against disintegration and the sources of it:

    (a) Drawing from the work of Klein (1946), as well as Fairbairn (1954), Erikson (1956), Jacobson (1964) and Mahler and Furer (1968), and his own version of object relations theory, Kernberg stresses that basic assumption processes originate in pre-Oedipal anxieties and defences in the context of early object relations. Pointing out that the focus of Freud's theory was really the horde and the mob rather than the group as such (but not considering the implications of this for his own subsequent hypotheses), and citing the contributions of Mitscherlich (1963), Anzieu (1981), Moscovici (1981) and

Chasseguet-Smirgel (1975) from within psychoanalysis, and those of Ortega y Gasset (1929), Canetti (1960) and Lasch (1978) from related disciplines, he (Kernberg 1998) argues that small and large groups promote regression because they lack an operational leadership and clearly defined tasks to relate them to their environment. The propensity to regress determines the threat to personal identity and the fear that primitive aggression will be activated, which motivates defensive operations that are typical of groups. It is implied that 'dissaroy' is primary and homogenisation secondary, and that homogenisation is based on the sexualisation of aggression associated with dissaroy. In other words, the dynamics of the desire to merge with the maternal object must be considered in their own right, and not only or even primarily in terms of the inability to negotiate the Oedipal challenge.

(b) Drawing on Redl's (1942) notion of 'role suction', Kernberg develops Bion's hypothesis that particular people will have a valence for the leadership of particular basic assumption groups, and Turquet's brief remarks about charismatic leaders. He argues that a spectrum of different types of *symbolic leadership* (my italics: that is, of basic assumption processes) reflects the degree of regression in the group. For example, the Dependency group tends to promote infantile narcissistic (and even psychopathic) leaders; the Fight/Flight group, a leader with paranoid characteristics; and the Pairing group, a leader who has a surfeit of hysterical features. Most importantly, Kernberg argues that the projections of pseudo-paternal ego-ideals into the leader of a Oneness group protect the group against archaic aggression towards the 'mother' of, and in, the Oneness group.

(c) With respect to the leadership of the work group, Kernberg (1994b) observes that, with certain exceptions, for example, Levinson (1968), Rangell (1974), Chasseguet-Smirgel (1985), Zaleznik (1979), Anzieu (1981) and himself (Kernberg 1991), psychoanalysts and students of group dynamics in general have neglected to study leaders and leadership of the work group as a pro-active process. He goes on to argue:

> ...The mature superego (is) derived from the post-Oedipal parental couple ...(involving) the rational, protective, moral functions of the parents, (which is the basis for) the symbolic meaning of the rational leadership of functional organisations ... (Rational leadership) is characterised by (1) high intelligence; (2) personal honesty and noncorruptibility by the political process; (3) capacity for establishing and maintaining object relations in depth; (4) a healthy narcissism; and (5) a healthy, justifiable anticipatory paranoid attitude in contrast to naiveté. The last two characteristics, namely, a certain amount of narcissism and paranoia, are perhaps the most surprising and yet the most important aspects of task leadership, already pointed to in Freud's 1921 essay. A healthy narcissism protects the leader from overdependency on approval from others, and provides strength to his capacity for autonomous functioning. A healthy paranoid attitude alerts the leader to the dangers of corruption and paranoiagenic regression – the acting out of diffuse aggression unconsciously activated in all organisational processes. He is also thereby protected from a naiveté that would prevent him from analysing the motivational aspects of institutional conflicts' (pp.65–66).

(d) Kernberg's contribution to the psychoanalytical study of group dynamics can be summarised as follows: (i) he develops Bion's ideas about 'leadership' based on valence by introducing Redl's implicit notion of role suction, and by analysing the attraction of people with specific kinds of psychopathology to the leadership of specific basic assumption processes in terms of the projection of super-ego constituents; (ii) he outlines some of the features of a rational leader of the work group, emphasising that a leader can influence the structures, functions and culture of his work group and wider organisation; (iii) he emphasises that what Turquet called 'dissaroy' is primary, and 'oneness' secondary, and based on sexualised fusion as a defence against aggression; and (iv) he delineates the 'narcissistic-dependent' features of what Turquet called the 'charismatic' leader of the oneness group.

This contribution is, however, not without flaws. For example, I have argued that pairing is a manic defence against depressive anxieties, in much the same way that hysteria is primarily pre-Oedipal in its origins. After all, it is not only the fourth basic assumption of mass psychology that is a matter for the Sphinx rather than for Oedipus. Like Bion and Turquet, Kernberg does not take sufficient care about generalising from the unconscious dynamics of groups, whether small or large, to those of more complex social organisations, especially societies. Nor is he clear about the aetiology of aggression: although he does not assume the existence of a death instinct, and does not explain all aggression in terms of envy, he continues to focus on projective processes, and neglects introjective ones. Kernberg also neglects the traumatogenic process: although he is aware of the real constraints of social facts on unconscious life, his brief reference to the absence of the good father in the context of post-war German society is the exception that proves the rule. In other words, like Bion and Turquet, Kernberg does not address the problem of failed dependency. For example, what happens to sexualised aggression when dependency fails, when a leader is deposed, when projections into the social context must be taken back, etc? Also, Redl (1942) argued that whereas the 'work group' has leaders, 'basic assumption groups' have 'central persons', and thus, a so-called 'leader' of a basic assumption group is really a kind of follower who is vulnerable to role-suction, especially in the case of the charismatic 'leader' of a Oneness group.[6] For groups who meet for the purpose of psychotherapy, these are vital observations. The group analyst must struggle to be the leader of the work group, while the other members of the group are free to be the central persons of basic assumption processes, although it is hoped that ultimately the members of the group will all become leaders of work group processes (Foulkes and Anthony 1964).

7. Lawrence (1993) and Lawrence, Bain and Gould (1996) are organisational and group relations consultants who have applied psychoanalytical ideas to the study of organisations. Following my preliminary formulation of a fourth basic assumption (Hopper 1989a, b) they proposed a fifth basic assumption of 'Me-ness', the opposite of what Turquet called 'Oneness'. In the same way that Isolates are defined as 'Me's, Not-you's', Me-ness is defined as 'Not-oneness'. This putative basic assumption of Me-ness is said to function as a defence against the anxieties associated with being a Membership Individual in a Oneness group, such as the fear of contamination. The basis for Me-ness is a developmental moment in the early life of persons.[7] The authors cite Winnicott's statement:

> The idea of a limiting membrane appears, and from this follows the idea of an inside and an outside. Then there develops the theme of a ME and a not-ME. There are now contents that develop partly on instinctual experience. (Winnicott 1980, p.68)

Curiously, it is also suggested that schizoid anxieties and defences (I suspect in the sense that Guntrip would describe them) are the basis of Me-ness which, in turn, is manifest in various forms of alienation, withdrawal and pathological narcissism.

It is indeed important that Oneness and Me-ness should be considered together. However, the argument advanced by Lawrence, Bain and Gould has certain inconsistencies. For example, whereas it is argued that Me-ness is not only a defence against the 'we-ness' of homogenisation, but also an expression of aggression against the whole, and involves attacks on linking, based on unbridled envy, such phenomena are also said to be 'socially induced', and to be typical of life in modern societies. These authors ignore the fact that Bion's theory of basic assumptions in general and Turquet's theory of Oneness in particular are predicated on the assumption that innate malign envy is an expression of the death instinct. They adopt the fundamental Kleinian tenet that fusion is a defence against envy, and that 'me, not-you' is motivated by an envious retreat from fusion. This is very different from the assumptions in a Winnicottian theory of human development that emphasises that in the beginning the infant is in a state of 'unintegration' within the context of a relationship with a mother that is characterised by a 'harmonious mix-up', and that 'disintegration' is a product of traumatic experience. Thus, although the authors nod in the direction of Winnicott, they think within the tradition of Klein, Bion and Turquet. It is curious, therefore, that 'me-ness' is not conceptualised as a characteristic of the singleton, who is associated with dissaroy, of which me-ness is the central feature. In other words, these authors have described defensive shifts from Oneness to what Turquet might have termed 'secondary dissaroy'.[8]

It follows that in the same way that Turquet was unable quite to conceptualise a fourth basic assumption, Lawrence, Bain and Gould have not quite conceptualised a fifth, primarily because they have not attempted to relate basic assumptions to basic psychotic anxieties within a context of a specific model of development. Actually, 'social induction' may be a kind of euphemism for traumatic experience and the traumatogenic process, which could not be described as such, because it is so difficult to develop a psychoanalytical theory of trauma, especially within the Klein/Bion tradition of psychoanalytical thought. In other words, although these authors refer to a process of 'social induction', they do not give this process much importance in the aetiology of psychic life, perhaps because unless the Klein/Bion/Turquet model is modified, it is impossible to integrate an emphasis on projective processes with an emphasis on social induction.

In sum, the psychoanalytical theory proposed by Bion and Turquet and developed by Kernberg and by Lawrence, Bain and Gould is especially illuminating. Although it does not provide a complete explanation of the phenomenon of incohesion in groups, it has drawn attention to various factors that have been neglected in other disciplines. Nonetheless, the main problem with this particular theory is that aggression is explained in terms of envy and, by implication, the so-called death instinct and, therefore, that threats to identity are explained in terms of the fear of retaliation from objects that have been invested with projected envy and aggressive impulses. From this perspective it is impossible to postulate more than three basic assumptions. Furthermore, the 'leadership' of basic assumption processes is not distinguished from the leadership of the work group, which curtails the application of this theory to clinical work and to consultations with organisations. Although these contradictions are insurmountable, certain modifications to the underlying metapsychology leads to my alternative theory of a fourth basic assumption, which negates the need to conceptualise a fifth.

Notes

1 It is noteworthy that 'On Introjection' was the title of Foulkes' (1937) first publication in English.

2 Instead, Bion stopped theorising group processes, and began to focus on the relationship between the body and the mind. Although he began to consider the nature of 'normal' projective identification, he also began to grant less and less importance to the external world. Could this development in Bion's thinking have been foretold in his not having cited the influence of Fairbairn on his initial formulation of the theory of basic assumptions? For example, a basic assumption process is similar to what I think Fairbairn (e.g. 1952) regarded as an 'interpersonal defence' against anxieties. Although his ideas were not very well worked out, and expressed cryptically, the notion of the 'inter-personal defence' was a milestone in the development of the psychoanalytical model of the mind, clinical technique, and the application of both to our understanding of groups. I suspect that Bion was influenced by discussions with Fairbairn when they met in Edinburgh during World War II, a view held by Sutherland (1985), who wrote: 'Fairbairn and Bion met on several occasions in Edinburgh, though in the circumstances of war with little chance of much sharing of work … In retrospect, the contributions of each can be seen … as needing (those) of the other, and … (the) tough theoretical work … (of each as) drawing … inspiration from the intuitive genius of Melanie Klein' (p.84).

I have often wondered why although Bion cited the influence on his ideas of Klein and Rickman, he did not cite the influence of Fairbairn.

3 These articles are very difficult to understand, partly because: Turquet coined various neologisms rather than use the concepts of sociology and social psychology; many of his concepts were 'residual categories', named but not elaborated; and the exposition of the argument needed a monograph, not merely a couple of articles which were hardly more than notes for lectures.

4 This hypothesis about Oneness and the charismatic leader seems to have been taken from Weber's (1947) discussion of charisma.

5 For example, having referred to the work of Bion, Turquet and myself (1977), Scharff and Scharff (1987) used their own notion of 'fission-fusion' in order to describe the fourth basic assumption. However, they have not addressed the problems that underpin Bion's and Turquet's theory. This compromise is typical of neo-Kleinian theory building in the United States, where clinical theory is more important than meta-theory.

It is sometimes said that Turquet remained uncertain whether Oneness really was a fourth basic assumption or was a part of Dependency or even a part of Pairing. Whereas in his (Turquet 1974) first paper he says that he '… would add a fourth basic assumption, … and call it oneness' (p.107), in his (Turquet 1975) second paper he does not even mention basic assumption theory, and he barely mentions Bion. It is possible that within the Kleinian school of the day, no one was allowed to improve upon the perfection of Bion. Yet I have often wondered why Turquet did not try to integrate his theory of Oneness with Bion's theory of basic assumptions in a more systematic way. Perhaps the answer lies in the same considerations that led Bion away from the questions about failed dependency and the importance of birth trauma, which are hardly 'Kleinian' questions.

Actually, Turquet's work should be read along with an important paper by Joffe (1969) on the nature of envy that was presented to The British Psychoanalytical Society a few months before Turquet presented the first version of his second article. The heated discussions of Joffe's hypothesis that envy should be seen as a function of helplessness and social relationships were reminiscent of the 'controversial discussions' in the British Society about Kleinian modifications to Freudian ideas (King and Steiner 1991). These issues have continued to preoccupy the scientific life of the Society. For example, in a discussion of a paper by Spillius (1992) 'Two ways of experiencing envy', I (Hopper 1992) commented that for Kleinians envy was still not seen as a feature of the relationship between analysand and analyst within a social context, but as an inevitable product of the so-called death instinct; and that (as I will argue in the next chapter) if in contrast envy were seen as an emergent defence against helplessness, and if helplessness were seen as a variable product of a particular transference-countertransference relationship, then it could be understood how envy could be iatrogenic (Limentani 1969). It could also be seen that in general envy was a variable, the aetiology of which could be traced to social facts rather than biological ones. Obviously, this observation applies to group phenomena as well as to the transference in full psychoanalysis.

Perhaps Turquet's attempt to distance himself from Bion may also have been influenced by another factor. His two papers are virtually identical to the little known and unpublished 'Uniformity and diversity in groups' by John Rickman (1938), edited by Pearl King from two public lectures that Rickman gave in a series sponsored by The British Psychoanalytical Society. In this paper, Rickman analyses the 'optimal cohesion' of societies and villages, using examples from Russia, Britain and the United States, in terms of 'heterogeneity', 'diversity' and 'unity', in contrast to 'homogeneity', 'uniformity' and 'fragmentation'. He gives special emphasis to the distinction between 'leaders', 'heroes' and what I would call 'anti-heroes', and suggests that 'helplessness' and 'frustrated desire and ambition' warrant at least as much attention as jealousy and envy. Pearl King (1997) and other colleagues believe that while at the Tavi, Rickman gave Turquet a copy of his paper, which contains the kernel of a non-Kleinian view of group process. Is it possible that Turquet felt that to have acknowledged Rickman would have been disloyal to Bion, and that the solution to this dilemma was not to acknowledge the influence of either? After all, although Rickman was analysed by Melanie Klein, and was Bion's first analyst, he was actually one of the fathers of the Group of Independent Psychoanalysts.

Similarly, in the first versions of his two articles, Turquet referred to 'personification' and 'polarities'. However, several years previously, Foulkes and Anthony (1964) discussed 'personification', and 'polarisation' as characteristics of both the normative and the interactive aspects of a group. Was it necessary for Turquet to ignore the work of Foulkes as well as that of Rickman? Was Turquet constrained by schismatic processes within The British Psychoanalytical Society? Might these tendencies reflect the unconscious constraints of the fourth basic assumption in the unconscious life of a traumatised Society?

6 Of course, Bion may not have been aware of Redl's work. However, it is judicious to cite here Scheidlinger's (1980) comments that Kernberg's discussion of the leadership of regressed groups should have taken account of additional work that was available to him, for example: Scheidlinger's (1952) own analysis of mature and immature leaders; Freud's (1931) delineation of libidinal types and their tendency to assume leadership roles; Bychowski's (1948) study of dictators; Alexander's (1942) and Erikson's (1948) analysis of mature and immature leaders; and Kohut and Wolf's (1978) discussion of the 'narcissistic group self'. I will cite this work in Chapter 3.

7 I would suggest that Oedipus is still alive and well, as can be seen in the fact that 'not me-ness' can be understood in terms of 'not my-ness', or as Coriolanus put it: 'One man's meat is another's poison'. It is always difficult to know just where to put the emphasis, i.e. on Oedipal or pre-Oedipal dynamics. After all, the Oedipus complex has a natural history, and both 'me-ness' and 'not me-ness' can be understood in terms of the oral Oedipus complex.

8 In the context of their argument, 'me-ness' refers to what Bion (1958) called 'secondary splitting', which I (Hopper 1991, 1994; excerpts of which are included as Appendix II of this book) have called 'secondary fission and fragmentation'. As I have written: 'As a consequence of processes of secondary envy and internal projections, the fusional and confusional introjected object is likely to be perceived as dangerous. As a defence against the anxieties associated with fusion and confusion with an object that is perceived to be dangerous, there is likely to occur a regressive shift back towards processes of fission and fragmentation' (1991, p.610).

CHAPTER 2

The Fear of Annihilation and Traumatic Experience

My theory of incohesion of groups and group-like social systems is formulated in terms of a fourth basic assumption, the component processes of which are personified by central persons whose identities can be described in terms of characterological protections against the fear of annihilation. Incohesion is a manifestation within the 'external' world of the fear of annihilation which, in turn, is a product of traumatic experience within the context of traumatogenic processes, and vice versa. Thus, incohesion is based on the continuing interaction of inter-personal and intra-personal processes within a wider and trans-generational social context.

In this chapter I will outline the aetiology of the fear of annihilation and its vicissitudes within the context of the traumatogenic process. In the next chapter I will examine the relationship between the fear of annihilation and the incohesion of groups and group-like social systems.

1. I have defined and discussed the fear of annihilation in my work on encapsulation (Hopper 1991, 1994, excerpts of which are included as Appendix II of this book). In essence, the fear of annihilation is experienced as the fear of intrapsychic fission and fragmentation, or of disintegration and dissolution. The first response to the anxieties associated with fission and fragmentation is introjective fusion and confusion with the lost, abandoning and damaging object. However, fusion and confusion are also associated with typical psychotic anxieties, for example: fear of suffocation, swallowing and being swallowed, being crushed, being entrapped, becoming a puppet, and

becoming petrified. In order to protect against the anxieties associated with fusion and confusion, a retreat occurs to the state of fission and fragmentation. The relationship between fission and fragmentation, and fusion and confusion, and then, in a secondary way, between fusion and confusion and fission and fragmentation, and back again to fusion and confusion is, therefore, one of pendulum like, non-dialectical oscillation, involving incessant psychic activity but no change and no development.[1]

The fear of annihilation is closely connected with the fear of separation, because separation from an object with whom one has fused is likely to be felt as losing a part of one's self. Also, one is likely to have fused with an object who has been lost prematurely and/or precipitously, especially at the phase of unintegration, when it is difficult, if not impossible, to hold in mind representations of the object. In effect, the loss of the breast is experienced as the loss of the mouth.

2. The fear of annihilation is a response to the experience of profound helplessness arising from loss, abandonment and damage within the context of the traumatogenic process which spans generations and involves the relationships between victims, perpetrators and bystanders, and patterns of responses to the traumatised:[2]

    (a) The experience of helplessness in response to loss, abandonment and damage may be understood in terms of: the Chinese water torture *strains* of daily life, the *cumulative* build up of small incidents into an overpowering wave of oppression, and/or the *catastrophic* violation of the safety shield. In fact, trauma has been classified as primarily either strain, cumulative or catastrophic. Trauma is always a matter of failed dependency on other people and situations for containment, holding and nurturing in both personal and social domains. A specific instance of failed dependency is the experience of losing a leader, at one extreme through his death or disability and, at the other, through his failure or incompetence. The loss of a leader is likely to be followed by panic, the degree of which depending on the ensuing threats to safety and the ability to realise various kinds of interests and goals (McDougal 1920).[3]

(b) Traumatic experience is ubiquitous. It is virtually impossible to imagine a life which has been protected from all traumatic experience from conception to death. In any case, we have all been born. However, traumatic experience is a matter of degree. Helplessness is determined by both the magnitude of the strain and/or catastrophe, and the maturity of the ego (which is only partly a function of chronological age). Although logically a trauma must be defined in terms of both the wounding agent and the susceptibility of a person to the wound (Brenner 1985), this is really more an axiom of psychoanalysis than an argument of substance. Perhaps it would be useful to distinguish (t)rauma from T(rauma), although in practice it is impossible to do so. It must be stressed that some events are so overwhelming that 'meaning' is likely to be a secondary and retrospective construction – interesting but virtually beside the point. (In clinical work, concentration on meaning may even offer defensive respite from listening to the details of a traumatic event.)

(c) It is nonetheless essential to understand why certain events are experienced as traumatic by some people but not by others, or at least as more or less traumatic. Clearly, it is necessary to consider a variety of mediating factors. One mediating factor is the content of a person's unconscious fantasy life at the time of the experience. The constraints of the unconscious Oedipus complex can hardly be ignored. The death of a friend in an automobile accident might be experienced in terms of an unconscious fantasy that the friend was a sibling; the sibling might be experienced in terms of unconscious aggressive wishes, and even the unconscious fantasy that the subject has murdered a sibling; moreover, the unconsciously hated and unconsciously murdered sibling might even have been killed in an automobile accident. Another mediating factor is the extent to which previous traumatic experience was encapsulated, so that subsequently the subject was unable to think about the experience, symbolise it and make it accessible to a fluidity of affects, which governs the extent to which subsequent trauma can be experienced in a more mature way. Many factors which influence the extent to which a particular experience is traumatic also influence the degree to which a person is likely to encapsulate the experience, for example: the amount of shame associated with the event; the relationship between the subject and the perpetrator of the traumatic experience; the ability and willingness of the perpetrator to acknowledge to the victims his culpability (Balint 1969); the ability and willingness of bystanders to acknowledge to the victims that what happened 'really happened' (Garland and Hopper 1980); attempts to prevent the isolation of the victim and to reintegrate the victim as quickly as possible into a caring community, and etc.

(d) A comprehensive classification of events that might be traumatic is impossible. However, events that have been traumatic can be seen in terms of whether they were primarily personal, random and idiosyncratic, or more patterned for large numbers of people. They may have been primarily social and political in nature or primarily natural or a mixture of both. For example, with respect to the coal slurry slide in Aberfan, although the Government could not have stopped the rains, the slurry did not have to be piled next to a primary school within a working class area of the village.[4]

(e) The predisposition both to experience events as traumatic and actually to seek traumatic experience, is known as traumatophilia (Abraham 1907). It involves both libidinal and aggressive wishes, including the desire for punishment as well as for revenge on others. It is based on the compulsion to repeat traumatic experience that has been encapsulated in the context of attempts to master the original experience, to bind up the continuing anxieties associated with it, and to expel, control and attack objects that are reminiscent of those that failed originally, as well as to communicate ineffable experience.[5]

3. The fear of annihilation can be located within a more general model of psycho-sexual development. In this connection I would like to propose a modification to the Klein/Bion theory that envy originates

in the so-called 'death instinct' and that fusion develops as a defence against envy:

(a) 'In the beginning' the primal emotion in psychic life is not innate, malign envy based on the death instinct, but 'grenvy' (Coltart 1989). This neologism is intended to convey a mixture of greed and possessive desire. (It is impossible to find an English word that connotes a mixture of greed and possessive desire that is not in essence malign and entirely instinctual, although such words do exist in German and especially in French and in other Romance languages.)

(b) I would suggest that on the basis of traumatic experience grenvy is split into greedy desire, on the one hand, and into malign envy, on the other. Malign envy is directed towards objects who are perceived as able but unwilling to help, and who are perceived as responsible for failed dependency, that is, failed containment, holding and nurturing. In other words, according to this perspective, malign envy is not innate, but develops as a defence against feelings of profound helplessness, which are a consequence of traumatic experience. Envy can be understood as a defensive response to the shame of narcissistic injury (Rutan and Stone 2000).

(c) Fusion arises as a defence against helplessness. Of course, fusion can also arise as a defence against envy, and helplessness can be a consequence of fusion, but these are secondary processes.[6] Furthermore, envy can itself be traumatic, because it leads to the destruction in fantasy of the bad object, but this too is a secondary process. My theory of envy and fusion is illustrated in Figure 2.1.

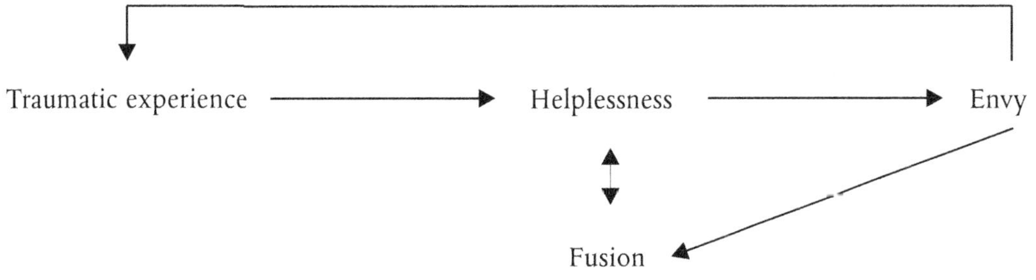

Figure 2.1 The Hopper Theory of Fusion

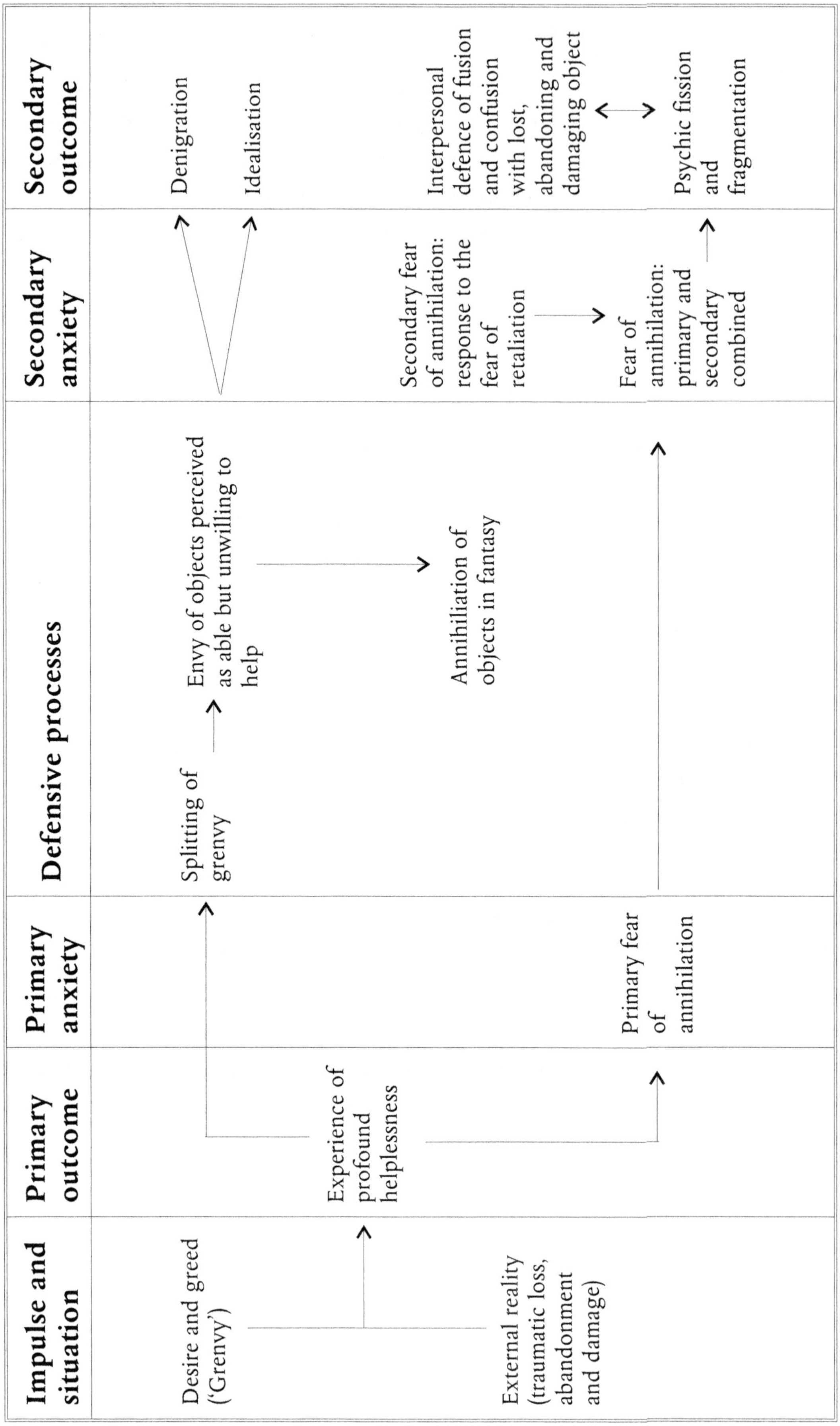

Figure 2.2 The Hopper theory of the fear of annihilation

(d) On the basis of the emergence of defensive, malign envy, paranoid/schizoid splitting leads to denigration and idealisation. Objects of failed dependency are then subjected to denigrating attacks, usually but not always, in fantasy. In turn, the denigrated objects of failed dependency are perceived to be retaliatory and, thus, a secondary fear of annihilation is likely to develop. (Sometimes, on the basis of projective and introjective identification, they actually do retaliate.)

(e) My theory of the fear of annihilation within the context of the traumatogenic process is summarised in Figure 2.2.

4. The traumatogenic process does not culminate in the fear of annihilation but in various forms of either pathological defences against it or attempts to make creative use of it. The main defence against the fear of annihilation is encapsulation. Basically, in order for life to continue and psychic paralysis to be avoided, the entire intrapsychic experience of the fear of annihilation and of oscillation between fission and fragmentation, and fusion and confusion, is encysted or encapsulated, producing autistic islands of experience, characterised by all encompassing silence and grotesque internal developments of aggregated objects.

   Encapsulation is associated with two autistic forms of self-protection: 'crustacean' and 'amoeboid' (Tustin 1981). A crustacean type may actually refer to himself in terms of crustacean imagery, for example, as a lobster or a tortoise or covered by a shell; and an amoeboid type, as a jellyfish, feeling utterly vulnerable, and as someone whose skin functions merely to distinguish what is felt to be a 'self' from a 'not-self', or a 'me' from a 'not-me' (Winnicott 1980). Amoeboid people find protection in merger and accommodation based on fantasies of vacuole incorporation.

   This distinction is virtually identical to that of 'contact-shunning' and 'merger-hungry' disorders of the self (Kohut and Wolf 1978) although, with slightly different nuances, several psychoanalysts have made similar comparisons. For example, especially important is Bleger's (1966) differentiation of Type I Epileptoid character disorders in which people protect themselves through profound withdrawal, from Type II disorders in which they protect themselves through hallucinated merger. This is similar to and overlapping with Balint's (1968) distinction between the philobat who loves empty spaces and avoids people, and the ocnophile who clings to people. Kernberg's (1975) systematic outline of types of borderline and narcissistic disorders with special reference to malignant narcissism can also be compared with these types of characterological defences. So, too, can H. Rosenfeld's (1971) distinction between thick and thin skinned narcissists, and Steiner's (1990) types of pathological organisation.

Both crustacean and amoeboid characters tend to use projective and introjective identification of malignant kinds, involving the repetition compulsion and traumatophilia, in the service of expulsion, attack, control and communication of that which would otherwise be enacted. After all, people who have had a history of traumatic experience are likely to have no other way in which to communicate. They are, therefore, exceedingly vulnerable to role suction. However, they also tend to create those roles which, if enacted, offer a sense of containment and holding, in that they bestow an identity within a field of turmoil and chaos.

Processes of role creation and role suction are connected with another fundamental defence or protection against the fear of annihilation, i.e. disassociation (Klein and Schermer 2000). Multiple personality disorders are based on disassociation, and maintained through encapsulation. It is as though various 'personalities' have developed from the initial fission and fragmentation of the self in response to traumatic experience (Hopper 1991, 1994, excerpts of which are included as Appendix II). It is possible that a crustacean personality oscillates with an amoeboid personality within the psychic life of the traumatised, although other, additional personalities may also develop in order both to protect the core of the self against the pain of trauma and to express and communicate the particular traumatic experience.

5. The fear of annihilation and various forms of protection against it are magnified by the inability to mourn adequately and authentically, and vice versa (Klein 1935, 1940). This is partly a function of the re-awakening of the anxieties associated with the depressive position and, therefore, of the regressive shift to anxieties associated with the paranoid-schizoid position. It is also a function of the use of manic defences against the pain of mourning, such as the triumphant

disparagement, repudiation and renunciation of the lost object, idealisation, various forms of externalisation, fantasies of omnipotence, omniscience and grandiosity, the denial of psychic reality, and compulsive attempts to control and to master both the object and the situation. Of course, it must be acknowledged that very often the circumstances of traumatic experience prevent adequate and authentic mourning.

The inability to mourn adequately and authentically is often both expressed and disguised, both individually and collectively, through various forms of pseudo-reparative mourning:

(a) Triumphant mourning, marked by the denial of grief and the commemoration of 'chosen trauma' (Volkan 1991). For example, on the occasion of ritualised Memorial Day celebrations, mourning is confined to one or two minutes of official silence.

(b) Sentimental and masochistic mourning, marked by compulsive and ritualised wailing and displays of grief. For example, the bereaved may adopt the garb of mourning and use reassuring clichés and aphorisms such as: 'Every cloud has a silver lining', 'Light follows darkness', and 'Spring follows winter'. (It is notable that the title of Khan's (1988) deathbed book was *When Spring Comes*, and that its publication led to his being expelled from The British Psychoanalytical Society for expressing his anti-Semitism, bringing the Society into disrepute.)

(c) Revengeful and sadistic mourning, marked by bitterness, blame and a refusal to forgive. For example, the Book of Lamentations is not only a story of failed redemption and the loss of the divine basis of justice, but also a long complaint, recounting horror and terror.

    Revengeful and sadistic mourning is closely associated with the experience of fission and fragmentation, and sentimental and masochistic mourning, with fusion and confusion, the two polar forms of the fear of annihilation. In fact, both individually and collectively, these two forms of defensive and inauthentic mourning may alternate with one another, in much the same way that in sado-masochistic disorders, sadism

> alternates with masochism. Moreover, each of these two forms of mourning have two forms: one is associated with the pole of fission and fragmentation; and the other, with fusion and confusion. For example, in connection with revengeful and sadistic mourning, the poetic structure of the Book of Lamentations reflects the relationship between the individual and the group when they have each been traumatised; the complaint shifts back and forth between the group tragedy and the personal tragedy, because at one moment the individual is merged with the group, and at the next he is isolated from it. Similarly, in connection with sentimental and masochistic mourning, the displays of grief can be affiliative and even contagious, but at the same time they can alienate the mourners from those who might offer help and support. This can be seen in the proverbial 'Aunt Sally' who keeps a special dress in the closet for funerals at which she continues to mourn the untimely death of her own young lover.

All loss must be mourned. Not only the dead. Not only the perfect breast. Not only the good enough mother. The loss of self-esteem, of certainty, of group charisma, of physical power, of the rights and privileges associated with a particular phase of life...must all be acknowledged. Only then is it possible to form a more or less realistic appreciation of what has been lost, and to integrate into the core of the self the psychic representations of their most desirable aspects. In this sense all growth and development involve the mastery of depressive anxieties associated with the metabolism of prior identifications. In other words, the ego is not so much a reservoir of 'the precipitates of abandoned object cathexes' (Freud 1923) as it is a compost heap to be used for the continuing nourishment and enrichment of the garden.

When adequately and authentically mourned, a death gives rise to a new and more stable identity for the living, associated with an increased sense of personal autonomy, tinged with slight sadness, which facilitates the development of a hopeful attitude, the capacity for trust and optimism, and a new or renewed commitment to law and order (Mitscherlich and Mitscherlich 1975). These qualities of personal and collective life lead to more satisfactory social adjustment – by which I do not mean submission and acquiescence – to the prevailing social, cultural and political conditions, allowing for attempts to change those conditions that are felt to be unacceptable, or in other words, to good citizenship (Hopper 1996b, 2000).

6. The importance of mourning can be seen in the institutionalisation of arrangements for helping people with their experience of death (Homans 1989). In some societies there are even professional mourners, which indicates that the traditional family system has been disrupted and, in turn, the mourning process retarded, often through natural catastrophes, wars, and/or high rates of migration. Normative beliefs define the 'natural' span of life and, therefore, what constitutes a 'natural' death and even a 'good' death. It is recognised that although death is not always peaceful, it should be 'just' and 'honourable', which is what the ceremonies of a Memorial Day are supposed to celebrate.

7. The refusal and inability to mourn adequately and authentically are likely to be associated with the transgenerational perpetuation of traumatic experience, usually organised around the group's chosen trauma, and a cause of the general paranoiagenesis of traumatised social systems (Jaques 1955; Kernberg 1993), which contributes to continuing difficulties in mourning and, in turn, further traumatic experience. Within traumatised societies, people tend to repeat traumatic experience within their families, schools, military, political and religious institutions and organisations, and within their groups generally.

   Children are especially vulnerable to being used as the container puppets of their elders' need to seek revenge. Immigrants, refugees and survivors of social trauma are especially likely to recreate their previous traumatic experiences in their new societies, for example, in those organisations that are important to their personal and social identities, especially when they gain positions of authority and power. This can be seen in battles for leadership and control over scarce resources, which may continue long after the initial insults and conflicts first occurred.

In sum, I have proposed that the fear of annihilation is rooted in traumatic experience, and that envy arises as a defence against helplessness and the shame associated with it. The phenomenology of the fear of annihilation involves non-developmental oscillation between fission and fragmentation, in the first instance, and fusion and confusion, in the second. Each pole of the fear of annihilation is associated with its own distinctive anxieties, and the phenomenology of each pole functions as a defence against the anxieties associated with its opposite. The main, overall defences or protections against the fear of annihilation and its vicissitudes are encapsulation and disassociation, which characterise various kinds of addiction and perversion. The two main characterological protections associated with encapsulation are the crustacean, based on fission and fragmentation, and the amoeboid, based on fusion and confusion. The fear of annihilation and the defences against it are magnified by the inability to mourn adequately and authentically which, in turn, is associated with the perpetuation of the traumatogenic process across the generations.

Notes

1 Drawing implicitly on the work of many psychoanalysts, perhaps in particular *The Divided Self* (Laing 1960), a similar idea is expressed by Giddens (1991) when he writes: 'Diffuse anxieties about...risks might contribute...to feelings of powerlessness...Where an individual feels overwhelmed by a sense of powerlessness...we may speak of a process of engulfment. The individual feels dominated by approaching forces ...haunted by implacable forces robbing him of all autonomy or action...caught up in a maelstrom of events in which he swirls around in a helpless fashion. At the other end of the powerlessness/appropriation divide...(we may speak of a process of) omnipotence ...The individuals' sense of ontological security is achieved through a fantasy of dominance: the phenomenal world feels as if it is orchestrated by that person as a puppeteer. Since omnipotence is a defence it is brittle...under pressure, it can dissolve into its contrary, engulfment' (pp.193–4).

2 Modern attachment theorists have conceptualised the effects of traumatic experience in much the same way (Marrone 1998). In fact, in my previous attempts to describe the traumatogenic process I should have considered the work of Bowlby in greater depth. I have outlined the structure of the traumatogenic process with special reference to encapsulation and to addiction in Hopper 1991 and 1995a, and I will draw on this work in the present discussion of trauma and personifications of the fourth basic assumption.

3 Although Freud (1921) agrees with McDougal's hypothesis about the development of panic following the loss of a leader, he emphasised the importance of the unconscious Oedipus complex in determining the degree to which panic would ensue, that is, how traumatic the loss of the leader would be.

4 I (Hopper 1981) have discussed the social sources of trauma and failed dependency in terms of anomogenic, blocking, and comparative reference group factors, for example, stagflation, high unemployment, inconsistencies between structures of stratification and education, etc. Similarly, Gutmann (1989) has written about the decline of traditional defences against anxiety, focusing on the failure of science, religion and other institutions to provide the protection that people have sought from them.

5 This view of traumatophilia is very different from the one that is at the core of what I would call 'romantic psychoanalysis', for example, as described by Auden to the effect that the so-called traumatic experience is not an accident, but the opportunity for which

the child has been patiently waiting – had it not occurred, it would have found another, equally trivial – in order to find a necessity in direction for its existence, in order that its life may become a serious matter. Although I would acknowledge that it is hard – if not impossible – to know whether traumatophilia begins before or after the first traumatic experience has occurred, it is reasonable to assume that such a quest for self-destruction is based on previous traumatic experience. At any rate, this axiom is a cornerstone of my own perspective in the study of traumatic experience. However, in terms of the logic of apperception, traumatophilia may be based not only on the experience of birth, but also on the propensity to abort imperfect zygotes (Sonne 1994a, b).

6 It is important to recognise that 'fusion' and 'confusion' are used here to refer to the defensive response to the anxieties that follow a ruptured primary attachment and the safety shield, and not to a 'harmonious mix-up' of the infant with the mother (Balint 1968) or to a state of unintegration in which infant and mother are not yet perceived to be separate objects (Winnicott 1965).

CHAPTER 3

The Fourth Basic Assumption

Incohesion: Aggregation/Massification or (ba) I:A/M

Groups and group-like social systems are likely to evince basic assumption processes, not only those adumbrated by Bion, but also those of a fourth basic assumption as outlined in a preliminary and partial way by Turquet, Kernberg, Lawrence, Bain and Gould. This fourth basic assumption is a manifestation of the fear of annihilation and its vicissitudes, which are universal and ubiquitous, but especially intense and pronounced among those people who have been traumatised. Thus, although this fourth basic assumption is also universal and ubiquitous in groups and group-like social systems, it is especially intense and pronounced within groups and group-like social systems who have been traumatised or whose members (or at least a large number of them) have been traumatised. What are the general features of this fourth basic assumption, and what should it be called?

People who have experienced the fear of annihilation and its vicissitudes, including the encapsulation of intra-psychic oscillations between fission and fragmentation and fusion and confusion with their lost, abandoning and damaging objects, are likely to form groups that are characterised by general processes of incohesion. These processes of incohesion are likely to be characterised by 'aggregation', in response to fission and fragmentation and, then, by 'massification', in response to fusion and confusion and, in turn, by oscillations between massification and aggregation. In other words, primary and secondary aggregation and primary and secondary massification comprise the bi-polar forms of incohesion. Thus, I call this fourth basic assumption 'Incohesion: Aggregation/Massification' or (ba) 'I:A/M'. (It is a coincidence, fortunate or otherwise, that these initials spell 'I AM', which can be taken as an assertion of personal identity by people who feel that their personal identity is threatened within a traumatised social system.)

I will now develop these hypotheses, and delineate the main features of aggregation and massification as the bi-polar states of incohesion.

1. Aggregates and masses are the two most simple, primitive social formations. They are not merely collections of people, but nor are they groups. They are not merely crowds, but nor are they audiences.[1] An aggregate is characterised by a minimal degree of mutual attraction and involvement among three or more people who are neither interdependent nor in sympathy with one another on the basis of shared beliefs, norms and values. In contrast, a mass is characterised by a maximal degree of mutual attraction and involvement among three or more people who are neither interdependent nor in sympathy with one another but who share the illusion of solidarity with respect to beliefs, norms and values, usually for a brief period of time.

   Although the members of a mass may feel otherwise, a mass is no more a group than an aggregate is. Whereas an aggregate has too much individuality to be a group, a mass has too little. An aggregate and a mass are each social formations, and each has its own dynamics. An aggregate is highly incohesive. A mass seems to be very cohesive, but in reality it is as incohesive as an aggregate. In fact, a mass is like an aggregate masquerading as a group, like an aggregate in drag or a transsexual aggregate. A mass should not be confused with a mob or a horde. Although mobs and hordes are especially likely to evince massification processes, they have their own typical structures and dynamics.

   A mass is characterised by the common investment of ego-ideals into the same person, ideas and values (Freud 1921). By definition, this person becomes the leader, and his ideas and values become dominant. On this basis the leader is likely to be the 'archaic father'. However, more fundamentally the leader is likely to be the 'archaic mother' (Chasseguet-Smirgel 1985; Kernberg 1998). Also important in the process of massification are 'twinning' (Kohut and Wolf 1978) and 'imitative identification' (Gaddini 1992). Through these processes of identification people attempt to merge with a 'perfect' group, in which all flaws, impurities and variations in any of its properties are obliterated. Unconsciously, the fundamental goal is safety within the smooth, white womb of the group-mother (Chasseguet-Smirgel 1985;

Schindler 1966). The perfect group requires total submission to impersonal law and order. The members of the group regard themselves as absolutely equal in terms of being a member of the group. Hierarchies and differences with respect to other qualities and characteristics are defined as 'unimportant', or at least they are supported by the rules of distributive justice.[2]

A mass usually consists of a large number of people, perhaps ranging from sixteen to an unknown number. Sixteen is the number of pieces in a chess team and, thus, the number that Turquet (1973) suggested would differentiate the dynamics of a large group from those of a small group. However, as a criterion for the formation of a mass, density of population may be more important than size, because the more that people can spread out, the larger the number required for the development of a mass. In other words, in a small room only a 'few' people may be sufficient for a massification process to occur.[3]

Metaphors for an aggregate are a handful of gravel, a piece of granite, a set of billiard balls, or even a plate of deep-fried whitebait; in contrast, metaphors for a mass are a slab of basalt, a handful of warm wet sponges, a chunk of faeces, a nice piece of stuffed fish, or a lump of dough. Another metaphor for a mass is a highly condensed bundle of burning candles, such that they melt into one, becoming a mass of hot wax, which is an image that is conveyed by the etymology of the word 'fascist' (Reich 1933). Many metaphors of this sort are used in exhortations to battle, for example, the strength of a bundle of arrows as opposed to the single arrow, the linked shields of a phalanx as opposed to a loose collection of soldiers, etc. The words and ideas associated with 'free-market capitalism' and 'managed-market socialism' are also metaphors for aggregation and massification, respectively.[4]

Aggregates and masses have equivalents within the animal world, for example, various kinds of swarms, shoals, herds and hordes. These formations almost certainly have survival value, depending on the challenges presented. For example, a flock of flamingos evinces a social pattern that is analogous to a mass, as shown in Figure 3.1.

This flock may be contrasted with a herd of walruses which evinces a pattern that is analogous to a social mass, as shown in Figure 3.2.

Figure 3.1 A flock of flamingos

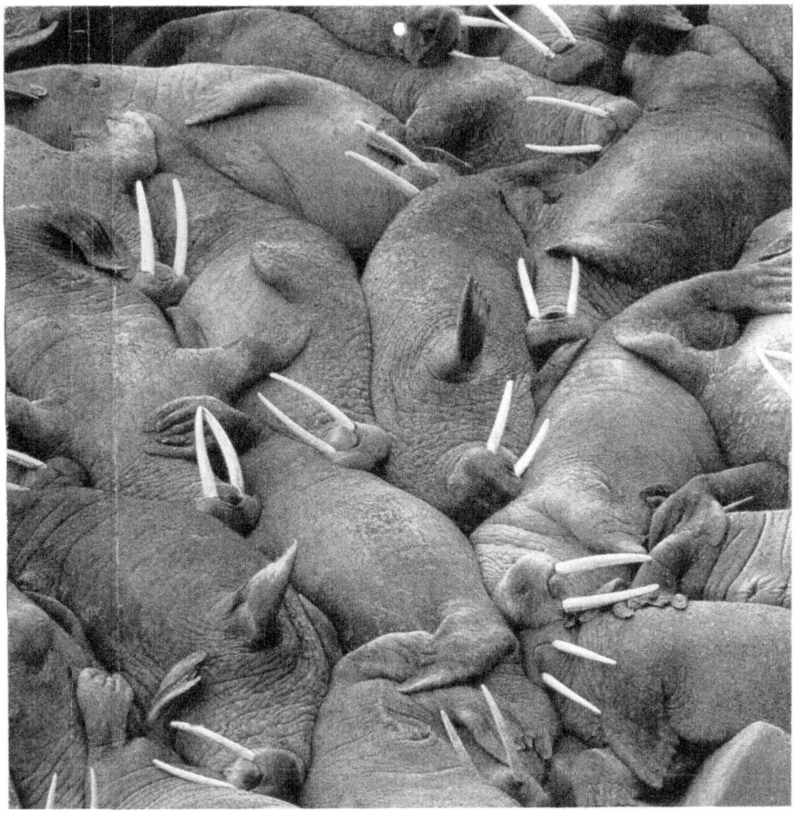

Figure 3.2 A herd of walruses

2. Aggregates and masses, like all social formations, are manifest in typical patterns of interaction, normation, and communication, as well as styles of thinking and feeling, and leadership and followership. In effect, aggregates and masses can be described as bi-polar syndromes of features of each of these dimensions of social formation. For example, with respect to interaction, the disintegration of an aggregate contrasts with the bureaucratisation or mechanisation of a mass; and with respect to normation, the insolidarity of an aggregate contrasts with the fanaticism, fundamentalism and idolatry of a mass. Both the disintegration of an aggregate and the bureaucratisation or mechanisation of a mass contrast with the integration of the well functioning work group; similarly, both the insolidarity of an aggregate and the fundamentalism and idolatry of a mass contrast with the solidarity of a well functioning work group.

I have listed many of these features in Table 3.1, using my own terminology and that of others who have sought to adumbrate the various dimensions of incohesion.

This Table may seem to be inaccessible, but actually it is very simple. The Table contains a great deal of information about the study of incohesion, and warrants careful study. The reader will be reminded of the extent and variety of attempts to understand incohesion in groups, and of how interesting, but partial, this work has been. Curiously, it is easier to understand my argument if this work has not been studied before, because the problems of 'one phenomenon: multiple concepts' and 'multiple phenomena: single concept' that beset this field of inquiry will not be so confusing. I will call attention to only three of the features listed in Table 3.1:

(a) With respect to normation, incohesion is manifest in patterns of 'insolidarity' or 'pseudo-solidarity'. In social systems characterised by aggregation, insolidarity is manifest in anomogenic processes. For example, aggregation generates ignorance and misunderstanding of norms, as well as inurement to them; and under extreme conditions, aggregation generates normlessness. When a group is characterised by ignorance and misunderstanding of the norms, inurement to the norms, and processes of normlessness, the levels of normative expectation tend to rise higher than the levels of achievement with respect to objects

Table 3.1 Some features of the fourth basic assumption of incohesion

Properties of social system / Basic assumption: Incohesion	Interaction (the basis for cohesion in a complex society) (5)	Normation (the basis for cohesion in a simple society) (5)	Communication: Incoherent (12)	Communication: Style of thinking and feeling
Incohesion: Aggregation (fragmentation) (1) (dissaroy) (2)	Excessive degree of role differentiation and specificity (5) Cross pressures (6) Polarities (2) Encapsulated sub-groups and countra-groups (7) Enclaves, ghettos and other enclosures (7) Isolation (6) Non-engagement	Forms of Anomie (6) Normlessness Ignorance Conflict Inurement Encapsulated Contra-cultures Sub-cultures (7) Normative taciturnity (6)	Bureaucratise Impersonal Excessive Abstraction Entirely verbal (numeral?) Euphemistic Battles over the choice of official language	Scientistic Encapsulated (7) Inhibited and secret Errancy (2) Either/and (13) Black humour and Sarcasm
Incohesion: Massification (oneness) (2) (3) (homogeneity) (2) (fusion) (4)	Imitation and Simulation Minimal degree of role differentiation (5) Excessively diffuse quality of interaction (5) Horde, mob, mass, crowd, etc. (8) Elements of homogeneity (2) or anonymisation (9) Scapegoating	Fundamentalism Total uniformity of beliefs (10) Enchantment (11) Elements of homogeneity (2) or anonymisation (9)	Cult speak Personal Argot and Jargon Non-verbal (music and rhythm) Speaking in tongues (2) Dominant and exclusive use of one official language	Magic and rites Group anniversaries, celebrations and rituals Inauthentic mourning Excessive display of pseudo-morale Affect contagion (14) Primary process using symbolic equations (15) No humour

(1) Springmann (1970, 1975)
(2) Turquet (1974, 1975)
(3) Bion (1961, 1967)
(4) Battegay *et al.* (1992); Bion (1961, 1967); Pines (1986); Turquet (1974, 1975)
(5) Hopper (1975)
(6) Hopper (1981)
(7) Hopper (1991)
(8) Battegay (1973)
(9) Main (1975)
(10) Rickman (1938)
(11) Agazarian and Carter (1993)
(12) Pines (1983, 1986); Steiner (1999)
(13) Britton (1994)
(14) Issroff (1979)
(15) Segal (1957)

that are valued as goals both compulsively and fetishistically. There is no shared basis for status hierarchies, and both rankings and differences become a source of invidious comparison. Power is not supported by authority, and administration becomes manipulative. Sub-grouping and contra-grouping become ubiquitous. People feel lonely and unsafe (Hopper 1981).

In contrast, in social systems characterised by massification, insolidarity is manifest in fundamentalism and uniformity of belief. Individuality and diversity are regarded as delinquent and rebellious. Cultural homogeneity is regarded as a collective achievement.

(b) With respect to communication, incohesion is manifest in patterns of incoherence. This is especially important for social systems that derive their cohesion primarily from communication, for example, in groups who meet for the purpose of psychotherapy. However, it is important to understand incoherence within the communication patterns of all social systems.[5]

In social systems characterised by aggregation, people tend to be 'isolates'. They wish to avoid the recognition of agency and responsibility and, therefore, tend to communicate in euphemism and bureaucratise, which eliminates the affect associated with words. In organisations this can be seen in the language of administrators and managers who may be frightened for their livelihoods and, in some instances, for their lives. In therapeutic groups the incoherence of aggregation is often associated with the language of 'either/and' (Britton 1994). It is also associated with profound silences which lack resonance, and convey a deep sense of isolation (Anzieu 1981).

In contrast, in social systems characterised by massification, people tend to be 'Membership Individuals' who define their identities by using cult-speak and by speaking in tongues. Words and catch-phrases have nuanced meaning only to the core-members of the group. Rumour abounds. Communication is laden with references to their common history, which must have been shared in order for statements to be fully understood. In organisations this can be seen in the way people use jargon in order to indicate their group identity, for example, in some institutes of psychoanalysis group identity is indicated by the use of 'split-off' rather than 'repressed'. Similarly, I have consulted to traumatised business firms whose managers are preoccupied with the latest buzz words from American management gurus. The Board of one large firm regarded 'community' to mean 'Christian'; thus, all the members of the Board, including a Moslem from Kuwait, wore gold crosses on their lapels. (My own bare lapel facilitated the shift from massification to work group functioning, but only after there occurred some very plain speaking, and the fears associated with traumatised aggregation were acknowledged.) In therapeutic groups the incoherence of massification is often associated with 'psychobabble'. However, such incoherence can also be associated with silence, but with that kind of silence in which the members feel that they are merged in such a way that mutual understanding does not require words, and the ambiguity of non-verbal communication is preferred. Such silences are not so much non-verbal as anti-verbal, that is, the non-verbal communication is used to attack and undermine verbal communication, which requires thought and shared rules of discourse.

(c) With respect to styles of thinking and feeling, incohesion is associated with an absence of a sense of humour and an appreciation of irony (which require the optimal cohesion of the work group, in which people can be both tolerant and amused). Aggregation is associated with black humour and sarcasm. The release of tension afforded by the mockery of pomposity and death is the glue of aggregated groups. For example, the gallows humour of concentration camps, as well as of the 'underground' in Nazi Germany (Hillenbrand 1995) was echoed by that of Prague after 1968, and by Moscow after Gorbachev. In therapeutic groups, aggregation is manifest in excessive abstraction and cold intellectualising, as well as in jokes made at the expense of other members of the group, as seen in sadistic teasing.

Massification, in contrast, kills humour, as it does art, which require a degree of psychological space and social distance between the subject and the object, and between the speaker and the listener. For example, it was very hard to hear laughter in the senior common room at the London School of Economics for a long while after the events of 1968–70. Similarly, it is rare to hear a joke in the informal gatherings associated with scientific meetings of our most august institutes of psychoanalysis, even when colleagues present papers about jokes. This is different from the early days of psychoanalysis when optimism and a sense of challenge prevailed, and Freud and his colleagues often shared jokes, especially so-called 'Jewish jokes'. In groups, massification is manifest in the expression of truisms with which all members of the group agree, and simple platitudes which pass as solutions to complex personal problems, as well as in jokes made at the expense of people who are outside the group, such as partners and large categories of people who are not represented in the group.

3. Aggressive feelings and aggression within aggregates and masses warrant special consideration. In the first instance it is important to stress several points:

   (a) Aggressive feelings and aggression may be unconscious.

   (b) Aggression depends both on the strength of the aggressive feelings, and on the normative controls over the expression of feelings in general and aggressive feelings in particular. However, the suppression of aggressive feelings is often associated with covert aggression (Hopper 1965).

   (c) The targets, functions and forms of aggressive feelings and aggression should be distinguished:

      (i) Targets. Aggressive feelings and aggression can be displaced from the body to the parts of the body, states of mind, reputation, the objects of collective identifications and their signs and symbols, the members of such collective identifications, such as the members of a family, ethnic group, and nation. Aggressive feelings may be diffuse and, therefore, detached from any particular object, in which case these feelings are liable to be mobilised towards a variety of targets.

(ii) Functions. The functions of aggression are numerous and various. However, in this context it should be emphasised that aggression is often used to maintain pressure on people and sub-groups to comply with and conform to various moral norms which are felt to be important to the identity of the group, especially when the survival of the group is threatened. General processes of social control become a form of punishment, and vice versa (Durkheim 1893).

(iii) Forms. Aggression can involve either verbal or non-verbal attacks, or both. However, people can be made to feel terrible through the projection of beta elements associated with raw, unprocessed sensations (Bion 1963); a raised eyebrow, a pursed lip or a certain kind of smile can be devastating; contempt can be more painful than a blow. Although gossip is a normal and important form of social control, it can become grotesquely distorted into forms of lying, rumour mongering, ridicule and other kinds of denigration. Aggression can involve actions that are immoral rather than illegal, marked by boundary breaking, exploitation, deception, corruption, seduction and complicity. For example, patients and clients may be confused 'perversely' and 'subversively' with family and friends.

In the context of aggregation, aggressive feelings and aggression are prevalent. They are manifest in indifference, hostility and withdrawal from relationships to the more open hatred and conflict of a 'free for all', in which each person is against each person, and each sub-group is against each sub-group, or in effect each sub-group becomes a contra-group. For example, in aggregated societies unconscious aggression ranges from what in Israel is called 'balagan' (that is, a totally confused 'cock-up') to boundary breaking and blurring, including 'gender-bending', perversion, moral corruption, and both serious and petty crime. The film *Cabaret*, based on Christopher Isherwood's (1954) *The Berlin Novels*, offers an entertaining but accurate depiction of covert, displaced aggression in an aggregated society. In aggregated organisations, aggression is seen in: the desperation of managers who claim 'This firm is unmanageable'; a culture which condones the exploitation of the 'expense account'; the self-destructive reduction of productivity; and in corruption, seduction and complicity associated with the pursuit of self-interest, for example, the stories of corporate life in the recent Enron and Arthur Andersen debacles. In aggregated large groups, aggression is seen in the way people tend to come late to a session and then choose seats that make it difficult for those who come even later to find seats in a way that does not call excessive and embarrassing attention to themselves, and does not disrupt the proceedings.

In the context of massification, in contrast, aggressive feelings and aggression are more covert, but when they are overt, they are regarded as justified, because they are in the common interest. For example, in massified societies, the regulation of aggression can be seen in various forms of nationalism which are associated with the purification of language, race, ethnicity, custom and even aesthetic values (de Mendelssohn 2000). In massified organisations those in power refuse to learn from other organisations, to recruit personnel with new skills, and to permit diversity in the service of the expression of individuality and autonomy, ranging from the imposition of dress codes to enforcing rules for extra-corporate social and domestic arrangements and styles. In large groups, the aggressive regulation of aggressive feelings and aggression can be seen in an over-emphasis by participants on the importance of the group-as-a-whole, and in their avoidance of recognition of, and interaction with, individual members of the group, which is justified by the cliché that the study of groups should focus only on the dynamics of the group and not on the properties of the members of it.

4. The regulation of aggression is typical of massified social systems, but such regulation is itself an expresion of aggression. Several processes of both the regulation and the expression of aggression are central to massification:

    (a) Targets of aggression are displaced from objects within the group into objects within the group's environment, especially into 'other' groups and their members, who are then perceived to be a source of pollution, denigrated as 'different', 'strange', and 'inferior' and, therefore, are repudiated as pseudo-species (Erikson 1968). This process may be called 'pseudo-speciation'.

(b) The development of a ritualised way of life, both in private and in public domains. Daily life becomes an expression of moral and religious perfection and purification. The pressures to conform and to comply are immense. The boundaries of a group are marked continuously, and personal identity is asserted in terms of membership of the group, i.e. the members of the group become Membership Individuals. The continuous assertion of personal identity in terms of group identity can be seen in the importance given to conforming to the norms of daily life.

(c) The 'sexualisation' of aggressive feelings. Aggressive feelings are diluted and made more manageable through their sexualisation or libidinalisation, which in extreme form is the basis of sadism: hate masquerades as love, and pain becomes inseparable from pleasure; ligatures are transformed into ligaments, and bonds into bondage. Competition is converted into banding, as seen in a 'band of brothers', in which homosexuality becomes problematic.

Pseudo-speciation and the ritualisation and sexualisation of aggression are rarely completely effective. What happens when these prophylactics against aggressive feelings and aggression towards targets within the group prove to be inadequate? In general terms, the answer is that aggressive feelings and aggression become more essential to the maintenance of massification. Four forms of aggression become ubiquitous:

(a) The development and maintenance of an attitude of 'moral superiority' by those who are at the core of the group towards those who are at the periphery of it (Hopper 1981). This is based on the manipulation of the norms that regulate moral judgements in order to ensure that the targets of aggressive feelings are defined as deviant, immoral and criminal. These judgements are then used to justify and to mobilise pressure to conform, to participate in various public rituals, and to comply with the expectations of those in authority.

(b) The development and maintenance of processes of 'anonymisation' (Main 1975). The essence of anonymisation is an attack on the personal identity of each individual member of a group, and on the confidence of each to have and to maintain a personal identity. To anonymise a person is to destroy his identity as a unique person. Anonymisation reduces the sense of personal responsibility for thought, feeling and deed, because action is felt to originate in the mind of an incumbent of a specific role within a group and not in the mind of a unique person who is required to interpret the constraints of the role. Anonymisation also eliminates the possibility of giving credit to individuals for their contributions. Paradoxically, although anonymisation is a form of aggression towards individuals, it also functions to reduce the envy of individuality and, hence, it helps to dilute aggressive feelings and aggression towards people who are able to retain their 'names'. People who feel frightened and helpless also tend to anonymise themselves in order to pre-empt envy from others (Kreeger 1992). Anonymisation is often used by dictators and the governments of totalitarian states against their citizens, for example, through substituting a number for a name, which occurred in concentration and death camps. In traditional bureaucratic organisations under threat, numbers are assigned to employees, ranging from the number 'one' to a chairman or chief executive officer to the 'last in the series' to a janitor who has been hired temporarily. In groups, both participants and leaders or conductors too often make interpretations that a particular person is carrying a particular feeling or thought 'for the group' without due consideration and respect for individuals and their diverse contributions.

(c) Shunning. People who are defined as deviant, immoral and criminal are likely to be shunned, that is, marginalised, peripheralised and ignored in order to deprive them of social and cultural sustenance. At one extreme, the shunned are merely ignored and deprived of a sense of being recognised; at the other, they are deprived of help and support, which is not only hurtful, but also dangerous, at least under certain conditions.

(d) Banishment. In the last resort, being shunned gives way to being banished from the group, being sent beyond the pale. In extreme, this may involve being regarded as 'dead', and becoming the object of rituals of mourning. Banishment is the ultimate expression of social and cultural purification.

Based on the development and maintenance of moral superiority, anonymisation, shunning and banishment, two additional and interrelated forms of aggression are especially prominent in groups who are attempting to maintain a state of massification, and are used both against targets within the group and in the service of pseudo-speciation:

(a) *Scapegoating* (Lewin 1948; Cartwright and Zander 1953; Scheidlinger 1982). In scapegoating, traditionally, pressures to conform and to comply with moral norms were intensified in order to propitiate the gods who were thought to have punished the group for its sins for having initiated the traumatogenic process by which the group is afflicted. This may still characterise scapegoating processes, but in more secular societies the general process is that the members of a group purge themselves of unacceptable and dangerous feelings, ideas, attributes and qualities by projecting them into particular people and sub-groups. These targeted people are then judged very stringently, and in absolute rather than relative terms, and perceived to be guilty. They are punished by being peripheralised and marginalised from the core of the group. Ultimately they may be shunned and even banished.

Scapegoating may involve an unconscious attack on the Father (Money-Kyrle 1929), who is perceived to have failed the group and/or to have stopped access to the Mother. From this point of view, people and sub-groups who are perceived to be either obstacles to merger with a perfect group and/or as impurities within the hallucination of perfection (Chasseguet-Smirgel 1985) are displacement from the Father.

Scapegoating also stems from helplessness and envy of the Mother and the mother-group, on the basis of which 'she' is split into good and bad objects. The 'bad' target is attacked and ultimately banished. However, the 'good' target is killed and eaten, or at least incorporated symbolically, thus initiating a process of atonement (Cohen and Schermer 2002; Maccoby 1982).

The targets of scapegoating may be more or less innocent, that is, as more or less deserving of the projections. They may even possess desirable and highly valued qualities or attributes, in which case the motive for the attack may be envy and/or punishment for acting as though they were gods or special kinds of human being, for example, for being too intelligent or for assuming that they do not need natural protection, such as the foreskin. Moreover, the scapegoat '...may respond *antagonistically*, by condemning or withdrawing from the community while, in contrast, exalting (himself)'; 'or *agonistically*, by joining with the community in both its condemnation of the scapegoat and exaltation of (himself)' (Cohen and Schermer 2002, p.93).

Although scapegoats are drawn from the ranks of singletons or isolates (Roth 1980), presumably because they are vulnerable and lack protective allies, scapegoats are always likely to be central persons who carry the group's thoughts and feelings. In other words, expectations of conformity and compliance are situated within relationships between people and sub-groups and contra-groups. Although the scapegoating process may be unconscious, it is always political. The dilemma is how to banish a person or a sub-group without losing qualities and attributes that are useful to the group.

The scapegoating process is rarely self-contained and self-limiting. Scapegoating breeds scapegoating, and those who actively personify and lead the scapegoating process are likely to become the passive personifiers and victims of later scapegoating processes in connection with guilt and blame for the aggression that was inherent in the previous scapegoating processes, which is always multi-phasic, and spans the generations.

(b) The *assassination* of people and their characters.[6] Obviously, actual assassinations occur less often than character assassinations, and actual assassinations are unlikely to occur within the context of organisations and groups compared with the society as a whole (no matter how some of us who are active in the politics of our professional organisations would wish). Nonetheless, groups who meet more than once do provide time and space outside their meetings for interactions between individual participants, sub-groups and contra-groups. Character assassinations occur between meetings of the group. This occurs in groups who meet for work within the context of a more complex organisation, such as a small team, or committee, as well as in other kinds of group, for example, those who meet for the purpose of psychotherapy. All members of a group may be subjected to character assassination, especially the central persons of the basic assumption processes, and the leader of the work group.

Both actual assassination and character assassination are used mainly to purge a group of obstacles to massification. They are also used in the service of pseudo-speciation in which the character of 'others' and their leaders are denigrated and stigmatised.

Actual assassination and character assassination are also used to provoke states of aggregation. Within a stable society, governed by the rule of law, an assassination of a leader violates expectations about personal and public life, and it becomes extremely difficult to maintain the morale of the work group. The loss of a leader into whom so many people had projected their ego ideals involves a loss of social glue, and anomie of norms that govern both social goals and the means for achieving them is likely to arise. People feel that law and order will not protect them. Isolation, sub-grouping and contra-grouping become ubiquitous.

An assassination is likely to delay the natural shift from aggregation to massification. Terrified and enraged people create terror and rage. Also, an assassination is very difficult to mourn:

(i) When the victim is a prominent public figure, assassination causes a heightened concern with matters of national security and public rituals of mourning. There is little time for more intimate mourning.

(ii) It is difficult to get the right balance between the private and the public. For example, a prime minister or a president may be assassinated and mourned, but Mr Rabin or Mr Kennedy is murdered but not mourned.

(iii) Usually a 'greater' person is killed by a 'lesser' one. Thus, the murder is regarded as illicit, illegitimate and devious, and the death is defined as bad, dishonourable, or at least without honour, and as a waste. There is a sense that natural justice has been violated and, therefore, a sense of grievance, bitterness and lamentation prevails (as occurs in other kinds of unanticipated death, for example, of a patient in hospital for a routine treatment, in a case of medical negligence, or in a case of an untimely death in general). An assassination is regarded as an illegitimate 'cutting down', associated with feelings of horror, terror and rage, in contrast to a death that involves a sense of return to the inner-sanctum and to the womb of the earth, associated with feelings of natural tenderness and protectiveness.[7]

(iv) Assassination tends to be followed by the suicide, murder, incarceration and/or execution of the person who is held to be responsible for it. The assassin may not be iconic, but he may have the sympathy of a portion of the population, who will have to choose who to mourn. It is not easy to mourn both the assassinated and his assassin. An assassination is, therefore, associated with personal and public confusion.

(c) Some types of actual assassination and character assassination are associated with scapegoating. The target of the assassination is the recipient of the projections of repudiated qualities and characteristics, not only in his own right but also on behalf of the group who he represents. The assassin is also the recipient of projections from those who he represents. Both the assassin and the assassinated are displacements from those who control them. Moreover, the subsequent suicide, murder, execution or incarceration of the assassin, which almost always occurs, can be seen in terms of the two stage process of scapegoating. For example, the gossip and monger of rumour eventually ruin their own reputations. Similarly, some assassins and terrorists actually participate in forms of ritualised purification, involving separation from their family and friends, and being excused from the social obligations of ordinary daily life, in such a way that all elements of contamination are projected into the other who is about to die, and the purified assassin or terrorist is then able to enter heaven, and to merger with a perfect 'mass'. The annihilation that is perpetrated through the assassination of a person or a group creates an aggregate, that is, the opposite of mass, which is created simultaneously for the assassin and his group. The entire activity is a kind of sacrifice.

5. Groups and group-like social systems who are under the sway of the fourth basic assumption of Incohesion are likely to oscillate between states of aggregation and of massification, for several reasons:

   (a) First of all, massification is itself an attempt to deal with aggressive feelings and aggression that are both ubiquitous in aggregation and typical of it.

   (b) Massification is, however, associated with its own distinctive difficulties. Massification is always transitory and fragile. It is highly dependent on the maintenance of enchantment (Agazarian and Carter 1993), and on the perfect fulfilment of its promise. For example, the larger the population of a massified social system, the more likely is it that a core group will become differentiated from peripheral groups, and that horizontal social distance will be transformed into hierarchy, which is inimical to the perpetuation of homogeneity, on which massification is based. Similarly, massification makes it difficult to accomplish complex tasks, which require flexible social organisation and the expenditure of scarce resources in a way that does not violate the prevailing norms of distributive justice. Thus, it is virtually impossible to utilise the variety of skills and idiosyncrasies within the population in order to provide for the greater good of the whole.

   The emergence of obstacles to perfect massification is, therefore, more or less inevitable. Sooner rather than later, latent and encapsulated isolates, sub-groups and contra-groups are likely to surface, and make rivalrous claims for various kinds of social, cultural and political goods and preferences, many of which are 'positional' (Hirsch 1977), and thus, by definition unavailable for perfectly equal distribution. In large, complex social systems, the elites always demand unequal rewards; and the emergence and maintenance of structure and hierarchy limit the duration and extent of the massification process, which relies on the romanticism of pure populism and eventually the terror of idolatry and fundamentalism. In addition, helplessness within peripheral groups is likely to generate envy of core groups from whom the former feel excluded. Of course, people also feel helpless with respect to the apparent pseudo-cohesion of massification, and unconsciously wish to prevent such 'coming together'. However, such envious attacks on 'parental intercourse' are likely to be a secondary process.

(c) In order to protect against the difficulties and anxieties associated with massification, a social system shifts back towards the state of aggregation, and the original anxieties and difficulties associated with aggregation are likely to re-emerge. 'Secondary' panic is also likely to arise. And the entire process repeats itself. In the same way that traumatised people who are overwhelmed by their fear of annihilation are caught in incessant motion, without possibilities of resolution, incohesive social systems oscillate incessantly between states of aggregation and states of massification. These oscillations manifest motion and process, but no dynamic, dialectical movement. Aggregation and massification are equally incohesive. Thus, an incohesive social system is in a state of social paralysis or social stasis.

6. Although social stasis can and does occur, so, too, do processes of social formation or development, and processes of social regression (Dunning and Hopper 1966). Although it is a difficult and lengthy process for either an aggregate or a mass to become a group, a group can become an aggregate or a mass easily and quickly. Similarly, it is a difficult and lengthy process for a group to become an organisation, but an organisation can become a group very quickly, despite some of its appearances to the contrary. However, a group that becomes an organisation in response to change and challenge, is very different from a group that becomes *like* an organisation while remaining a

group, in which case the group is likely to have regressed towards a state of aggregation, and not to have developed into a more complex social system.

Incohesion is likely to emerge in all groups and group-like social systems, but it is especially likely to emerge in social systems that have been traumatised and/or in social systems the members of which have been traumatised. For example, within a family group the traumatic loss of a parent through death or even through the loss of parental authority is usually followed by intense, unbridled rivalry among siblings for the 'place' that has been vacated; the resulting family aggregate is likely to massify only in competition with other families or with 'outsiders' in general. Similarly, when the production managers and progress chasers who supervised the construction of the Tower of Babel were perceived to have failed the dependency placed on them by the members of their work groups, the organisation was likely to have regressed into a group-like social system, and to have begun to evince oscillations between aggregation and massification. Following the loss of a war or after massive immigration, conflict among ethnic groups can be understood in terms of the aggregation of the regressed society, and its attempts to shift towards massification. Incohesion is especially likely to occur in large groups in various kinds of training conferences, not only because the members of large groups are especially likely to regress, but also because they experience the requirement that they participate in such groups as manipulative and abusive, and feel traumatised by the staff and the management of the conference.[8] Incohesion is ubiquitous in small groups of people who have been traumatised, as seen, for example, in small therapeutic groups in prisons and in therapeutic communities for people with 'personality disorders', in bereavement groups, and in debriefing groups for survivors of massive social trauma, including for the leaders of these groups.

The emergence of any basic assumption indicates that a group has regressed, and that its work group is under threat. However, the emergence of the basic assumption of Incohesion indicates that the survival of the group is in doubt.

7. It is beyond the scope of this inquiry to address the problem of work group development in complex social systems.[9] However, by way of a brief comparison of a group characterised by the basic assumption of

Incohesion with a group that is functioning as a work group in a state of optimal cohesion, I have outlined some of the features of an optimally cohesive work group in Table 3.2, which warrants careful study.

Table 3.2 Some features of the work group: optimal cohesion (or heterogeneity) (1) (2)

Properties of Social System			
Interaction: (The basis for cohesion in a complex society)	Normation: (The basis for cohesion in a simple society)	Communication: Language is coherent (4)	Communication: Style of Thinking and Feeling (5)
Integration, based on interdependence for goods and services Optimal degree of role differentiation and specificity	Solidarity, based on similitude of beliefs, norms and values, but tolerating a degree of difference and disagreement, individuality and non-conformity Diversity (2) Sub-cultures and pluralism Nomie (the norms exist, are known and understood; not characterised by conflict; people are committed to them) (3)	Level of abstraction and jargon is task appropriate People 'speak the same language'	Secondary process Functional symbolism Sense of continuity: memory and anticipations are in balance Confidentiality High morale Humour and irony
(1) Turquet (1974, 1975)	(2) Rickman (1938) (3) Hopper (1981)	(4) Pines (1983) (5) King (1969)	

As is the case with all basic assumptions, virtually by definition, Incohesion prevents the development and the maintenance of the work group. Aggregation and massification are grotesque versions of processes of authentic diversity and unity that are necessary for the optimal cohesion of the work group. 'Heterogeneity' is sometimes used to refer to the optimal cohesion of the work group, but this concept is ambiguous, and stems from Turquet's brief discussion of the homogeneity of Oneness in contrast to the heterogeneity of the optimal cohesion of the work group. For this reason, I refer to the 'cohesion' of the work group, and think in terms of high, low and optimal degrees of cohesion. For example, under conditions of optimal cohesion, the work group manifests a 'good' sense of humour, tolerance and respect for differences, including differences of opinion, a degree of disinterest that facilitates a scientific attitude towards data and techniques, etc. High morale and passionate commitment to the achievement of collective goals are possible, and not to be confused with the pseudo-morale of massification. Optimal cohesion is based on an appropriate degree of personal autonomy.

In small groups, especially in those who meet for the purpose of psychotherapy, it is possible to use interpretations of underlying anxieties and defences in order to facilitate the development of the work group. Obviously, in larger, more complex social systems, this is very difficult, if not impossible, although working with large groups within organisational settings can be very effective.

In sum, I have postulated the existence of a fourth basic assumption in the unconscious life of groups and group-like social systems. I call it 'Incohesion: Aggregation/Massification' or (ba) 'I:A/M'. Incohesion is manifest in patterns of interaction, normation and communication, as well as in styles of thinking and feeling and styles of leadership and followership. States of aggregation, on the one hand, and of massification, on the other, can be denoted in these terms. Aggregation and massification are associated with, and are an expression of, distinctive patterns of aggressive feelings and aggression, and distinctive patterns of the sexualisation of aggressive feelings and aggression. Incohesive social systems tend to oscillate between bi-polar states of aggregation and massification. Aggregation includes dissaroy and me-ness, and is more extensive than the binary splitting that characterises Fight/Flight. Of course, Aggregation and Fight/Flight are each characterised by attacks on linking and by moves towards isolation. Similarly, Massification includes 'homogenisation', and is more extensive than the affiliative submission and compliance that characterises Dependency. Of course,

Massification and Dependency are each characterised by the sexualisation of aggression as seen in mergers and instrusions. Although groups and group-like social systems evince processes of Incohesion: Aggregation/Massification, the frequency and the intensity with which this fourth basic assumption emerges is a matter of degree. It is especially chronic and intense in groups of traumatised people and/or those who have been traumatised.

Notes

1 Although 'aggregate' and 'mass' are technically correct, these two social formations have been described by social scientists and social philosophers from many points of view, using a variety of terms and concepts. Within the 'European' tradition, especially useful is the work of Reich (1933), Geiger (1969), who discusses the 'atomisation of mass society', and Baschwitz (1938); within the later 'American' tradition, special attention should be given to the work of Cooley (1909), Giddings (1924), Sumner and Keller (1927), MacIver (1937) and Kornhauser (1960).

2 For people who cannot abide even one tall poppy, massification is very desirable. I gather that in some countries this syndrome is based on fields of other flowers, e.g. in Israel it is the 'tall sunflower syndrome'.

3 This point was developed by Ferenczi (1922) in his discussion of *Group Psychology and the Analysis of the Ego*. He says that based on 'suggestibility', the aetiology of which is uncertain, massification processes can occur in a small circle of people, a family or even a relationship between two people.

4 The development of these social, cultural and political forms followed the horrendous social trauma associated with industrialisation, the effects of which are still underestimated, because the benefits of industrialisation have also been so great. Of course, this dilemma and contradiction was discussed by both Marx and Durkheim, and continue to be discussed by their many descendants. Although it is impossible to consider such general trauma within the present context, it remains pertinent to cite Marx's *Communist Manifesto* and his essays on alienation, and Durkheim's *Division of Labour and Suicide*, which were not merely attempts to formulate abstract theories.

5 George Orwell (1949) was instructive about the politicisation of language in totalitarian states, and many centuries ago Thucydides (1954) described the linguistic style of Spartans in terms of the corruption of language.

6 Although much is known about various cases of actual assassination (Elliott 1999; Hudson 2001), comparatively little is known about processes of assassination in general. It may be helpful to define 'assassination' and to indicate certain aspects of it. 'Assassination' refers to taking the life of a public figure through treacherous violence. Assassination can be distinguished from murder in general in terms of its characteristic elements of surprise, secrecy, and sense of triumph over the victim. Assassination is usually planned by a group but precipitated by one person, either a hired emissary or a willing volunteer. However, an assassination may be carried out by a group. Although it is often assumed that assassins are male, assassinations have been perpetrated by females, who used to be called 'assassinatresses', e.g. Lucrezia Borgia. Traditionally, assassinatresses used poison as their weapon of choice, perhaps because they had an affinity for murder by feeding. However, they also had more access to poison than to other weapons, as did

male and female house and kitchen slaves in the Caribbean and elsewhere who are known to have assassinated their owners by poisoning their livestock and food in general.

'Assassin' is derived from the Arabic word for 'hashish eater'. 'Assassin' was first used in the Middle Ages in the Middle East to refer to young men who dedicated themselves to the murder of European crusaders who had come in search of the Holy Grail and in order to penetrate the Holy City of Jerusalem. They ate hashish in order to become high, ecstatic and close to God before abandoning themselves to acts of murder which would almost certainly be followed by their own death, usually suicide. These desperate and dangerous men were sent forth by their sheikh (the Old Man of the Mountains). When referring to these Ismailiyah sectarians, the word is capitalised, i.e. 'Assassins'. Through their actions Assassins were able both to triumph over their enemies and to receive the love of their sheikh and, thus, were able to ensure their merger with God and their entry to heaven. I assume that in this context 'God' was a male object, and 'heaven' a female one.

Contrary to many assertions within the academic disciplines of history and political science, an assassination is never a 'meaningless' act of idiosyncratic aggression. For example, in the only assassination of a prime minister that has ever occurred in England, Spencer Percival was shot and killed in the House of Commons in 1812 by John Bellingham, who is generally regarded as merely an isolated 'madman' who had applied in vain to the Prime Minister for redress of a personal complaint against the Government. Although in England this particular assassination is always relegated to historical insignificance, it is likely that this deranged citizen personified widespread feelings of helplessness connected with the loss of economic power and status among certain groups of people in connection with various international affairs, including the war of 1812, which is associated with the loss of colonies in the Western world, thirteen of which developed into the United States of America.

The notion of assassination implies that the murder of the public figure occurs in a society in which succession to leadership has been institutionalised, that is, in a comparatively stable society, in which the rule of law prevails and is widely regarded as just. For example, in 1880, in his *History of England*, Macauley wrote that '... the English regard assassination with a loathing peculiar to themselves ...', suggesting not only that England had become more stable than other European nations, but also that Englishmen had begun to hold these other nations in profound contempt.

During the seventeenth century, various writers, such as Dryden, began to use 'assassin' and 'assassinated' to refer to the murdering of the character or reputation of a person. Before this time, the word was used only to refer to actual murder by stealth. Character assassination may be as – if not more – effective than actual assassination. Certainly, character assassination may be more painful than actual assassination, especially in professional organisations and voluntary organisations in which the development and maintenance of reputation is virtually all that is at stake. Moreover, whereas an actual assassination may remove a particular person from the scene, it may not affect the role that is vacated, and may even create a 'martyr', thereby enhancing the reputation of the person who has been murdered, and giving emphasis to the values and interests that he represented. In contrast, a character assassination is likely to render a person powerless, and to weaken the social, cultural and political structures in which his role is embedded.

There are many kinds of assassination processes, but I will not attempt here to distinguish one kind of assassination from another. Similarly, assassination differs from terrorism, but this too is beyond the scope of the present discussion.

7 In this connection, the English analyst Mary Chadwick (1929) introduced the terms 'mother death' and 'father death'. Although we no longer make such distinctions, because they seem so phallocentric and neglect the possibility of female violence, it is possible to regard assassination as a kind of father death. However, in the context of the basic assumption of Incohesion, it would be more accurate to think in terms of two different kinds of mother death, one associated with aggregation, and the other with massification.

8 Turquet mentioned that the participants in large groups in training conferences are likely to feel overlooked and unheard, or in effect to feel narcissistically injured (Ganzarain 2000). However, such experience was regarded as important because it promoted regression, and not because it was traumatic.

9 Some idea of the enormous scope of such a task can be seen in *Inequality and Heterogeneity: A Primitive Theory of Social Structure* by Blau (1977) in which Simmel's insight about the significance of numbers to social life, which have been used largely in studies of small groups, are applied to the analysis of entire societies.

CHAPTER 4

The Personification of Incohesion: Aggregation/Massification

People who have been traumatised, have experienced the fear of annihilation, and who have developed protective encapsulations are likely both to create processes of aggregation and massification, and to be vulnerable to the constraints of roles associated with them. People who have experienced the fear of annihilation are desperate for the holding and containing provided by roles that offer an identity which can be substituted for the one that has been threatened, fragmented or even lost. Such roles are like new skin; perhaps a costume and mask is an apposite metaphor. Contact-shunning, crustacean characters are likely to personify states of aggregation, and merger-hungry, amoeboid characters are likely to personify states of massification. However, there are mixtures of types of personification, as there are mixtures of and rapid shifts between aggregation and massification, especially in large, complex social systems.

In this chapter I will discuss the concept of personification of basic assumption processes, as opposed to the 'leadership' of work groups. I will also develop these hypotheses about the personification of Incohesion: Aggregation/Massification, with special reference to aggressive feelings and aggression.

1. Personification is usually defined as a literary device in which an author uses the action and personality of a particular person in order to represent abstract qualities, principles and more general processes and problems in the course of his narrative. However, the concept is apposite for the discussion of valence and role suction. The 'narrative'

mode is very important in group analysis and in some schools of psychoanalysis, in which maturation involves an increasingly accurate and truthful rendition of a life history, as well as an opening up of new and transcendent possibilities for the authorship of future chapters (Hopper 2001b).

People with a particular pattern of anxiety and defence are likely to 'personify' those roles that are unconsciously constructed in association with particular basic assumptions.[1] However, 'personification' emphasises the possibilities for the active interpretation of a role to which a person has a valence, or a heightened sensitivity to its suction. The concept implies that a role can be enacted with many individual idiosyncrasies, and that it permits a range of interpretations.[2]

Personification is based on a complex mixture of projective and introjective identification, as well as other forms of externalisation and internalisation. The object of one's identifications is always seen within specific roles and sets of roles within a wider social context. Personification is always a social and cultural process that involves the group as a whole as well as individual members of it. This is partly what we mean when we say that the individual and the group are two sides of the same coin, and that the individual is permeated through and through by social and cultural factors and forces, and vice versa.

Personification is part of making identifications at all phases of life. However, it is most noticeable during adolescence and young adulthood when making serial identity substitutions is rife, because one is leaving the family and school friends and entering the wider world of further education and work. During these transitions, identifications with Father give way to those with heroes of myths, to those with heroes in popular films, to mentors, and so on.

Personification processes are also seen in the ways in which certain groups become associated with certain activities and stereotyped styles of thought and feeling. For example, it might be argued that in Germany Jews personified the knowledge component of the development of the work group, while Nazis personified the industrialised application of knowledge.

Personification processes can be pathological, especially when they are associated with compulsive identity substitutions associated with social roles and categories. For example, I am not Mr X but a Jew, or I am not Mr X but a psychoanalyst, or I am not Mr X but a schizophrenic, etc. rather than the other way around, that is, I am Mr X to whom being a Jew is an important part of my life and central to my identity, etc. (Volkan 2001). People whose personal identities are under threat attempt to circumvent their conflicts and confusions by taking on the identities associated with a particular social role or the identities conferred by being a Membership Individual. In other words, they attempt to 'correct' a lack of identity or a very limited and diffuse identify by taking on a role or a 'biography supplied by cultural sources' (Kris 1956). It is important to understand such cultural objects, but it is as, if not more, important to understand how people use such objects in the service of both expression and protection (Winnicott 1953).

Related to personification are the concepts of figuration and fractal. Norbert Elias (1938) introduced 'figuration' in order to describe the interlocking social, cultural and personal aspects of a particular pattern of action. A figuration can be analysed from various points of view and on many levels, ranging from the constraints of social facts, on the one hand, to the constraints of intra-psychic unconscious fantasy, on the other. This is especially important in the elucidation of the social unconscious (Gfaller 1996).

The concept of fractal is borrowed from the new information and computer sciences in which the discovery has been made that in many realms of the universe parts seem to manifest the same fundamental structures as their wholes, thus illustrating the old idea that the universe can be found in a grain of sand. When applied to the social and psychological domain, it is possible to think of a person and his intra-psychic life as being a fractal of his immediate group, which in turn can be seen as a fractal of the group's wider social context. (Lawrence 1993; Scharff and Scharff 1998). However, I am sceptical about the use of 'fractal' to describe the personification of a group process, because it is too 'over-socialised', and ignores the idiosyncrasies of the interpretation of roles and processes by particular individuals.

The focus on an individual person as a fractal or as a figuration is exactly that, a matter of focus. This is consistent with Bion's idea that binocular vision is necessary in attempts to understand group process, and with the emphasis given by Foulkes to maintaining the tension

Table 4.1 Some features of the personification of the fourth basic assumption of Incohesion compared to the leadership of a work group with optimal cohesion

Properties of social system / Basic assumption: Incohesion	Personification 'Leadership' Representation Types of 'central person' (14)	Followership	Bystander-ship
Incohesion: Aggregation	Crustacean (1) Contact avoiding (2) Austere/purist Anti-hero Lone Wolf Outsider (3) (4) Space Cadet Narcissistic (5, 6) Epileptoid: Type I (7) Immature leader: Type I (12)	Singletons (8)	[to be continued]
Incohesion: Massification	Amoeboid (1) Merger-hungry (2) Charismatic-narcissistic (5, 6, 8, 9) Dependent-narcissistic (7, 15) Destructive-narcissistic (16) Hero Warrior Magician Cheerleader Morale Booster Insider Merchant of Illusions (10) Epileptoid: Type II (7) Immature leader: Type II (12) Dictator (13) Perverse (17)	Membership Individuals (8)	[to be continued]
Work Group with optimal cohesion	Leadership Crystallizers Makers of meaning Citizens (11) Mature leader (12) Rational and mature (5) Reparative-narcissistic (6,15)	Individual members (8) Citizens (11)	[to be continued]

(1) Tustin (1981) (2) Kohut and Wolf (1978) (3) Wright (1953) (4) Camus (1983) (5) Kernberg (1978) (6) Volkan (1980, 1981)	(7) Bleger (1966) (8) Turquet (1974, 1975) (9) Zaleznik (1979) (10) Anzieu (1981) (11) de Maré (1991) (12) Alexander (1942) Erikson (1948)	(13) Bychowski (1948) (14) Redl (1942) (15) Volkan and Itzkowitz (1984) (16) Post (1991) (17) Chasseguet-Smirgel (1985)

between the figure and the ground of the gestalt. Thus, in group analysis patients can be seen in terms of a figuration or a fractal of the group, on the basis of which it is not only entirely justifiable but also clinically appropriate to engage an individual patient within a group. The patient is regarded as personifying a particular process which, in turn, may be a function of the 'matrix' of the group, including its 'foundation matrix' (Foulkes and Anthony 1964). In other words, the patient is a nodal point in the matrices of the group, which is always an 'open' system (Hopper 1975).

2. Several types of the personification of aggregation and massification are outlined in Table 4.1, which also lists some of the types of leadership and followership of work groups who have developed optimal cohesion. I have cited the work of scholars who have studied some of these features, using their own terminology as well as my own.

   This table warrants careful study. However, I will call attention to only a few points:

   (a) Aggregation processes are likely to be personified by crustacean, contact-shunning, Epileptoid Type I, philobatic, thick skinned narcissistic characters, and massification processes, by amoeboid, merger-hungry, Epileptoid Type II, oncophilac, thin skinned narcissistic characters. Turquet might have said that aggregation processes are personified by Isolates and Singletons, and massification processes, by Membership Individuals.

   (b) Aggregation and massification processes are also personified by people with particular kinds of perversions or perverse characters, based on the 'core complex', the distinguishing characteristic of which is the fear of annihilation (Glasser 1979). Although some kinds of perversions would seem to lend themselves to the personification of the cold and distant patterns of the alienated detachment of aggregation, other kinds of perversions are associated with the hot, clinging and virtually parasitical mergers of massification, which are marked by the desire to subvert all 'natural' differences between the sexes and the generations (Chasseguet-Smirgel 1985), including the differences between the living and the dead (Money-Kyrle 1978), and by the compulsion to confuse all that would 'ordinarily' be regarded as 'appropriately' separate. (I would argue, however, that 'natural' and 'appropriate' are matters for negotiation.)

(c) Addicts evince a mixture of pronounced crustacean and amoeboid features, and oscillate between these extreme states of mind. These oscillations can be confusing, because they can be precipitated by the experience of intimacy, which is welcomed one moment but feared the next. Various kinds of addiction can be understood in terms of the addiction syndrome, the elements of which include somatisation, perverse sexuality, homosexuality and gender confusion. Moreover, a history of traumatic experience is so typical of addicts and people with perversions that it would be just as apt to describe a trauma syndrome in which addiction and perversion were crucial elements, as it would be to describe an addiction or perversion syndrome in which traumatic experience was crucial. Traumatophilia may lead traumatised people into the addiction syndrome through any one of its components. The use of drugs within specific social contexts offers many opportunities for traumatic experience. In fact, within communities of drug addicts, the producers and dealers (perpetrators), the secondary profiteers (collusive bystanders), the addicts and their main partners (collusive victims) are united in individual and collective traumatophilia (Hopper 1995).

(d) The personification of aggregation and massification reflects a multi-generational cycle of perversion in which victims become perpetrators, and vice versa, and the majority collude as bystanders. Under such circumstances 'innocence' is inauthentic. Those who have been treated as vermin become the persecutors of those who they regard as vermin. The collusive creation of these roles, and the propensity to fill them, involves the recapitulation of early life experiences within the matrix of the family and its surrounding social groups, as well as 'later' sources of the fear of annihilation, such as war, terrorist activities and high rates of unemployment, within the context of traumatogenic processes.

(e) An exhaustive inventory of the character types associated with the personification of the fourth basic assumption is yet to be made. Jungian Analytical Psychology offers many examples in terms of archetypes. The 'scientist' of aggregation might be compared with the 'magician' of massification. Similarly, the 'Apollo' of the work group might be compared with different kinds of 'Dionysus' figures, such as the one who personifies merger, and the loss of self, and the other who personifies the subversion of structure and the loss of social trust. The characters of many great books and other works of art are especially illustrative, for example, consider the cast of *Julius Caesar* and *The Tempest.* In the film *Viva Zapata*, Zapata was played by Marlon Brando as an amoeboid character who personified massification process, and the Trotsky-like fellow traveller was played by Joseph Wiseman as a cold crustacean character who personified aggregation process. Lévi-Strauss (1961) refers to the representation of cold and hot cultures, which might be compared to states of aggregation and of massification, respectively. In clinical group analysis, alienated schizoid 'space cadets' and 'lone wolves' can be contrasted with 'cheerleaders' and 'morale boosters'.

3. Much that has been written about leaders and leadership actually pertains to inadequate leaders and leadership, or at any rate to the leaders and leadership of the work group that is threatened by basic assumption processes. Actually, it is sometimes difficult to distinguish the inadequate leadership of the work group from the personification of a basic assumption process, that is, a 'leader' from a 'central person'.[3]

With respect to the adequate leadership of the work group, Turquet would have said that a work group can be led only by people who have succeeded in becoming 'Individual Members' of it. Similarly, Kernberg (1991) argues that 'rational and mature leadership' is essential, and that one of the most important elements of this is the ability and willingness to maintain ethical codes of conduct and to resist corruption and complicity. Following the work of de Maré (1972), I (Hopper 1996b, 2000) have argued that the leaders of work groups should also be able to take the role of 'citizen', and to give meaning to this role. In fact, maturity can be defined not only in terms of the capacity to work and to love, but also, to function as a citizen. Of course, good followers, who are essential to the optimal cohesion of a work group, must also be good citizens.

When social systems are characterised by Incohesion, their work groups are likely to be led by charismatic leaders. The psychic stability of the charismatic leader depends on his receiving recognition and other narcissistic supplies from the group, and on his functioning as the individual embodiment of the group and their collective self-object. This is denied by both the leader and his followers. Instead, they feel that the psychic stability of the followers depends on their being recognised by their leader.[4] This may account for both the compulsive need for sexual gratification that overwhelms many charismatic leaders, and their sexual attractiveness to their followers.

There are various kinds of charismatic leader and of leadership (Barker, Beckford and Dobbelaere 1993; B.R.Wilson 1975). Some are more stable than others, and some are actually reparative rather than destructive (Post 1991). However, charismatic leaders are especially vulnerable to the role suction of basic assumption processes and, therefore, they are likely to become personifiers rather than leaders. Some, however, are likely to be severely split between a competent, rational self and an extremely anxious and vulnerable self and, therefore, likely to be both leaders and personifiers, and perhaps to oscillate between these two roles and functions. For example, some evidence suggests (Steinberg 1990) that Hitler might be regarded as a competent charismatic leader who was also an amoeboid character who personified massification processes while Germany was recovering from the aggregation associated with the trauma of World War I; only later, when Germany began to lose the war and aggregation again prevailed, did Hitler shift to his more basic crustacean personality in order to protect himself from being overwhelmed by his psychopathology. In contrast, Mussolini might be regarded as a competent charismatic leader who continued to function as an amoeboid character who personified the massification processes of Italian fascism until the very end. Similarly, Stalin was a competent leader who was also a crustacean character who personified aggregation processes that were magnified by the challenges presented to the government of a large territory containing extreme social and cultural diversity (Rickman 1938; Tucker 1992). Personifications of aggregation and massification processes also existed within the groupings around Hitler, Stalin, Mussolini, Churchill and Roosevelt. Within the context of such speculative observations it might be said that, in contrast, Truman was primarily a work group leader who lacked charisma.

4. Crustacean and amoeboid characters are especially likely to personify the malignant and malevolent forms of social control associated with Incohesion. They are highly susceptible to the suction of roles that characterise aggregation and massification, which provide them with self-definition, protection, and normative support for their feelings. This is especially important because they have great difficulty in acknowledging and experiencing aggressive feelings, both in themselves and in others. However, when crustaceans become angry, they become cold and over-contained; and when amoeboids become angry, they become intrusive and engulfing, based on their tendencies towards vacuole incorporation.

   Crustacean and amoeboid characters are unconsciously compelled to try to communicate the story of their traumatic experience. These personal stories have structure and rhythm, and must be told in a particular way. When traumatised people are unable to tell their stories in a particular way, or when they have no one to listen to them, they attempt unconsciously to communicate through enactments. Projective identification is an important element in such enactments. Other people are forced to collude with both the narrative and the narrator.[5] This can be seen in the way that traumatised children feel compelled to repeat particular stories without realising their symbolic significance (Barrows 2001), and in the way that addicts feel compelled to entertain specific fantasies, which can be traced to screen memories of their traumatic experience (Hopper 1995). Moreover, 'doing drugs' requires the adherence to rituals. In a sense, the need to 'do drugs' indicates the inability of addicts to communicate, that is, to find anyone who can and will both listen to them and hear them, and to respond appropriately to their needs. Although the fantasies of traumatised addicts are highly personal and idiosyncratic, they involve highly sexualised scenarios that are usually taboo. However, these are the stories that the group needs to be told and to hear, which may be why these vulnerable people arouse such intense ambivalence, as seen in the attitudes of traumatised groups to deviant heterosexualities and homosexualities, that is, in the group's polarisation between acceptance and condemnation.

Within the context of Incohesion in general, crustaceans and amoeboids are likely to be both perpetrators and victims of aggression. They acquire identity through both attacking and being attacked. They may even set themselves up to be victimised, which is more satisfying and safer than being completely overlooked and ignored. This involves contradictory processes, some of which occur simultaneously, and some, at different phases of the oscillation between aggregation and massification:

(a) Within the context of aggregation, crustaceans, who are prone to assert their identities as singletons and isolates, are likely to attack the group and its members by withdrawing their affect and involvement from them. They repudiate the group, and they refuse to 'join in'. However, amoeboids, who are prone to assert their identities as membership individuals, are likely to regard crustaceans as responsible for the group's inability to 'come together', for the common experience of empty, silent and cold meaninglessness and for other anxieties associated with aggregation. Hence, amoeboids are likely to attack crustaceans.

(b) Within the context of the early phases of massification, when the compulsion to protect against the psychotic anxieties associated with fission and fragmentation and, hence, with aggregation, is most intense, the people and sub-groups who are perceived as having maintained the idiosyncrasies of identity and who, therefore, stand out from the crowd, are likely to be regarded as 'mavericks', and 'loose cannons'. They must be shunned, and even banished. Hence, amoeboids are likely to attack crustaceans.

(c) Within the context of the later phases of massification, when the psychotic anxieties associated with fusion and confusion are most intense, the people and sub-groups who are perceived as responsible for the loss of autonomy, freedom and individuality, the experience of cultural suffocation, and for various other anxieties associated with massification, are likely to be regarded as 'conformists', who must be replaced. Hence, crustaceans are likely to attack amoeboids.

Charismatic-amoeboid characters are especially vulnerable to being attacked, because they are highly unusual objects of envy. As a defence against the full recognition that they have suffered special predicaments and catastrophes, they both perceive themselves and are perceived by others as having special contact with God or the 'sacred' in general, as being touched by grace, and as having been given a unique 'blessing', which excuses them from ordinary social and cultural constraints, and from the need for ordinary protections. They have been 'chosen' for special treatments and special dispensations. They are beyond cause and effect, which technically is what 'charisma' means. Thus, they both perceive themselves and are perceived by others as being able to violate 'natural' laws and to be able to 'get away with it', for example: to evince a surfeit of bisexuality; to be unnaturally self-sufficient in general; to contain their own parentage and, in effect, to have given birth to themselves specifically; and to be unnaturally youthful or in possession of a charmed combination of youth and maturity, which is not subject to the normal processes of ageing. The son or daughter part of these parent-child combined and amalgamated objects is denigrated, and the father or mother part or parts is idealised, and/or vice versa. Other combinations of gender and generation may also be denigrated and idealised simultaneously in terms of judgements such as competent/incompetent, intelligent/stupid, feared/fearful and worshipped/worshipful, or in other words, in terms of a 'magician' and a 'Mario'. Moreover, even if the illusion of being 'special' and 'chosen' is supported through collusion, it is experienced as exceptionally arrogant, which magnifies the envy aroused by the illusion in the first place, which more or less ensures that the people and sub-groups who maintain this illusion will be chosen for special 'treatment'.

5. Within the context of Incohesion in general, the leaders of the work group and the sub-groups associated with the realities of structure and hierarchy and of positional and relational goods are especially vulnerable to being attacked, for several reasons:

   (a) Leaders are expected to be perfect. A kind of 'Rebecca myth' almost always constrains the group's valuation of them in terms of an idealisation of previous social and political arrangements that have been lost but unmourned (Gouldner 1955). When dependency fails, leaders are likely to be perceived as responsible for the woes of the group, to have betrayed the people, and to be singularly responsible for their feelings of group disgrace. In fact, leaders are always midgets, like Gulliver in the land of Brobdingnag. Hence, it is dangerous to be a bad leader.

   (b) Leaders must make people conscious of the need to make choices within the context of scarce resources, the inevitability of partial failure, the need for realism, and of the constraints of various kinds of social dilemma. Very few decisions can ever be made and realised without some degree of tension and conflict. Moreover, all leaders must have a degree of detachment and aloofness which allows them to resist the romantic idealisation of power, which makes them obstacles to the harmony, enchantment, and magic of massification, which has been collusively promised and expected. It is ironic that when massification prevails, the better the leadership of the work group, the greater is the desire for its elimination. Hence, it is dangerous to be a good leader.

   (c) Male leaders tend to be perceived as fathers or parts of them, who are adored by the mother group and, therefore, as an obstacle to 'her'. Thus, a good leader may be experienced as a 'bad father' who prevents merger with a 'good mother' group (Gibbard, Hartman and Mann 1974; Ruiz 1972). Similarly, female leaders tend to be perceived as mothers or parts of them who are adored by the father group and, therefore, as an obstacle to 'him'. This might apply to both male and female leaders, because in all relationships in which transference predominates, a female may be experienced as a man and a father, and a male, as a woman and a mother and, therefore, the actual sex of the leader may not determine the configuration of Oedipal fantasies about the group and its leaders, especially in the context of compulsions to merge with the perfect mother-group.[6]

(d) People want to be close to a powerful leader, and attacking a leader offers a way of doing this. Such attacks may be associated with homosexual feelings and the paranoid dread of them. The desire to be close to a powerful leader may be based on homosexual feelings which are then blamed on the object who is regarded as responsible for having created the desire: the victim becomes 'bad', and the perpetrator 'good' through eliminating the offending homosexuality both from the victim and himself (Socarides 1979). However, the desire to attack the leader may arouse an erotic defence, that is, a desire to be close to the object of hatred. Again, the homosexual transference to a female leader may involve very similar feelings and defences against them.

The powerful leader who appears to be bisexual may be especially at risk. For example, consider the cases of Prime Ministers Thatcher and Gandhi, and presidents Kennedy, Reagan and Clinton. Two of these leaders were actually assassinated; two were subjected to character assassination; one was ruined while still in office, and one was unceremoniously pushed from office; and one was the victim of an attempted assassination.

6. The leader of the work group who is also charismatic, or in other words, who is both a leader of the work group and a personifier of the massification process, is even more vulnerable to being attacked than the leader of the work group who is not also a personifier of massification process. Usually, these roles are shared between either a leader and a central person, or two leaders with complementary skills and qualities, or among a group of leaders and central persons. Such relationships are difficult, because they are subjected to splitting attacks, and the leader of the work group becomes envious of the admiration and adoration of the charismatic personifier of the

massification process, and/or vice versa. Thus, historically, very few people have been able to fulfil the requirements of these combined roles, at least not for very long.

The constant attacks on charismatic leaders are likely to unsettle their sense of competence, mastery and gender identity. Their frustration and aggressive feelings may be neutralised through sexual gratification, and their sense of impotence may be abated through exploitative coupling. I suppose that although the public would hardly agree that several unnaturally youthful and sexually vigorous presidents of the United States were in any way uncertain about their masculinity, the reports of their compulsive womanising, especially when they were under pressure, suggest otherwise, as do reports about the sexual exploits of charismatic leaders in other nations and in other political systems, e.g. Mussolini. Actually, it is surprising that charismatic leaders are not charged with sexual harassment more often than they are. In this context 'exploitative coupling' might be considered within the context of 'perverse pairing', which is typical of incohesion.

7. The personification of forms of aggression within the context of Incohesion in general can be considered in connection with assassination and terrorist violence. However, if little is known about processes of assassination, still less is known about assassins and terrorists themselves. Biographies of them usually stress that they are indistinguishable from other people who are not assassins, at least in terms of the criteria selected for the comparisons. However, some material suggests that assassins possess a unique mixture of contact-shunning, crustacean characteristics and merger-hungry, amoeboid characteristics. Young, single, intensely committed to one fundamentalist ideology or another, they are likely to be shy, withdrawn 'loners', attracted by the possibilities for stealth and deviousness, and by the opportunities offered for the experience of triumph over their enemies, who may be perceived more in terms of their personal, internal objects than in terms of prevailing political sentiments. Hence, they are marked by a diffuse, weak identity that makes them unusually susceptible to being seductively recruited for the role of assassin, which may strengthen their existing identities, but is more likely to offer a new identity which is valued and respected by the members of the group, who are likely to engage in acts of

reparation towards these vulnerable people and their families (Biran 1995; Forsyth 1971; Mosley 1972; Reeves 2001 and Volkan 2001). These hypotheses are consistent with observations such as that before assassinating John Lennon, John Chapman sought and obtained his autograph, and is quoted afterwards as having said, 'I was a nobody before I killed a somebody'. The data also suggest that the assassins of John F. Kennedy, Robert Kennedy and Martin Luther King, that is, Lee Harvey Oswald, Sirhan Sirhan, and James Earl Ray, respectively, all struggled to maintain the integrity of their personal identities, as did Jack Ruby, who was Oswald's assassin. Torturers and interrogators within the military and police institutions within societies in crisis can be described in these terms (Lifton 1986; Welldon 2000), as can some Hamas suicide bombers and other terrorists in Ireland and the Middle East.

This psychological profile of the assassin is drawn with great subtlety in *Julius Caesar*, in which Shakespeare, who knew everything, arranges for the first cut to Caesar's body to be made not by Brutus and not by Cassius, but by Casca, who is the least known male character in the play. Before striking the first blow, his only action is to offer corrective information about the time on the ides of March that the sun illuminates a particular spot, which suggests a particular cast of mind and preoccupation. When Brutus enquires from Cassius about Casca's reliability as a member of the assassination party, Cassius replies that he knew him at school, when he was particularly concerned to be liked and to be 'one of the boys'. In other words, it is implied that Casca is a highly vulnerable, merger-hungry, amoeboid character (in contrast to Caesar, who is depicted as a once highly competent leader of the work group who is now merely a charismatic central person).[7] Thus, Casca is given an identity as a member of the assassination party, which he gladly substitutes for his highly fragmented and ambiguous personal identity. As a Membership Individual he becomes very self-important.

In sum, the roles associated with processes of Incohesion: Aggregation/Massification are likely to be personified by contact-shunning, crustacean characters, and merger-hungry amoeboid characters. The former are likely to be sucked into the roles that are typical of aggregation, and the latter, into the roles that are typical of massification. These patterns of personification are typical of traumatised groups and group-like social systems. Types of personifiers and personification of basic assumption processes should be distinguished from types of leader and leadership of the work group. Some charismatic leaders are also likely to personify basic assumption processes: aggregation, by charismatic crustacean characters, and massification, by charismatic amoeboid characters. Within the roles offered by the processes of incohesion, crustacean and amoeboid characters are likely to be both perpetrators of aggression and the victims of aggression from others. Within the context of massification processes, the work group leader is also vulnerable, especially when he is charismatic leader, and likely to be blamed for both the imperfections of the massified society and for the suffocating fundamentalism and idolatry which are characteristic of it. These distinctions are absolutely central to our clinical work in groups with difficult patients, because they are likely to personify the roles that are generated by the processes of incohesion.

Notes

1 Modern biography is often a study of personification, as seen, for example, in *Foot Steps* by Richard Holmes (1995), whose biographies of Coleridge offer insights into the society and culture in which he lived. Within the sociological tradition, Bendix (1966) offers simultaneously a biography of his father and a social history of the legal profession in conjunction with a particular social class within a particular region of Germany at a particular phase of its history, also shedding light on the structure of the family, gender roles, and political power. Similar ideas were explored by Canetti (1935, 1980).

2 Foulkes (1968) used this concept, which was common parlance in socio-drama, e.g. Blatner (2000). Turquet (1975) once referred to the personification of homogenisation by a charismatic leader. However, I suspect that this is a perfect example of Kreeger's editorial gloss on the manuscript that Turquet 'submitted' for his chapter in Kreeger (1975).

3 For example, Turquet (1975) wrote that Oneness groups are likely to be led by 'charismatic' people; Kernberg (1994a) described such leaders as 'narcissistic-dependent'; Anzieu (1981) referred to them as promoters or merchants of illusions; Freud (1931), to the narcissistic libidinal type; Scheidlinger (1980), to the immature leader; and Kohut and Wolf (1978), to the leader who was in search of his narcissistic group-self; etc.

4 This collusive unit of charismatic leaders, followers and bystanders was described in *Mario and the Magician* by Thomas Mann (1933), as noted by Margaret Rioch (1971).

5 I suspect that this was recognised by Coleridge (1798) in *The Rime of the Ancient Mariner*, in which one is never certain whether it is the mariner or the wedding guest who deserves the greater amount of sympathy.

6 Authoritarian leaders use a scapegoating process in order to displace aggression directed towards themselves as 'bad' father figures onto still more vulnerable targets (Scheidlinger 1952). Hence, the propensity to attack the 'bad' father and the 'bad' mother leaders is not always apparent.

7 *Julius Caesar* also illustrates the continuing, phased and virtually cyclical pattern of the emergence of the fourth basic assumption of Incohesion: Aggregation/Massification, as seen in the inability to mourn the death of Caesar, in the subsequent oscillations from massification to aggregation and back again to massification, and in their respective personifications by various central persons who comprised the assassination party, before the work group was eventually restored.

CHAPTER 5

The Treatment of Difficult Patients in Clinical Group Analysis

The Personification of Aggregation by Pandoro

In this and the next two chapters I will illustrate my theory of Incohesion as the fourth basic assumption in the unconscious life of groups with clinical data from twice weekly group analysis, which involves, in effect, the application of the study of group dynamics to clinical work in groups. I will also consider one of the reasons why group analysis is especially useful in the treatment of difficult patients, and when and why we can and should address particular individuals, even at some length, within the treatment modality of group analysis.

1. By 'difficult patient' I mean those with pronounced borderline and narcissistic elements in their personalities and characters. 'Difficult' is not a particularly precise diagnosis, but many clinicians prefer to use this broad, ambiguous working category. Nonetheless, it must be acknowledged that whether in dyadic or group forms of treatment, all patients can be difficult, and patients who are difficult for some therapists may be easier for others, at least for some of the time (Gans and Alonso 1998). As outlined in Chapter 2, difficult patients have been described in similar but slightly different ways by authors such as Balint (1968), Bleger (1966), Anna Freud (1946), Zetzel (1958), Kernberg (1975), Kohut and Wolf (1978), Tustin (1981), H. Rosenfeld (1971), and Steiner (1999). The distinguishing features of difficult patients are their fear of annihilation, specific anxieties

associated with fission and fragmentation and fusion and confusion, and the encapsulation of their traumatic experience and disassociation from it. It is useful to think in terms of two main types of difficult patient: those with contact-shunning, crustacean character structures associated with the phenomenology of fission and fragmentation, and those with merger-hungry, amoeboid character structures associated with the phenomenology of fusion and confusion. Such patients manifest the main features of multiple personality disorder, and it may be apposite to think of them in terms of the 'Osiris complex', which refers to an unconscious syndrome of impulses, fears, fantasies, and relationships associated with feeling fragmented, and with feeling that one has fragmented others (Ross 1994).

I presented clinical vignettes of a number of such patients in 'Encapsulation as a defence against the fear of annihilation' (Hopper 1991, excerpts of which are reprinted as Appendix II of this book). I will remind you here of their clinical 'feel'. With respect to contact-shunning, crustacean characters, consider the case of a man of twenty-nine years of age who was referred for help with his compulsive promiscuity, inability to 'settle down' in his career, involving several very promising freelance pursuits in artistic fields of work which he could never actually complete, and the excessive use of illegal drugs. I call him 'Pandoro', a masculine version of a name that refers to the very essence of narcissistic and borderline suffering (Tuttman 1990). Pandoro was referred to me for help with his urticaria and addiction to marijuana and compulsive abuse of other illegal substances, such as cocaine and occasionally heroin:

> He was the second of five children who were born approximately one year apart. His mother was hospitalised in connection with the difficult pregnancy of a younger brother. Subsequently, she was very depressed, and treated by a psychiatrist for 'post-natal depression'. She has spent the rest of her life in and out of hospital for a variety of what would seem to be psychosomatic illnesses. Both the patient and his mother had a history of skin ailments.

These data are taken from sessions during the sixth year of a four times a week psychoanalysis:

> After a 'night on the tiles' in an all Black area of the inner city, he confessed being both hung over and still high from smoking a lot of dope. He planned more of the same for the weekend. I interpreted that he was withdrawing

> from me and into the urban jungle, because he was hurt that I would be unavailable to him for the weekend, and soon for an entire month. After a long dreamy silence during which he seemed to have faded away, he said that while 'doing dope' early that morning, he had a fantasy that he was in a clearing in the African jungle, looking into an enormous black hole within the foliage that threatened to envelop him. He had an African type of javelin spear that he threw into the centre of the black hole. He followed that javelin through the hole up to the point where it landed. He discovered that it had pinioned me to my chair. As I stared transfixed across the room, he sat down next to me and stroked my hand in a very gentle way.

Although this material sounds very exciting, the mood of the sessions was dull, even boring, and certainly inconsistent with the contents of the verbal communication. In fact, flatness of affect is one of the distinguishing characteristics of patients with encapsulations. The clinical 'feel' of their material, especially during the early phases of treatment, is like a knot in an otherwise well cut plank of wood, or the sensations of running one's fingers over a piece of silk, linen or tweed and perceiving that a few threads are broken, miswoven or missing.

In the analyses of such patients I focus primarily on problems of helplessness and powerlessness, loss and separation, fear of damaging and being damaged. I focus on rage and impotence, shame and humiliation and unbearable guilt. Only secondarily do I try to analyse envy, and eventually various kinds of negative therapeutic reactions that usually arise only in association with termination. When I do analyse envy it is as a defence against feelings of helplessness, usually in the context of the transference to me as someone who could be of help but who will not.

2. There is an extensive literature on the treatment of difficult patients in groups and in conjoint and serial combinations of dyadic and group modalities.[1] This literature can be summarised by a list of ten reasons why treatment in groups is thought to be helpful for our most difficult patients:

    (a) The group provides a holding and containing environment, which is supportive, facilitating and encouraging. Some think of this in terms of Winnicott's concept of the 'environmental mother', but others prefer the concept of an 'archaic good mother'.

    (b) The group provides opportunities for experience with transitional objects and transitional phenomena, because it is so clearly a 'me-not me' object, and, therefore, it helps an individual to individuate and separate from archaic, negative maternal objects.

(c) The group provides opportunities for safe play, that is, for trying on and taking off various gloves of identity without serious consequences.

(d) The group provides opportunities for realistic feedback from people who are heterogeneous in their social and personal qualities.

(e) The group provides opportunities for the negotiations of personal and social boundaries both between self and other and within oneself, and in this connection to test reality and to understand the difference between psychic and social facts.

(f) The group offers opportunities for benign mirroring and echoing, with many 'witnesses' and 'referees' who help to limit the intensity of negotiations about psychic and social truths.

(g) The group offers protection and shielding from tough but necessary confrontations. Although scapegoating occurs, the conductor can usually bring some objectivity to this process, and help the various members reclaim those parts of themselves that are projected. Actually, intensive scapegoating by an entire group of only one member is fairly rare, except when it happens to the group conductor.

(h) The group provides opportunities for intimacy with males and females, but in general intimacy is more diffuse and, therefore, less frightening to the vulnerable patient, who usually suffers from a degree of confusion in his or her gender identity.

(i) The group offers opportunities for altruism, that is, patients can simultaneously both help and be helped, and this greater degree of symmetry and interdependence between patients and the group conductor provides opportunities for reparation and forgiveness, and for moderating the experience of destructive envy and rage.

(j) Face to face interaction with peers and the therapist is especially suitable for anxieties associated with shame, which is more than merely an archaic form of guilt.

The tenth reason in the list is especially pertinent. Although many regard shame as merely an archaic form of guilt, I take a more traditional view that shame is primary to guilt, and is inherent in the interpersonal nature of the human condition. As Winnicott (1971) has commented, seeing and being seen cannot be reduced to a matter of having displaced the experience of the breast upwards into the gaze, or of having projected desires to attack the breast into the gaze of others, including that of third parties. Shame in psychoanalysis and group analysis has been discussed at some length by Pines (1987), who works within the tradition of self psychology.

This list is not meant to replace Yalom's (1975) 'ten curative factors in group psychotherapy', which has been corroborated by clinical data, although the search for an eleventh or even a twelfth factor has become an industry in its own right, as have attempts to reduce this list to several key factors (Scheidlinger 1997; Piper 1995), especially in connection with the issue of whether the analysis of group dynamics should be considered when assessing the value of therapy in a group (Munich 1993), as I think it must. Some of these factors are derived from the object relations 'tradition', and some from self psychology, but they are all derived from contemporary psychoanalysis, and developed for our work in groups. For example, the concepts of 'transitional phenomena' and 'environmental mother' (Winnicott 1971) are consistent with theories of the group as mother (Scheidlinger 1980).

Most of the reasons listed why experience in a therapeutic group is thought to be important are similar to the reasons that I would list why experience of psychoanalysis and of dyadic therapy is important and, of course, both group and dyadic modalities can be cold, sloppy and uncontained. What therefore does group analysis offer that is unique, especially in the treatment of difficult patients? I believe that the essence of an answer to this question lies in the help that the group can provide the group analyst with his countertransference and general affective responses to his most difficult patients. This view is completely consistent with the theory of group analysis, in which it is recognised that we may become immobilised or blinded, hopefully on a temporary basis, with any and all of our patients, but especially with those who are most difficult for us.[2]

I would like, however, to consider another factor that is unique to group analytic treatment generally, but especially for our most difficult patients.

Group analysis presents opportunities for working in a contained way with the personification of the roles associated with unconscious basic assumption processes, and in particular with those associated with Incohesion: Aggregation/Massification. Our most difficult patients are particularly likely to personify these roles, mainly because helplessness, envy and aggression are especially troublesome for them. They are highly vulnerable to role suction, because they tend to communicate through processes of malignant projective and introjective identification. The basic assumption of Incohesion is also likely to have characterised their early and continuing family life. Group analysis affords opportunities for the unconscious repetition of such processes, and for their unconscious personification. Although this is a source of various technical problems within 'difficult groups', these processes can be used to provide insight and opportunities to work through fundamental intra-personal and inter-personal conflicts.[3]

3. I first described my clinical technique or orientation in group analysis in 1982 in 'The Problem of Context'. However, over the years I have become more 'transparent' and 'supportive'.[4]

   Usually, my groups have nine patients, four men and five women plus myself. People stay for an average of five or six years, and some have stayed longer than twenty years.

   I do not think in terms of 'individual versus group' modalities of treatment. What I used to recommend only for my most difficult patients, I now recommend for them all. I prefer to see people first individually, for as many times per week as possible, given the exigencies of cost, times, constraints of living and working within an urban conurbation, etc. for at least two years, and then in a group for an indefinite period of time.

   Early on in the negotiation of the terms of dyadic treatment, it is agreed that eventually we will explore the possibility of coming into one of my twice weekly groups. I usually arrange a transitional phase during which a patient reduces the number of individual sessions per week, and then enters a group, followed by a period of time during which he has both individual and group sessions. This latter phase can last from six to eighteen months or longer, by when he is usually able to manage in a group without the help of individual sessions. Naturally there continues to be a transference to me, but within a group new elements of the transference emerge. Also, the transferences to members of a group, to their relationships, to sub-groups, to a group as a whole, etc. gradually take precedence over the transference to me. On occasion, it is necessary for a patient to come back into individual treatment, particularly when new members have entered a group. During the lengthy introduction of a new patient, the members of a group are generally very co-operative and helpful, although they are not always pleased to share a group's and my time and attention.

Some of my group patients will have had psychoanalysis or psychoanalytical therapy from a colleague who does not share my clinical orientation. In this case, group analysis is usually offered as a kind of complementary or perhaps supplementary form of treatment, but on occasion it has offered an antidote.[5]

4. This clinical vignette is from a mature, heterogeneous slow-open group of adults who meet twice weekly for the purpose of psychotherapy. The patients in this vignette are no longer in the Group, and I have altered some information in order to protect confidentiality. It would be best to describe group process in terms of data from at least two observers with respect to all the dimensions of a group as a social system, and in terms of information about the feelings of the therapist and other members of the Group. However, like most authors, I will emphasise the content of the communications, primarily because it is easier both to present and to grasp, and it is most relevant for clinical work.

With respect to the treatment of difficult patients in group analysis, I will focus on the personification of Incohesion by Pandoro, a compulsive abuser of various illegal drugs, who evinced both crustacean and amoeboid characteristics. He personified both the yearning for isolation, which underlies Aggregation, and the yearning for merger, which underlies Massification. Pandoro was in the second, group phase of his therapy. The Group helped Pandoro and me to tolerate the aggression in my countertransference to him. They provided a degree of holding and containing that enabled me to get in touch with various feelings in the Group and in myself, and enabled Pandoro to hear what I was saying to him, and to make use of it. The Group also tolerated my failures and imperfections, which enabled me to think more deeply about myself, and to become a little less critical of myself and, therefore, of Pandoro in particular and other patients more generally.

With respect to the theory of Incohesion, this vignette is intended to illustrate a number of points: the development of aggregation in response to helplessness precipitated by the experience of failed dependency; a tentative shift towards massification in an attempt to seek protection; and, on the basis of interpretation of complex transferences to myself and to the Group as a whole, the tentative recovery of work group functioning and optimal cohesion. The intrusion of frightening and hateful elements from the environment of the Group made it very difficult to project fear and hatred into the environment, which delayed a protective shift towards massification. Instead, a gender based contra-group developed, which then became a social encapsulation. (In the wider social context this would be called an 'enclave' or a 'ghetto'.) The patterns of aggression are particularly clear. Typical of aggregation, the members of the Group rejected one another, and as the leader of the work group, I was attacked for both failing the Group and attempting to hold it together. I was then attacked as an obstacle to massification, specifically as a flawed paternal object who prevented attempts to merge with an hallucinated maternal object.

The clinical vignette

One evening in August, shortly before I would be taking my holiday, the Group began with a sullen silence, as if they had been talking a lot but stopped abruptly when I entered the room. Several minutes later a 'buzzing' developed. Buzz, buzz, buzz, buzz. At first it was intermittent. The Group and I ignored this noise, and the session continued. However, over the next few sessions the buzzing became louder and more continuous. Still, no one acknowledged that what had begun as a kind of irritating 'background noise' had become increasingly intrusive and disturbing.

Although I, too, had ignored this sound, I was the first to become really aware of it. This is hardly surprising. Not only was the basic ecology of the Group my responsibility, I was in the room for many hours a day, and certainly in between the group sessions. I had noticed that a yellow-brown stain had appeared at the corner of one of the two symmetrical windows of the consulting room, but now a yellow-brown liquid had begun to drip from the wall from where the buzzing was loudest. Upon inspection, the wall was warm to the touch.

The development of aggregation

> When the Group next met, they acknowledged the buzzing, the stain and the drip, but they seemed petrified to discuss this 'turbulent event at its boundaries' (Agazarian and Carter 1993). Instead, they sat in silence. Occasionally, they looked at the wall, and punctuated their silence with brief comments. I realised that the buzzing, stain and dripping had become even more pronounced than I had allowed myself to acknowledge. I felt a little anxious that I had not taken more care to protect the Group from real danger from the 'outside'.
>
> Pandoro broke the silence: 'This is a wasps' nest. By "wasp" you know what I really mean: " WASP", White, Anglo-Saxon, Protestant. Ha, ha, ha'. This joke was not all that funny, but the Group continued to make these kinds of remarks. Pandoro laughed much more than anyone else.

Before I indicate how I interpreted this material, I will consider the question of the 'location' (Bernfeld 1929; Foulkes and Anthony 1964; Winnicott 1967) of meaning of communications within the matrix of the group. I (Hopper 1996b) have argued elsewhere that it is necessary in both individual and group work to interpret the transference and counter-transference in the 'Here and Now' in terms of all the cells in the time/space paradigm, namely: 'Here and Then' of experience during infancy; 'There and Now' of extra session experience in the social and cultural context of treatment; and 'There and Then' of the experience of parents, grand-parents and others in previous generations. In order to understand such constraints, it is necessary to think in terms of concepts such as the 'social unconscious' and of 'equivalence', and to be especially sensitive to anxieties associated with personal and social powerlessness. Although ultimately the 'complete interpretation' requires work within all four cells, at any one moment the analyst must trust his intuitive sense of where it is hottest, and where the Group cannot or will not go without interpretive help and facilitative 'nudges'. All basic assumption processes and their personifications can be taken up in terms of the unconscious constraints of social and cultural factors, as well as of more universal aspects of infancy and childhood, which are in any case completely intertwined. This is especially true for aggregation and massification, because they are responses to the fear of annihilation associated with profound personal and social powerlessness.

The clinical vignette is from the Group that I (Hopper 1982b) first presented in 'Group Analysis: The Problem of Context', in which I described the emergence of anti-Semitic sentiments based on feelings of helplessness and defensive envy, which was interpreted or 'contextualised' in terms of the unconscious constraints of social, cultural and political processes of the wider society, or in other words, in terms of the foundation matrix of the group (Foulkes and Anthony 1964). The Group came to recognise that they had created a matrix that was 'equivalent' to the arrangements of the wider society, of which they had been 'socially unconscious' (Hopper 1996b).

However, I regarded Pandoro's jokey communications about wasps and WASPs as an attempt to escape from the emotions of the 'Here and Now'. Actually, they were not so much an escape as they were an attempt to entice me into a discussion of racialism in Britain in order to divert our attention from attempting to deepen our experience and to explore the full range of possible explanations of it, including the repetition of more personal, infantile conflicts. Culture and meaning are, of course, the essence of persons-in-relationships, the basis of human society (Hopper 1991). However, I felt that it would have been defensive for me to examine, for example, references to a 'wasps' nest' as a metaphor for an inhuman state of affairs, a society without culture and, therefore, without meaning. Thus, I proceeded in a more traditional, psychoanalytical way.

An interpretation from the group analyst

> Without much hesitation, I interpreted these 'teasing' remarks about WASPs in terms of what I believed was an envious attack in response to the helplessness that they felt about my taking a holiday in a few weeks' time, and specifically in terms of the cutting and stinging of separation anxiety. I said that their attack was expressed in their understandable preoccupations with the brown stains and yellow liquid, which involved unconscious projections of their desires to make anal and urethral attacks on my eyes, which were displacements upwards from my analytical breasts, as symbolized by the windows. The Group wanted to do to me what the wasps were doing to my wall, because I was leaving them in the lurch, as they had wanted to do to their mothers during their infancies, when they were so often so badly let down by them. They felt disappointed by my taking a holiday, but more importantly they felt that I had failed to protect us from these wasps.
>
> I emphasised their anxious fear about hurting me because, despite my imperfections, they felt very dependent on me and on the Group, and did not want to destroy us, or to make me feel reluctant to return after the summer break. In other words, I stressed the sequence of the traumatic effects of failed dependency, fear of annihilation characterised by extreme helplessness, defensive envy expressed in their desire to make anal and

> urethral attacks, anxiety about destructiveness and retaliation, partly converting their sadistic and destructive impulses into teasing and a joke, and partly projecting their impulses into the nest of wasps behind the wall near the window. I stressed the anxieties as much, if not more, than the aggressive and sadistic impulses. I also said that the wasps had no alternative but to follow their instincts, that is, the wasps were being wasps and doing what wasps do, but that as human beings we had choices.

I did not express these ideas in such complex and abstract terms. I used 'experience near' vernacular. I referred to 'shit' and 'piss'. Gradually, I returned to using more neutral, clinical language in keeping with a shift from emotional experience to reflection.

> During the remainder of the session the Group associated to their difficult relationships with parents who they felt were always preoccupied with people other than their children, or who were so obsessed with regulating their children's lives that they felt invisible as unique individuals. One member said that she had felt like a figment of her mother's imagination. The Group acknowledged their destructive feelings towards their parents. I said that it seemed easier to discuss such feelings towards their parents than towards me.

The persistence of aggregation

> At the next session it became clear that in their attempts to acknowledge their destructive feelings, the Group had become very frightened. The nest of wasps was still there, as were all the signs of its vitality. (I had rung the Council, and was assured that in due course 'someone' would call. I had not had a chance to bring in a private exterminator, and I had not wanted to deal with this dangerous nest of wasps by myself.) The Group were again silent, mesmerised by the buzzing of the wasps which were entirely invisible. I wondered about the Group as 'wasps', and about my internal 'wasps'. I also started to comfort myself with thoughts about a paper I had given about 'mediating objects'. My thoughts were interrupted by two or perhaps three interjections about the impending holiday break, but the Group kept lapsing into silence, unable and unwilling to build communications. Their silence was again sullen, characterised by mutual alienation, averted eye contact, occasional but affectless efforts to talk about any topic that might break the silence.
>
> During this and the next two sessions people continued to stare at one another or at the table or at the wall or the ceiling. The buzzing area of the wall and ceiling had become part of the Group's space. I was no longer in its

environment. From time to time someone would stare at me in a distancing manner. I tried to facilitate a discussion of the mood and the patterns of interaction and communication. I was hardly acknowledged. My efforts to interpret envy and anxiety about separation were met with silence. Occasionally someone giggled.

Another interpretation by the group analyst

I said that perhaps we shared some uncertainty about where the wasps really were, what the 'real' wasps really were, and what kind of exterminator was required. I suggested that by taking a holiday I had become the exterminator of the Group, and that the Group wanted to exterminate me. It was hard to see this because the wasps behind the wall were so scary. I was well aware of the constraints of the social unconscious, but this was not, I said, a matter of WASPs as exterminators, or of the wasps as the exterminated not, at any rate, primarily.

The personification of aggregation

Suddenly, Pandoro said, 'What a bloody waste of time. We really ought to have stopped at Whitsun, and started after the August bank holiday. The summer is always a dead loss. I have better things to do with my summers. I am going to get stoned out of my head until the summer's over. At least the people I'll be with won't sit around giggling and staring at one another. Actually, I don't want to talk to anybody here anyway'.

After a brief silence, I said, 'I have the impression that you do with your friends precisely what you say you don't want to do here, that is, you sit around giggling and staring at one another. The difference is that here you don't do dope'.

Lighting up a joint that he took from behind his ear, he replied, 'Why don't you get one of the women to protect you from the wasps? Even my father knew how to deal with this sort of problem'.

In a stilted and slightly defensive way, I replied, 'I suspect that you can't decide whether you want to sting me or protect me, possibly from my wife and children with whom I will be taking my holiday, as you know, and that you are very disappointed with my inability to protect you and the rest of us, including myself, from these wasps. But I am sure that the most dangerous wasps of all are the ones inside us all'. After a brief silence that I felt was attentive and thoughtful, I went on to say, 'Perhaps it is easier for you to opt out altogether. But I bet that you are waiting for one of the women to come between us, as your mother and older sister used to do when you fought with your Dad, so that you never had any contact with him'. However, none of the women volunteered. It was unclear whether they refrained on the basis of their sensitivity to Pandoro's need to relate directly to me, or of their fear of coming between us.

I tried with some success to convey to Pandoro that he needed his drug induced fantasies of homosexuality as a way of protecting us from his violence, but it was worth thinking about whether he really needed to smoke dope in order to regulate his homosexual fantasies, and really needed his homosexual fantasies in order to regulate his violent feelings towards me. Pandoro took a couple of tokes, and provocatively offered his roach to the others. Two men took drags. Pandoro stubbed out the roach, and became a bit glassy-eyed and withdrawn, staring off into the middle distance. I doubted whether he was as stoned as all that! The men looked at the table.

The emergence of an engendered contra-group

The women smiled at one another. Then, one of the women said that this whole problem could be acknowledged and thought about by the women in the Group. Another woman agreed, and said to Pandoro that like his father, I was from another generation, and most probably had never even tried dope. Yet another woman explained that I was not really as old as I seemed, but most probably had been some sort of prodigy who had missed out on his adolescence.

At the next session the women talked only to one another. They ignored Pandoro, the other men and me. Actually, they shunned us. When I asked the women about this, they said that fundamentally this was how they had been treated by men. One of the women said that she would not return in September. Another woman said that she did not blame her, and that she would leave at Christmas. I thought to myself that if she thought that she could wait until Christmas, we would all be able to get through this Group trough. The Group lapsed into silence, but the women were silent in a merged, communicative way. They continued to ignore the men. The men were silent in an alienated, withdrawn way. They continued to ignore everyone, and became a collection of isolates and singletons.

Yet another interpretation from the group analyst

I then made two interpretations. First, I said that I could imagine that the women were feeling rivalrous with the men, especially Pandoro who, like a little brother, had received a lot of attention from their father-analyst, although in fairness he did not deserve this, because he had behaved in a delinquent way. Their anger at us led them to want to leave the Group. Second, I acknowledged my failure to protect us from the wasps, and my preoccupations with other, more personal matters, which had involved a kind of denial of the danger that we were in. Although I had failed their expectations, I was determined to do the best I could. I added that perhaps we were all involved in a kind of denial of our various sorrows and tears which had become concretised in the weeping window.

In reply, a woman said that I was 'only human'. A man said that he had really only been teasing, and had wanted to provoke me into making more contact with him. I said that I was not asking for their forgiveness, but acknowledging their right to be disappointed and angry. However, I would not let them destroy the Group. One woman said that she thought that she had miscarried during the previous few days, but that no one knew that she was pregnant. The session ended in thoughtful silence.

A shift towards massification

Everyone returned to the next session. From time to time we discussed the nest of wasps, and how it was hoped that over the holiday I would attend to this. We accepted that the turmoil was both within and without, and that I had to share responsibility for it. We began to feel that we shared a very special event, from which we would learn a great deal. A sense of pride began to develop. Although these communications indicated a degree of recovery of work group functioning, I felt that the Group had begun to communicate with clichés. In fact, a tentative shift to a state of massification could be seen in the references to our unique experience, and to our belief that no other group in the world would ever have such an experience. The emphasis on being 'special' suggests a nascent process of pseudo-speciation. The Group ended with a lengthy, hypnotic silence, both the opposite from and identical to the buzzing sound from the nest of wasps.

During the summer break, with the help of the Council's exterminator, I did manage to exterminate the wasps.

The tentative re-emergence of the work group

After the break, the Group began as they had stopped: in silence. Eventually, Pandoro took a deep breath, and said that we should acknowledge that we had survived a danger brought on by my failure to protect them. We began a slow, patient exploration of the location of the danger. As the autumn passed, the Group focused on my weaknesses and flaws, sometimes with perception and concern. I again acknowledged that although during the summer I was not as sensitive to the Group as I would have liked, we were still together and still trying to help ourselves understand more about our internal worlds and about how we both affected and were affected by other people. I said that I had an important part to play in this achievement. I thought but did not say that we worked through a painful experience of aggregation involving feelings of extreme loneliness and isolation while being in the company of people whom we trusted and knew very well.

Pandoro said that he seemed no longer to feel like one of a number of balls on a billiard table (which is the source of my metaphor for aggregation being like a set of billiard balls). As the Group continued, I wondered about the foundation matrix. I suggested that the Group might wish to think about the kind of society in which they were living, and in which they wished to live. Was it possible, I asked, that the current view within the Government that there was no such thing as a society but only a collection of individuals was more disturbing than they realised? Was it possible that they were confused about how to establish connections and relationships that allowed them to identify with one another's sorrows as well as successes? Was the idea of a nurturing man an oxymoron? The Group began to explore issues of gender identity and homosexuality in an exceedingly honest way. They referred to homosexuality among public school boys who had lost their mothers so early in life. One man said that he would rather be the Queen than Prince Phillip. A woman said that Diana would never really be happy.

As the autumn gave way to winter, the Group explored addiction as an essential element in the personification of the foundation matrix. They discussed addiction and eating disorders. They explored how various features of failed dependency had led to states of aggregation and massification within the wider society of which the Group was a microcosm.

Notes

1 Among the most comprehensive and insightful volumes are Roth, Stone and Kibel (1990), and Schermer and Pines (1994). Among the most useful articles are Kauff (1991), Schlachet (1992) and Roller and Nelson (1999). These books and articles include extensive bibliography.

2 Although comparatively little has been written about countertransference in group analysis, the following examples are helpful: Foulkes and Anthony (1964), Hopper (1982b, 1985), Kauff, (1991), Roth (1980), and Yalom (1989).

3 Shapiro and Zinner (1979) were among the first to apply early developments of basic assumption theory to the treatment of difficult patients within family groups. They implied that the fragmentation of the families of borderline patients is inter-related with

their psychic fragmentation, and that parallel processes are involved. However, as noted in Chapter 1, Scharff and Scharff (1987) conceptualised these parallel processes in terms of a fourth basic assumption; and as noted in the Introduction, Battegay (1973), Springmann (1975), Pines (1986) and Ganzarain (1989) have all discussed the development of 'fusion' groups as a defence against the anxieties of borderline patients, and Wexler *et al.* (1984) referred to the 'one-ness' groups of schizophrenic patients. However, I maintain that rather than focus only on 'fusion' or 'one-ness', it is essential to understand the emergence of the full range of processes that comprise the fourth basic assumption of Incohesion in the unconscious life of groups, including primary and secondary aggregation.

4 My work is consistent with the guidelines established in Roberts and Pines (1991), but I continue to learn from other psychoanalytic group therapists, such as the contributors to Klein, Bernard and Singer (1992).

5 I am reminded that during a special panel for the American Group Psychotherapy Association meetings in San Antonio, 1991, Dr Otto Kernberg asked me, 'Why don't you just go on seeing these patients individually in analysis and work towards termination?' At this time I had six patients in four or five times a week traditional psychoanalysis, and perhaps three of them were rather 'difficult'. I answered, 'The culture of modern urban society simply does not support psychoanalysis, and by 'support' I do not mean merely financial support, which is one reason why the couch is at sea' (which was a reference to his 'The Couch at Sea' (Kernberg 1984)). Although I still believe this to be true, it is not the heart of the matter.

CHAPTER 6

The Personification of Massification by Pandora

In this chapter I will present a further illustration of the fourth basic assumption of Incohesion in the unconscious life of groups. I will focus on the personification of Massification by a merger-hungry, amoeboid character. It is hardly surprising that I will call her 'Pandora'.

Background

Pandora was thirty-eight years old. She contacted me after an unsatisfactory experience in a once weekly group conducted by a colleague who had died suddenly. She was shocked by his death, but not saddened. Actually, she was relieved, because this gave her the chance to leave the group, which somehow she had not been able to do. Among her presenting symptoms were shame of her history of periodic phases of bisexuality, an intense persistent monophobia of cancer which was virtually an hypochondriasis with respect to a single disease, leading her to seduce many doctors to perform various medical investigations, excessive drinking, and the abuse of a number of other addictive substances:

> Following the hospitalisation of her mother for a depressive illness, this patient was looked after by family friends from approximately three months of age, for approximately six months. Her mother was hospitalised again when the patient was two years of age and she was looked after by these friends for approximately six months. During these periods of time, she saw her father only rarely.

I accepted her into a full psychoanalysis. After seven years she decided, with my agreement, to reduce the number of sessions from five times a week to four. This decision was made in the spring. In June she became aware of a fistula, which was successfully removed in July. We took a break in August. The analysis resumed in September:

> In the very first session she introduced the image of Pandora's box as a metaphor for her rigid, hard, muscular and bony body. (She did not look that way to me.) In addition to other associations to the myth and to the box she was convinced that her Pandora's box contained powerful insects such as bees, hornets, and other 'stingy little creatures'. They were all dangerous but she felt well protected, because she could suffocate them with poisoned aerosol sprays. She felt that I would stop treatment if I knew how vulnerable I was to her inner dybbuks.
>
> In the next session she dreamt that her disreputable gynaecologist used a laser to remove from her cheek a birth mark mole with hairs growing out of it, and another mole from her buttock. In her dream the mole on her face turned into a pseudo-pod that stepped into my stomach where it became rooted in such a way that if she had to leave me it would have to be ripped out like a tumour or insidious weed. She associated these moles to stigmata of punishment for stealing and eventually for killing the unborn babies of her mother. We understood this material in terms of the encapsulation manifest in her recent fistula, the reparative surgery, separation and the loss of a session and her fantasies about the other patient(s) who had taken her session, and who would soon replace the space that she had vacated.
>
> During the autumn we focused on her fear that I had abandoned her and that her abandonment of me would soon lead to further cutting of her sessions. Obviously she was experiencing an intense fusion and confusion of her traumatised infantile self with her early maternal object, and with me and her analysis itself.

In January, after the Christmas break, we decided to reduce her sessions from four to three after the spring break, and from three to two after the summer break, when she would also join one of my twice weekly groups. The plan was that slowly she would terminate her dyadic sessions, but continue in the Group for an indefinite period of time.

When Pandora joined the Group, each of the seven members had been in psychoanalysis or lengthy psychoanalytical psychotherapy with me. Each person had a history of early traumatic experience, for example, one woman had been badly scarred by boiling water when she was four years old when her mother dropped a kettle while preparing her tea, and one man had a brother, two years younger than himself, who at six years of age was sexually abused and murdered.

Some idea of the intensity of the group process and the vulnerability of the members of the Group can be seen in how they responded to the impending summer break and my having told them that Pandora would be joining the Group in September. Although I gave this information in early June, in late July, right before the break, a Black woman, who had come to London when she was ten years old, and who had been in the Group for sixteen years, announced that she felt ready to terminate in the autumn. Another woman said that if her husband did not seek therapy she would separate from him. A third woman told the Group that her seventy-seven-year-old mother had been diagnosed as having breast cancer, and would have a mastectomy during August. A man who was grieving for his partner who had died from an Aids related disease said that he was going to have a blood test because he was feeling tired all the time. Another man who had survived a concentration camp, and who had been in the Group for three years and had been seeing me individually for eight years, told the Group that we had decided to stop individual sessions. The two other men, one of whom was a student at The Institute of Group Analysis, remained silent.

An outline of the process

The following clinical vignette illustrates all phases of Incohesion. In the first instance the Group responded to my reminding them of the forthcoming spring break by becoming very regressed and, in effect, by becoming an aggregate. The Group then transformed itself into a mass. Pandora personified the massification process. Also apparent is the emergence of an engendered contra-group, and the expression of aggressive moral superiority against the members of it, who were scapegoated for their doubt and scepticism about the value of group analysis. The massification process was supported by pseudo-speciation and denigration of various other groups, and by the character assassination of their conductors. Later the Group reversed this process, and became angry towards those who personified the massification process. They eschewed the temptation to become a massification cult. This was connected with my ability to resist their demands that I become a cult leader. Eventually, on the basis of interpretations offered by members of the Group, the participants regained their capacity to recognise and to accept their diversity and their imperfections. The work group began to reform itself, and made important efforts towards the resolution of various conflicts. The cohesion of the Group increased.

The clinical vignette

Aggregation

> As I sat down, I sensed that the Group was feeling overwhelmed with anxiety. The mood was sullen, the atmosphere heavy. The Group stared at one another in silence. I remembered that in the previous session the Group responded with hostile silence to my reminding them that I would soon be taking my usual spring break for three weeks for the Easter and Passover holidays. While reflecting on their reaction, which was based on a virtual denial that they knew that this would soon occur, I became aware that actually I was worried that the Group would disintegrate, and that some of us were unlikely to return after the break. I thought that their pattern of communication was a response to their anxiety following their having become more fully aware of the impending holiday break. In effect, they evinced a kind of silence that is typical of an aggregate.
>
> As the silence continued, I tried to think about my own anxiety, and about who in the Group was feeling what on behalf of whom. I became aware that the Group had seated themselves in an unusual pattern. I was aware that group analysts are inclined to read meaning into the seating patterns that have occurred by accident, largely influenced by where the second member of the Group sits, and so on, until all available places are filled. However, on this occasion the pattern defied statistical calculation. As the Group stared at one another, I counted to myself seven variables on the basis of which the Group had polarised and formed into sub-groups, contra-groups, and singletons. The data suggest that they formed a pattern of interaction that is typical of an aggregate.

The seating pattern of the Group is illustrated in Figure 6.1.

In Figure 6.1 each circle indicates the seating arrangement with respect to a particular variable; the broken line indicates one category, and the unbroken line, the other. I have included only those variables of which I became aware during the session. In retrospect, the group polarised with respect to several other variables as well, for example, various personality characteristics and even hair colour.

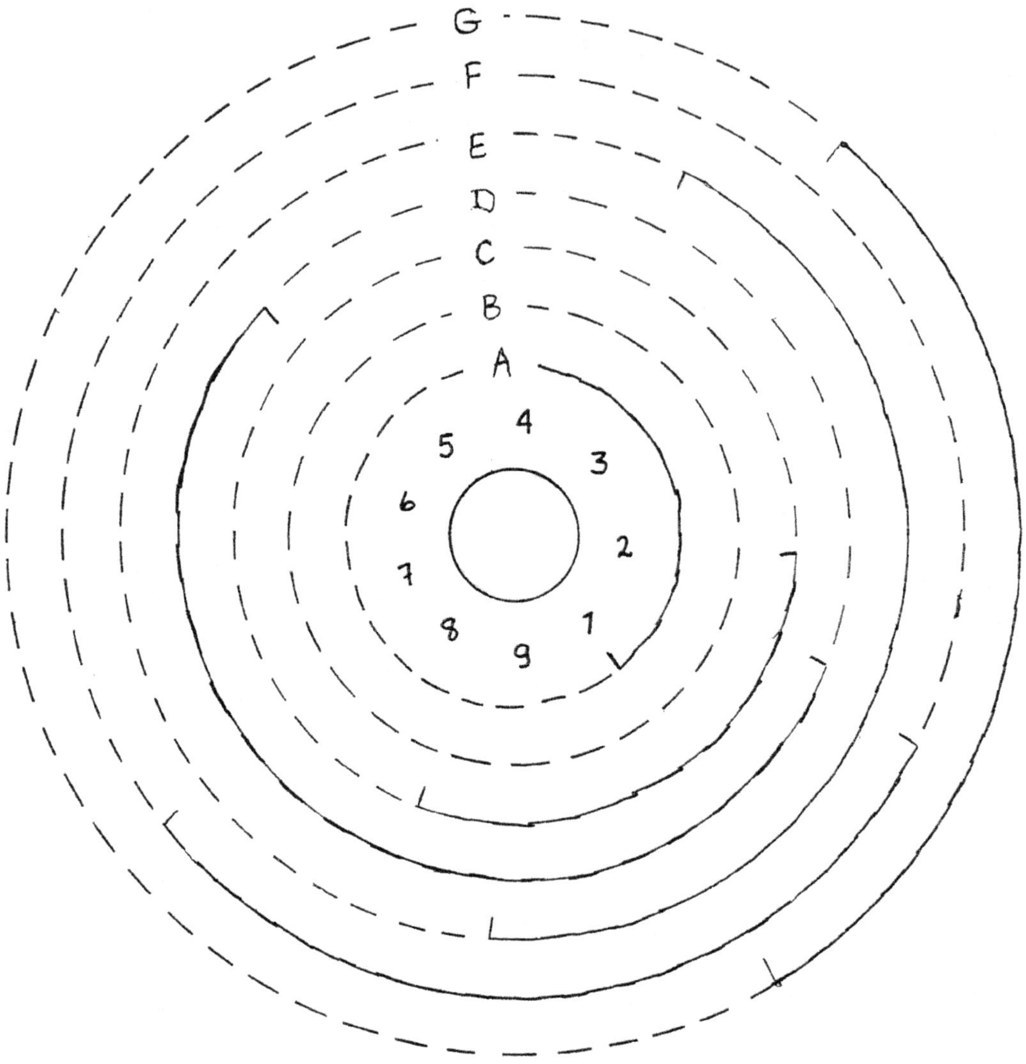

A	Religion:	Jews – non Jews (dotted line)
B	Clinical History:	Have been my individual patients – have not been my individual patients (dotted line)
C	Profession:	Therapists and candidates – neither therapists nor candidates (dotted line)
D	Sex:	Males – females (dotted line)
E	Age:	Older – younger (dotted line)
F	Country of Birth:	Abroad – UK (dotted line)
G	Marital Status:	Married – unmarried (dotted line)

Figure 6.1 An illustration of polarisation and aggregation in the seating pattern of the Group

The session continued in desultory silence. Various people attempted to 'get things going', but their attempts to communicate were not followed by a response or even an association. There was some social chit-chat. At least two people commented on the impending holiday. They said that they welcomed the extra time for themselves. There was no sense that these people were in a Group with a history and a future, let alone a present. It felt that I was in a collection of people who lacked a common culture. In other words, the Group evinced a pattern of normation characterised by 'insolidarity', which is typical of an aggregate.

Massification and its personification

In the next session the Group suddenly shifted towards massification. This was intense and surprising. The process was personified by Pandora, who was in the second, group phase of her therapy. She had not seen me individually for about two months. Although Pandora had found it very difficult to share her new Group with me, and to share me with her new Group, especially with those who had become her favourite rivals, her so-called 'figures' for a younger brother and a younger sister, she had begun to settle. Nonetheless, Pandora was especially anxious. She tried to disguise this by trying to generate an inauthentically cheerful, slightly manic atmosphere of pseudo-morale. She said that the members of the Group should really join one another in becoming more aware of their successes in life and of how they had been helped by their therapy.

In turn, people began to acknowledge that as a result of their participation in this particular Group they had made marvellous achievements and had no need to fear the impending holiday break. They had been helped far more than by psychoanalysis, and far more than they could have been helped by other group analysts and their groups. The men said that it was a great relief to be able to be aggressive in an open way. These communications became a frenzied but almost rhythmical litany of idealisation of the group and of me, coupled with denigration of my colleagues and their groups.

Pandora said that she adored me, and had nothing but contempt for a particular colleague of mine. Another woman agreed with Pandora. In other words, Pandora became a cheerleader, which is a typical massification role. Not only was she sucked into the role, but she also helped to create it. Although I remained silent, I felt myself to be a willing participant in this process of pseudo-speciation and cult formation.

The persistence of an engendered contra-group

The massification process was, however, not completely perfect. Two female patients formed a contra-group. They were a little less enthusiastic about how well things were going, at least for them. However, the rest of the Group attempted to silence them and to split them from one another. When they attempted to talk about their fear of the impending holiday they were attacked. When they tried to discuss a couple of my imperfections, they were ridiculed. They withdrew into a silent somewhat conspiratorial partnership which they maintained through non-verbal communication of eye contact and mutual raising of eyebrows. One man referred to them as 'sexually dysfunctional lesbians' who were unable to show respect to a man in authority, namely me. This insulting and hurtful comment was so outrageous that it did not feel as aggressive as in retrospect it might have been, but certainly the two individual members of the contra-group were stripped of their personal identities.

An interpretation from the group analyst

I became aware that I was on the receiving end of projective identification in the service of sucking me into the illusion of my perfection, based on idealisation, envy and, above all helplessness, most probably in connection with the forthcoming break. I wondered aloud if the refusal to allow any differences of points of view, or any expression of individuality, and if the need to maintain a continuous pep-talk, were attempts to avoid the fear that we might all go our individual ways never to return and, thus, that the group would dissolve and fall apart. Surely, I could not be so much better than the other group analysts, and our group so much better than the other groups. After all, they too took holiday breaks. I also suggested that Pandora might have been so contemptuous and critical of my colleagues, because she was worried that the Group would criticise her for having had such a close relationship with me during her long analysis. I said that perhaps there was an unspoken view or even an unconscious fantasy that we had been inappropriately close, that is, had broken boundaries. The Group replied with silence. However, the silence was thoughtful.

During this silence, Pandora was in the forefront of my mind because, on the basis of seemingly good advice, she had recently undergone yet more surgery. She had a mole removed from her lower lip. I looked at her and said that I remembered that she had surgery for a fistula which had also developed at a time of separation. I asked her if she might be a little more worried about the break than she was prepared to acknowledge both to us and to herself.

Pandora, continued

She replied that actually she had forgotten that last night she was awakened by a kind of nightmare. She had been looking forward to the session in order to be able to talk about it.

She was standing outside a large house with many rooms and many windows, but unable to get into it. No one was at home, and no one answered the bell. She began to throw pebbles at the window and then chose to throw rocks, but there was still no response. Finally, she threw one big rock that was somehow not really a rock but a very explosive strong weapon of some sort. There was a white light, not quite an explosion. She became very frightened. The rock bounced off the window and started to come back at her. Nonetheless, a transformation had occurred. 'Mercifully', this so-called weapon-rock turned into a thousand tadpoles which became very slimy and tried to get into her mouth, her ears and her body. Some more energetic than others, these tadpoles searched for 'appropriate openings'.[1]

Before I continue this vignette, I would like to give some basic information. My consulting room is in a flat in a 'mansion block'. In my consulting room I have two small containers with lids on which there are oversized handles shaped like frogs. They are made from clay with a translucent green glaze. I collected these objects many years earlier when a patient in the Group who was a potter began to play with the wish of turning me into a frog, and of my transforming the Group from frogs and other vermin into princes and princesses.[2] While she was in individual treatment Pandora had been preoccupied with these objects, and had often associated to them. Pandora did not know anything about the origins of these objects.

The re-emergence of the work group

I felt frustrated on two counts. Firstly, I wanted to be alone with Pandora in order to analyse the dream with her, which was obviously very interesting. After all, I had worked with this patient for so many years and wanted to explore her desire to merge with the Group, and her need to sexualise her aggression, which was the basis for the massification processes that she was personifying. However, I was so tempted to get into this material, that I assumed that I was involved in the introjective identification of Pandora's frustration and anger with her rivals for my attention, and that this was connected with my countertransference to her in terms of my own mother and maternal objects, that is, I wished to eliminate all rivals to our relationship.

I remembered how determined she was never to be blocked from a space in which she felt that she would be protected and looked after, and in which she would not have to communicate with words in a grown up way. Her experience of maternal space, including the flat to which she had been taken when her mother was hospitalised, had been transferred to my body, the Group and my consulting room.

I decided to remain silent. I wanted to let the Group respond to Pandora, and to allow the collective transference to develop more clearly and strongly. I was also aware that I was not thinking clearly, which, under these circumstances, was a common enough experience. I became preoccupied with my own early experiences of failed dependency.

The Group were very responsive to me in that they began to do their work, thereby giving me more time to think. They took charge, so to say. The man who was a candidate at The Institute of Group Analysis talked to Pandora about her rage and pointed out that although it was reactive it was quickly projected and re-introjected. Another said, 'That's sexy stuff, Pandora. Clearly those tadpoles were sperm'.

As hysterical as she was, Pandora was surprised that she had reported a sexy dream. It is likely that she felt sexually aroused. This was unusual for her. Although she could talk about sex quite freely, she was rarely aroused. Pandora then told us with feeling about her being alone and feeling empty inside. She described her own sense of despair as a female, and her envy of male creativity. She felt caught in a dilemma that as she came to accept herself more and more as a female she would not feel creative unless she had a baby, but if she felt herself to be female and had a baby she would lose her sense of herself as a male, which meant that she would have to sacrifice other things in her career, which could be described as a 'narcissistic investment'.

By this time I had regained my ability to think, possibly because she used the term 'narcissistic investment'. She had learned quite a lot over the years. I commented about retaliation from the house-mother, who did not let the weapon break into her. In fact, the weapon was rejected and transformed into a thousand tadpoles which, if they symbolised sperm, might not be expected to come from the mother. In any case, her aggression had been sexualised protectively. I wondered about her image of her father as a fertile man, and what sort of access to him she felt her mother had allowed her, and had allowed him to her. I had worked with her on this sort of material a thousand times, but somehow it all felt very fresh. After a brief silence, I said that maybe there was some confusion about her mother as a father and her father as a mother. A woman said that we could be certain that fathers do not menstruate. I replied that whereas that might be so, the impending holiday was like a menstrual period. After another brief silence, I said that sometimes the loss of perfection, creativity and hope was not mourned, but replaced by an imaginary, protective inner circle and the compulsion to enter it, and to remain in it for ever and ever.

At the next session, the Black woman, who had decided not to leave the Group after all, offered an interpretation of the group process and the personification of it. She said that somehow the Group had been recreating what Pandora had told them about her having felt shut out and kept out of her mother's life, and about her not having been helped by her father. She added that although Dr Hopper may have helped Pandora, she did not have to treat him as though he was Billy Graham and the Group a prayer meeting, because this suggested that she was still unhappy about a lot of things, especially the way her younger brother was able to have a 'normal' relationship with their mother, and because her brother was her father's favourite child. She added a few points of her own: she said that she had had enough of this revivalist bullshit; she stopped going to church with her mother a long time ago; and she did not want to turn the Group into a prayer meeting – Hampstead was not Brixton; and she had had enough of The Institute of Group Analysis, as well. The man who was a concentration camp survivor added that Pandora talked about her family after the birth of her brother as though it had been perfect, and as though he had everything, and she had nothing. He said that he used to feel this way about his English foster family. However, the only way he could be part of it, and obtain the warmth and support that he craved was to idealise his foster parents and express his gratitude all the time, even though this never felt natural and truthful. Moreover, he wondered whether his foster siblings had not been obliged to sing their parents' praises more than was actually warranted. The family was generous, but because they needed to be, more than because they really were.

In response to all this Pandora spoke of her fantasy that during the holiday I would see one of the patients who was training as a group analyst at an event at The Institute of Group Analysis. She was furious about this, which was 'totally unfair'. I said that I understood that the Group generally felt hurt and angry about the holiday break and also felt frightened both about their ability to function without too much anxiety and about their impulse to express such feelings to me, because they might hurt me and themselves. I also said that Pandora felt this very strongly, and that she had transformed her fears about falling apart into a desire to make the Group totally and absolutely whole and to put herself inside it, and to attach herself to the Group and to me, as she felt the male training candidate would be able to do, because he was my ideal boy-child and her younger brother. I went on to imply, but not to spell out, that she had a fantasy that only a boy could really do this, or at any rate a girl with a penis, which she thought was the only creative sexual organ. Pandora acknowledged this, and then became a little angry at the male candidate and the Group, which she had not been able to do before. She was, in fact, hardly ever able to be angry openly. Another member of the Group said that it was obvious that she was treating this man as though he were her younger brother. Several members of the Group then reminded her of her achievements in the field of the arts, which were considerable.

Contra-grouping and the persistence of massification

One of the women who was a member of the engendered contra-group said that she was thinking about the coming Passover holiday. Her family would have a Seder. As a child her favourite passage was using her little finger to take out ten drops of red wine from her glass while naming each of the ten plagues through which God took vengeance on Egyptians, including the Pharaoh. I commented that by being so cryptic, she was attempting to establish a special relationship with me, because she knew that I was a Jew and that although I would understand her, most of the others would be left out of this. Another member of the Group said that actually she was attempting to establish a relationship with me that was similar to the relationship that Pandora had with me.

We asked her to tell the story a little more fully in order that the non-Jews in the Group would know what she was talking about. She said that Passover takes its name from the arrangement that God made through Moses that the Jews in bondage in Egypt should mark the doorposts of their houses with the blood of a lamb in order that the Angel of Death would pass over their houses when fulfilling God's command to kill the first born son of all the families in Egypt. On the basis of this tenth and most horrific plague, Pharaoh let Moses and his people go.

Pandora said that preceding plagues included polluting the Nile with vermin and frogs, as in her dream. The Group offered various associations to Pandora's dream and to the Bible story. I suggested that the river Nile was an unconscious reference to the maternal group, and that Pandora wished to turn the male student at The Institute of Group Analysis into a frog, or perhaps she experienced him as a frog who polluted the water. It was, therefore, important to purify the water. I also suggested that she experienced him as the foetus of the Group, or as my foetus in particular, and that it was important to exterminate him. I wondered if Pandora was expressing these thoughts and feelings only on her own behalf or on behalf of the Group?

During the ensuing silence, I suggested that the reference to the tenth plague might be an expression of some confusion about me as a powerful male conductor of the Group. Was I a Pharaoh who had enslaved them, or a Moses who was trying to help them become more independent? Should I be punished or should I be thanked? I wondered if the Group had a sense of what a good father was like. Was a good parent always a mother, and a bad parent always a father? Somehow I doubted that this was true, although it may be in keeping with their experience.

The re-emergence of the work group

At the next session Pandora asked one of the members of the two-person contra-group to tell more about their feelings of doubt and scepticism about me. Pandora was actually enquiring about the feelings of others with whom she was in competition, but she was using their feelings as a way of being more aggressive towards me. This led to some anger and sadness and memories of having been let down repeatedly during childhood, an experience shared by the entire Group. The non-Jewish member of the engendered contra-group began to articulate her feelings that the Group was too focused on me as a father figure, whether a good one or a bad one, and this was hardly different from being focused on as a little baby brother. When Pandora said that finally she understood *some* aspects of the negativity towards me, the contra-group began to dissolve.

In this and in the previous chapters, I have attempted to illustrate my theory of 'Incohesion: Aggregation/Massification' or (ba) 'I:A/M' as the fourth basic assumption in the unconscious life of groups with clinical material from two twice weekly groups of adults in which traumatic experience was prevalent. I have argued that group analysis offers all patients, but especially our most difficult patients, unique opportunities to personify basic assumption processes, and the processes of Incohesion in particular. By focusing on personification it was possible to give special attention to individuals whose internal worlds most closely matched the patterns of interaction, normation, communication, styles of thinking and feeling and styles of leadership and followership that had developed within the Group, thus allowing all members of the Group to become involved in this process. They made connections between their present functioning in the Group and their previous experiences, both during infancy and later phases in life. Although Pandoro and Pandora had each experienced a long period of psychoanalysis, and psychoanalytic psychotherapy, the experiences within the Group offered new insights. Despite profound threats to the cohesion of the therapeutic work group, reciprocity and complementarity were recovered. The Group responded to my own difficulties with sensitivity and insight. They gave me the space that I needed in order to regain my own ability to think.

Most group analysts are familiar with processes of aggregation in groups within conferences, workshops, courses and other training activities within the mental health field. Such groups are time-limited, and the participants are likely to be more mature than ordinary patients. Even when mental health professionals have a difficult, regressed experience they are determined not to leave, and their groups may remain intact while containing many fissiparous tendencies. The 'lone wolves' of training groups are virtually archetypal!

In contrast, however, very few group therapists have experienced aggregation within slow-open groups who meet for the purpose of psychotherapy, because these groups tend not to evince aggregation processes for very long. If they do, they disintegrate. With an occasional exception, for example, Zelaskowski (1998), therapists and patients work very hard to prevent these painful, explosive processes. However, aggregation should not be feared. It presents an ideal opportunity for working with processes of intra-personal and inter-personal unintegration and disintegration, especially within institutions such as hospitals and prisons, and in those societies who have been founded in traumatic experience, such as Australia, Northern Ireland and Israel, and in those who have been plagued by natural disasters, wars, tensions and political instability in general.

Massification processes are much more troublesome than those of aggregation. Massification masks feelings of rage and destructiveness. The pseudo-morale of massification is deceptive and perverse. This is true not only in fundamentalist societies, but also in therapeutic groups. Group analysts are vulnerable to collusion with massification, because it allows them to escape from feelings of helplessness, not only the helplessness of aggregation, but also the helplessness of offering solutions other than 'sharing' and 'understanding'.

It is very important for the group analyst to maintain a sense of connectedness to all parts of the 'maternal body'. The peace of the work group requires the maintenance of diversity and autonomy. However, all members of the Group must have equal access to its holy places. This requires the exercise of benign authority.

Notes

1 I would like to draw attention to the kind of experience that so often occurs when working with difficult patients. The night before I presented some of this material in a lecture, I had a strange experience in another of my twice weekly groups. One patient was reassured that she was a frog princess who would be changed by her group experience. Another patient dreamt of tadpoles, gardens and a flock of birds who ate five out of the six tadpoles that she had put in her garden leaving only one survivor, who became a frog. Only one person in the Group knew that I would be giving a lecture the next day, and that the phrase 'difficult patient' was the title of it. Some Jungian analysts would describe this in terms of 'synchronicity'. In any case, it is obvious that Pandora's tadpoles had penetrated my mind. Perhaps, deep down, she knew that one day I would write a paper about her. Certainly she must have wanted me to.

2 This particular patient came from a family who was associated with the extreme right wing of the political life of the nation, although without doubt many members of whom were highly talented, creative and liberal minded people. Is this a matter of irony or synchronicity?

CHAPTER 7

An Illustration of Incohesion: Aggregation/Massification in the Extreme

A Group of Child Survivors of the Shoah[1]

Whereas aggregation and massification are ubiquitous in regressed groups, these polarised states of Incohesion are likely to be both chronic and acute within a group of people who have been severely traumatised. This can be seen very clearly in my slow-open groups of adults who were children in Nazi concentration camps, death camps, and/or in hiding in continuously frightening circumstances. Therefore, I will illustrate my theory of (ba) I:A/M with a clinical vignette from a group of child survivors who represent an 'extreme' case of a group of traumatised people.

Before turning to the clinical vignette, I will first consider several special features of group analysis for a homogeneous group of Shoah survivors:

1. Despite the spate of publications during the last couple of decades, knowledge of therapy for Shoah survivors is shared more within the oral tradition than the written one, possibly because the depth of their suffering defies scientific discourse. Survivors can be described in terms of the elements of the addiction/trauma syndrome, but this would not add much to an appreciation of their suffering. Some would not hesitate to acknowledge that they have perpetuated much pain on members of their own families, who they love and need, and who love and need them. Many survivors are not easy, gentle people, although

many have developed such personae. Diffuse feelings of guilt and shame are chronic. This can be understood in terms of 'survivor guilt', i.e. about having survived while others did not (Krystal 1968), but 'survivor shame', i.e. about helplessness, powerlessness and humiliation, may be even more important (Garwood 1996).[2]

2. When presenting my work with survivors of the Shoah, whether in talks or in writing, I always feel anxious. One reason for this is that survivors object most strongly to how their therapy has sometimes been turned into a kind of 'industry', and to how this has often been exploited in the fundraising and other charitable activities of the Jewish community, which can easily be confused with the social activities of its establishment (Finkelstein 2000). Over the years my groups have devoted many sessions to the discussion of the Shoah industry and to their feelings about it. For example, to some participants the Jewish establishment in England is an object of intense resentment, because they remember feeling patronised and treated as objects of interest by the people and agencies who offered them charitable help. Some survivors say that they were hurt more by how they were treated, for example, in orphanages and foster homes than they were during the war. Basically, they felt used, and continue to feel this way. I have acknowledged such concerns by asking this Group's permission to use material from their sessions in order to illustrate hypotheses about group process and trauma generally. Permission was granted only after I said that this might be of help to other traumatised people.

   I also feel anxious because in this specialised field professionals compete for accolades, even more than usual. Why? Basically, because we want our mothers to be proud of us. We want to be favourite children. Guilt and the need to make reparation are powerful forces, especially when combined with sibling rivalry (the underlying dynamics of which, ironically, also underpin chronic anti-Semitism). I feel a greater need than usual for the acceptance and approval of this work, because any audience is a surrogate mother.[3]

3. I conduct groups of survivors in the same way that I conduct other slow-open groups. However, I am more transparent and flexible around boundary issues, because with certain exceptions the members of the Group have not defined themselves as 'ill'. Most Shoah survivors do not accept that they suffer from 'post traumatic stress

disorder', which is in any case more a nosological category than it is an acknowledged disease. They are aware that they have problems, and that they want help in solving them, but this is not the same as defining themselves as *ill*. Many feel that to identify with illness is to submit to those responsible for traumatising them in the first place. Nonetheless, being able to accept the role of 'patient', in the best sense of the term, that is, to be allowed to relinquish for a while a degree of responsibility for one's identity in order to be able to reflect on one's life, is an essential element in the experience of psychoanalytical psychotherapy, especially for people who have been traumatised, because they must feel very safe and very strong indeed before they consider the state of their internal worlds, especially at the time that they experienced Shoah related trauma.

Clinical flexibility is also required because groups of Shoah survivors overlap and inter-penetrate many social groups within organisations in the Jewish community, for example, special centres for survivors, mental health centres, various leisure and study groups, fund raising activities for charities, etc. not to mention local authority activities in residential areas in which Jews tend to reside. In fact, at any one time it is difficult to know precisely what groups are actually meeting, e.g. a group of survivors of the Shoah or a group of people who are members of a particular synagogue or social centre. This is not only true in England, but also in the United States, Australia, Israel and elsewhere.

Ordinarily, groups with osmotic boundaries require very careful, tight regulation and management, but in my experience this is virtually impossible with groups of Shoah survivors. After all, the members of these groups are not professionals within the mental health field. They do not appreciate what seems to them to be administrative rigidity. This is perceived as 'Germanic', and reminiscent of their experience in the camps. It is ironic that although my groups *demanded* flexibility from me, when I attempted to apply the usual professional guidelines of group analysis, I was regarded as a Nazi. Clearly, their identifications with the aggressor are very complex.

Although I include Shoah survivors in my heterogeneous groups, many survivors report that in previous psychotherapy they were unable to talk about themselves as survivors. Within the context of a positive transference they wished to protect others from hearing about their worst experiences. In homogeneous groups survivors do not feel ashamed to talk to one another about their profound suffering. They trust one another to be able to hear what they are saying. Another reason why survivors prefer homogeneous groups is that people who have not had the same kind of experience are often envious of their suffering and their legitimate right to bear the consequences of traumatic experience. Such envy can effectively silence non-survivors, but it can also silence survivors as the targets of envy. Although the dynamics of hierarchies of suffering exist within my homogenous groups of survivors, usually this can be worked through.

It must be acknowledged that homogeneity also contributes to the maintenance of various kinds of defensive structures that resist interpretation. For example, my groups sometimes wish that some of their members were Christians, not only Christian victims and 'righteous Gentiles', but also Christian Nazis. Many survivors want to be able to hate with impunity. This cannot be understood only in terms of the refusal and inability to acknowledge impulses and fantasies that are easier to project into enemies. In my experience, most survivors need the defences offered by homogeneity, and I have learned that it is unwise to be overly zealous in the interpretation of such defences. It is sometimes best to accept that the projection of bad objects into the wider society, both now and then, is necessary for the mental health of traumatised people, especially those over sixty years of age.

4. My groups of child survivors met for five years: one group, once weekly for the first year and twice weekly for the next three; and the other group, once weekly for five years. The groups began with eight people, four men and four women. During the five year period, several members left, and new members came in. The groups stopped, one consisting of only four members, and the other of only three, because it was too difficult to maintain an appropriate flow of referrals, which would allow people to leave when they felt ready to do so without feeling guilty about damaging the groups, and which would allow new people to join before they began to feel excluded and frustrated.

The dynamic administration of my groups was challenged by the relationship of survivors to the wider community and its charitable mental health organisations. All therapy programmes for Shoah survivors, and perhaps for survivors of trauma in general, are fraught with difficulties and conflicts, and many groups do not last as long as they should. Such problems go beyond the personalities of key figures in the community who are often held responsible for the success and failure of particular programmes. Child survivors are more aggressive and demanding than older survivors, and the administration of their groups is especially difficult. However, it is possible that the experience of the survival of near death following trauma is constantly enacted.

5. In order to remind you of the kinds of experiences that are reported by people who were children in concentration and death camps, and in hiding in extreme conditions, I will present a few details from the case histories of the members of the group, although in order to protect confidentiality I have slightly modified this material:

   (a) A woman, at the age of three or perhaps five, was locked in the cellar of a convent for two and a half years. She was not clear about how old she was at the time, because she really did not know exactly when she was born. Her only contact with people was when the Mother Superior or one of the other nuns brought her food and water, in much the same way '... as one would feed a good dog'. She was later given to a band of partisans who protected her but also molested her, and at close quarters she witnessed many sexual acts.

   (b) A man, at the age of four, was brought from one section of a concentration camp where he was kept with his mother to another section in order to identify the dead body of his father, who he remembers as having a thin, bruised and bloody face. He was then sent back to his mother to tell her what he saw.

   (c) Another woman was in hiding with a band of adults and a few other children in a forest in the town from which they escaped. She was sold to a local farmer who hid her in his barn for 'a very long time', perhaps two years, and used her for sexual favours. On many occasions she was beaten up by the farmer's wife, although she co-operated with her husband's efforts to hide the 'Jewess'. This patient remained grateful to the farmer and his wife, and continued to visit the very elderly woman after her husband died.

I am aware of the phenomenon of screen memories, and of how necessary it is to work with them. Nonetheless…

I will present material from sessions during the third year of one of my groups. Among the processes that are most clearly illustrated are, in order: intense aggregation in response to the trauma of failed dependency; the repeated personification of aggregation in the form of personal anecdotes of horror and despair, punctuated by the tentative re-emergence of the work group; a protective shift to massification with attempts to create a cult-like group with me as its 'leader'; the personification of massification; and a tentative re-emergence of the work group. Also apparent are the expression of aggression in the form of anonymisation and the development of an engendered contra-group. Especially poignant is the somatisation of intrapsychic encapsulation.

The clinical vignette

Towards the end of a session I told the Group that I would be away for a spring break for almost four weeks. This was longer than usual, because the break would include both the Easter and Passover holidays. This information was noted and then ignored, perhaps denied.

Intense aggregation

The next session was dominated by an intractable silence. The Group had become unresponsive to me. Eventually they entered into a pattern of conversation which seemed to be an attempt to fill the silence rather than to communicate.

The personification of aggregation

Suddenly, a man said, 'I remember feeling so thirsty and so hungry. I had lost contact with my parents. I had depended on them to get me a little water sometimes, or a little food. They couldn't. I had no one to look after me'. Of course, he was speaking to people who knew. He said that one of his earliest memories was of finding a small bent fragment of a metal tray behind a wooden hut, into which rain water would drip off the roof. He would go there in order to be by himself for a few moments, and to drink water. He said that he would get down like a dog and drink the water out of the fragment of metal, which was the only way he could figure out how to drink the water. Once he turned it over and found a lot of woodlice. He said that he ate the woodlice, because he was so hungry. In retrospect, they may have saved him. This place became his secret space where he could be alone, drink water and eat woodlice. He had never told anybody about this. To my surprise, the Group did not express much sympathy or even interest. However, he went on to say that for some reason the most shameful thing that he could remember was his secret attempts to be by himself. The Group responded to this part of his confession. They all remembered feeling ashamed about wanting and trying to be alone. In general, the Group remained alienated from one another and from me.

Eventually, I wondered aloud if we were really a group or a society of woodlice, little bugs who digest life's debris, specialising in rotten wood and in the elimination of waste, with shells like cockroaches or beetles, who scattered for safety when put into light. Slowly we began to work with my tentative but provocative interpretation. Later I suggested that woodlice live in an aggregated way, without culture, but with a very primitive form of sociation, even more primitive than those of bees or ants. Woodlice personified, or in this case animalised, the whole ethos of the 'final solution', based on a process of dehumanisation. We explored the possibility that the Group felt that as Jews they were like woodlice, and that as woodlice they were like Nazis. This was a very primitive type of introjective and projective identification with aggressors, which is not uncommon in the sado-masochistic relationships between victims and perpetrators.

In the next session, a member of the Group continued with this theme. He had read that people who have eaten things that were supposed to be inedible continued for a very long time to feel ashamed and frightened of punishment. Another member said that he had heard that people who were in Japanese prisoner of war camps continued to feel this way. I interpreted their feelings of despondent and shameful alienation as a response to their feeling rejected by me, as a repetition of their sense of despair and betrayal connected with their Shoah experiences. I said that feeling so 'let down' led to the fear of annihilation, or more precisely to protections against it. I hoped that they would not have to resort to eating woodlice during the spring break, or to becoming like woodlice in order to get through the spring break, especially because they had fed me with ideas about the human condition. I wondered to myself whether the Group really understood what I was saying, but I knew that they felt that they had fed me, and that this would not be possible unless they also felt that I was trying my best to understand them. A woman said that shellfish were not kosher, and that most probably neither were woodlice.

After a lengthy silence a man told us about a dramatisation of Kafka's *Metamorphosis* that he had seen a few nights previously. He described how crustacean stick insects and other kinds of beetles were located on the stage in an aggregated pattern around the central character of a praying mantis. This reminded him of the Group. The Group identified with this statement of despair, but they also tried to disidentify with it, primarily by insisting that suffering could be understood by others who had not suffered directly to such an extent, namely me. I started to formulate in my mind some thoughts about the collective transference to me as a praying mantis, but before I could get this clear, I noticed that it was time to stop.

In the next session a man said, 'I remember my father, who was a jeweller. We were together in the camp. This woman...this woman who...in Auschwitz...she has a name...I forget her name just at the moment...she would come with a dog...a German Shepherd...and have the dog...you know...would set the dog on people. And the only way we could buy her off...she loved jewellery...was to make jewellery for her. And of course there were various stashes of rare gems and so on...'. Another man joined in, 'We scoured the camps looking for bits of rubbish, a bit of glass, a bit of wire, a pretty pebble. My father would then make them into a brooch'. And he described the brooch: 'Each bit of glass was treated like a small jewel, although they were really only rubbish. They were set in a frame that was welded together from the bits of wire. We would always put one real gem in the middle of the brooch'. From time to time the boys would give her a brooch '...so that she wouldn't set the dog on us...'.

An interpretation from the group analyst

I thought that the Group had the unconscious wish to set the dog on me, as they felt I had done to them by making them hungry for the sessions and for me. I remembered the man who said that he drank rain water from a bit of metal like a dog. I considered interpreting the transference to me as the father of the Group, and even as the executive nipple of the fragmented group breast. Instead, I took up this material in terms of the transference to me as the only real gem in the 'Group brooch'. I said that they felt like they were slivers of sharp glass, welded together into a Group brooch that was no substitute for the whole world that they had lost. I said that they wished that they were each authentic and special jewels, not merely 'survivors', without individuality. Eventually, several members of the group acknowledged their envious hatred of me. One member said that he resented my being able to feel so good and helpful at his expense. It was very difficult for me to take their envy and admiration.

A shift towards massification

Following the expression of these thoughts and feelings, one member stressed how privileged they were to be having this unique experience. I sensed a touch of irony. However, other members joined in. One said that actually he did feel very special compared to other child survivors who were unable to join the Group. The majority of the Group would not permit any dissension. Two women tried to distance themselves from this protection of pseudo-morale, but they were quickly silenced. The Group said that I was an 'honorary survivor'. Another woman said that she had read in the *Jewish Chronicle* that our Group was the only one like it in England, and that somehow I was chosen to lead it. (In fact, this article did not exist.)

I tried to get across the idea that in their having built and sustained a group for the purpose of therapy they were attempting to make creative use of their predicament, in much the same way that some of them had made creative use of the bits of rubbish that proved essential for their survival. This made them very different from a society of woodlice. However, although this was a special experience, it was cold comfort indeed! I added that selection into the Group might also have reminded them of selection into the gas chambers, as well as of the consequences of being members of the Chosen People, both good and bad.

The personification of massification

During the last session before the holiday break, the Group seemed pleased to be together. One of the women who had tried to individuate from the massification process asked me if I knew how she survived the sewers of Lubov, involving particularly harrowing periods of hunger and loneliness during which she was subjected to various kinds of torments and sexual abuse. I said that I did want to know about this. It would help me understand her better, and it would also help me understand all traumatised people. She replied that she had read that it was really only a matter of luck, and that typically survivors tell stories about their survival, and that they invent theories to explain it, ranging from absurd hypotheses about the survival of the fittest to hypotheses about special relationships to God. '(However)', she said, 'I used to think about the white tablecloth of the Sabbath meal. I would close my eyes, and look at the pictures in my mind. I would remember the shapes of things on the white cloth, and their colours. The challah, glasses of wine, candles, specific foods, mainly the gefilte fish. When things were really tough I would remember our Passover Seders: the Passover plate, the place settings, the people around the table. I would just think about this, and I would somehow eat my pictures. Over and over again. I would also think about my mother opening the door for Elijah. Of course, this was all before the Nazis came'.

The Group joined in with their own memories. They discussed the variety of Passover rituals. Some talked about how they would be organising their own Seders in a couple of weeks' time. At some level we all realised that the shared reports/fantasies/memories and plans for the Seder were a screen memory for the maternal body, and an expression of their wish to be held and contained by a good enough mother in the context of a good enough family within a troubled but intact Jewish community within larger European cities, towns and villages, both 'There and Then' and 'There and Now'. I was fairly quiet. I did not feel a need to interpret the material in terms of their wish that we would not be stopping the group for the break, and that we might have our own Seder. In fact, I felt that an interpretation might have killed their shared feelings.

The tentative re-emergence of the work group

The woman who introduced the Passover theme was speaking on behalf of the Group. She was connecting herself to the meaning of the springtime Passover holiday and rituals in terms of freedom from slavery and oppression, in which all alternatives can only be imagined but not realised, and in which hope is very difficult to sustain. She was identifying her current state of mind with the prayer or perhaps ritualised toast that Jews make during the Seder: 'Next year, in Jerusalem!' In other words, the 'Here and Now' of the group was pregnant with the future, and to her the future involved being part of what she regarded as her homeland and her people. Although 'Jerusalem' was primarily a symbol of a 'new beginning', to visit Jerusalem, and even to emigrate to Israel, was also a realistic possibility for each and every member of the Group. In fact, the Passover symbolises freedom from slavery, and the entire Seder could be regarded as a ritualisation of optimal social cohesion and cultural solidarity in which individuals have the freedom to find an appropriate identity and space. After all, does not 'Seder' mean 'order'?

The Group spoke about what they imagined were my own circumstances. Although they knew very little about me, they reconstructed my personal history with uncanny accuracy. They were very sensitive to my being so far from home, and they reached a consensus that they had

> provided me with a kind of home away from home. I became aware that in a way this was true. I felt very grateful to them for helping me become aware of aspects of my life and of my character that somehow I had managed not to know. I expressed my gratitude to them for being so sensitive to my needs.
>
> Towards the end of the session I said that they had tried to provide me with a Seder, because they assumed that I did not have one, and that I was alienated from the community of Jews. They also tried to provide me with a Friday night meal. I said that the braided Sabbath challah was a symbol of the Group. It was also a symbol of me, who they idealised as a 'rescuing figure', even if I was not a 'Messianic' one. In a sense, they ate from us both. It seemed that we would survive the holiday break, even though they were not allowed to eat the bread of group analysis. It seems that although the Group and I were hardly a substitute for the real thing, we were at least barely satisfactory, at least some of the time, despite the fact that they often wanted to tear us apart. As the session ended, the woman who had recounted her strategy for survival said that 'incidentally' she had discovered a cyst in one of her breasts, and would have it seen to during the break, and that she hoped that it was benign. We were stunned by this news. I was aware of the deep ambivalence that resided in her having fed us. However, I decided that the last few minutes before the break was not the right time to interpret this.
>
> The Group ended with our acknowledging that we were deeply affiliated to one another, and that we shared one another's sorrows and hopes.

In this context I will not consider the details and processes of such rich material. For example, I will not discuss aspects of my countertransference or the attempts to work through particular defensive structures both for the Group as a whole and for those who personified the processes of incohesion. It is important here to see that the shift from aggregation to massification was followed by more thoughtful and reflective work, and that this occurred as the result of interpretive interventions. Their increased sense of authentic affiliation and sharing was associated with the development of the space in which it was possible to imagine a more satisfactory way of life. We did not eliminate the psychic pain of survival, but our ability to imagine a 'new beginning' was part of a transcendent, creative response to our traumatic experience of loss, abandonment and damage. We discovered or perhaps rediscovered the possibility of mature, resilient hope, based on authentic mourning, and on a sense of order and unoppressive regularity. We began to work in the 'If and When' (Hopper 2001b).

It is difficult to analyse the obstacles to the development of optimal cohesion within any kind of social system, including a group who meets for the purpose of therapy. However, it is possible to help people make creative use of their own traumatic experience. Making connections and relationships that allow people both to share one another's sorrows, pains, and failures, and to identify with one another's successes, is the essential ingredient in our struggle to build our groups, organisations and societies from bricks rather than straws, and to maintain them. Rituals performed with love are helpful. The bereaved say that at least one year must go by before they begin to feel better, because all anniversaries and all seasons with the person who has died will have been remembered at least once. Survivors of the Shoah need more than one year. Many more. Nonetheless, the Sabbath is repeated each week, and the Passover each spring.

I will conclude by quoting Bettelheim (1979) who, referring to a poem by Celan (1971), writes that if with empathy and compassion, we dig towards those who have so completely given up all hope that 'there is earth in them', this will bind us together and we both will awaken: they from their living death; we from apathy to their suffering.

Notes

1 'Holocaust' refers to purification and burnt sacrifice, which conveys the intentions of the perpetrators rather than the victims. 'Shoah' is Hebrew for castastrophe or disaster. I prefer 'Shoah', as do many others.

2 The traumatic experience of survivors is discussed in detail and with great insight by Jucovy (1992). With special reference to children, Kestenberg (1989) focuses on the loss of identity and distortions in super-ego functions. Gampel (1996) stresses the importance for psychic survival of 'treasured objects', which are similar to what I (Hopper 1991, excerpts of which are reprinted as Appendix II of this book) have called 'positive encapsulations'. The experience of hidden children is described by Reijzer (1996). The treatment of survivors in groups is discussed by Danieli (1981, 1982) and by Fogelman (1989). Van der Hal, Tauber and Gottesfeld (1996) discuss countertransference and the life and death issues that are typical in group psychotherapy with child survivors. All these articles also provide extensive bibliography. For the most recent discussion of group psychotherapy for survivors of trauma in general, see Klein and Schermer (2000a).

3 For a thorough summary of countertransference problems that are ubiquitous in the psychotherapeutic treatment of Shoah survivors, see Danieli (1980).

CHAPTER 8

Summary, Invited Critical Commentaries, Discussion and Suggestions for Further Research and Applications

I will now summarise my theory of Incohesion: Aggregation/Massification or (ba) I:A/M as the fourth basic assumption in the unconscious life of traumatised social systems. I will then present excerpts from critical commentaries invited from several senior British and American group analysts and psychoanalysts, and address some of the concerns that they have raised about matters of theory and matters of clinical technique. I will conclude by suggesting several topics for further research and applications.

Summary

My theory of Incohesion: Aggregation/Massification or (ba) I:A/M is outlined in Figure 8.1.

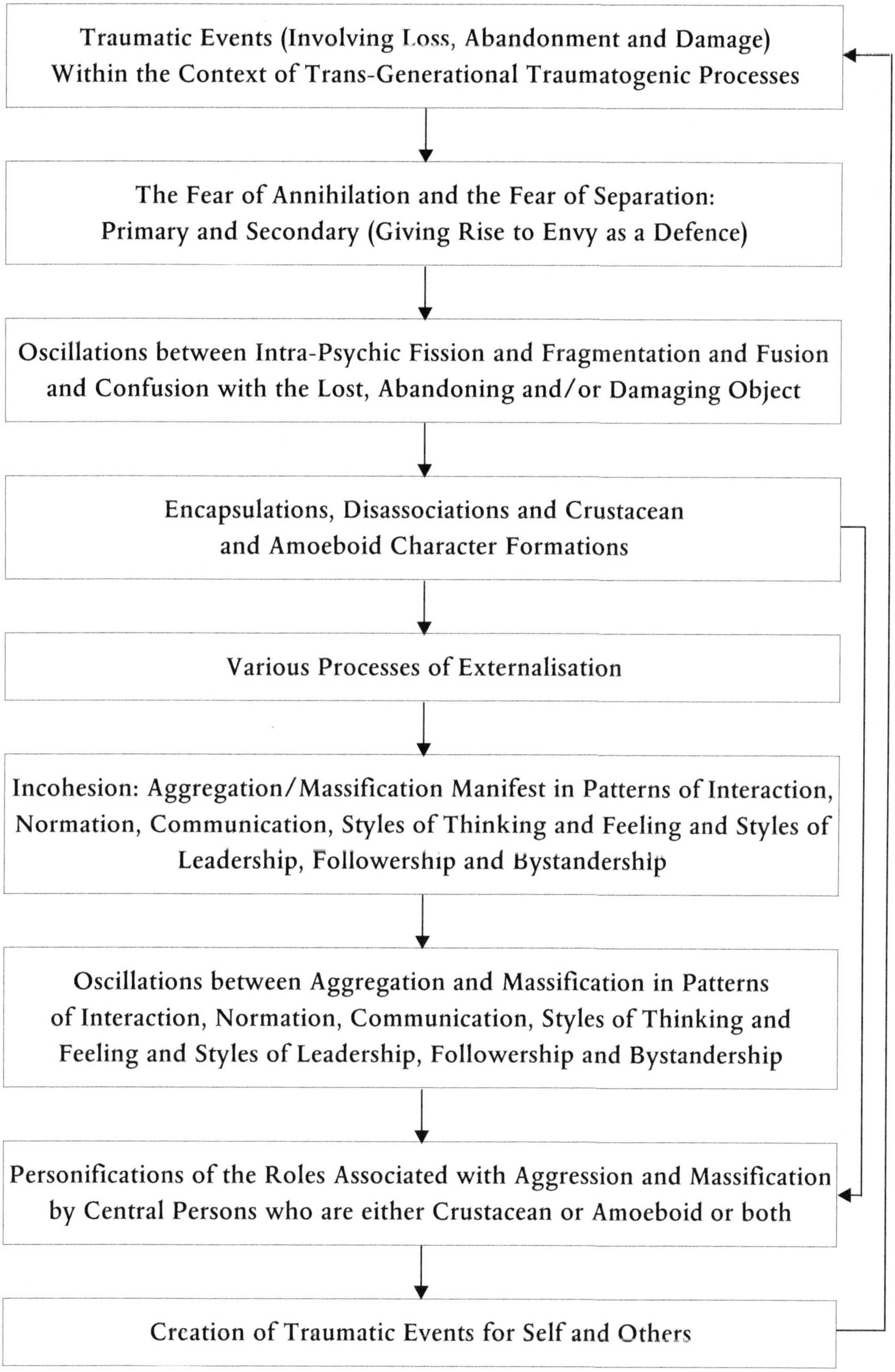

Figure 8.1 A summary of the theory of Incohesion: Aggregation/Massification or (ba) I:A/M

It is shown that (ba) I:A/M develops within the context of traumatogenic processes within a trans-generational social, cultural and political context in which traumatised people create situations in which others are traumatised. Traumatised people personify the roles within the processes associated with the fourth basic assumption which they themselves have created. On the basis of their internal oscillations between fission and fragmentation, and fusion and confusion, traumatised people unconsciously create aggregates and masses and oscillations between them. Within this context it is, therefore, extremely difficult to develop and maintain work groups characterised by optimal cohesion.

This theory of the incohesion of social systems is not intended to explain all incohesion in all social systems at all times. The theory focuses on traumatised social systems, and it emphasises traumatogenic processes. The theory is 'group-analytical' in that it draws on both sociological and psychoanalytical perspectives. The theory is recursive with respect to inter-personal and intra-personal processes within all cells of the time/space paradigm.

When groups who meet for the purpose of psychotherapy are constrained by (ba) I:A/M it is highly likely that the group analyst will fail the dependency demands of the groups. Thus, traumatised people are likely to form traumatised groups and, of course, vice versa. It is extremely difficult for such groups to maintain an optimal degree of self-doubt, containment and holding, and to strive to understand and seek meaning of their past and current experiences. However, the restoration of the cohesion of the work group following regression into basic assumption processes is clearly associated with the restoration of self-esteem and personal maturation. The personification of the fourth basic assumption is an important example of how a better understanding of group dynamics might be used for a specific patient population. Incohesion in small therapeutic groups of traumatised people is of special interest for specific sections of the patient population, for example, survivors of incest, disasters and social trauma, and in therapeutic communities and prisons. However, from time to time the fourth basic assumption appears in all therapeutic groups, and all patients benefit from understanding how they are likely to personify the roles associated with it, and how they may participate in the development of it.

Invited critical commentaries

Parts of my theory of the fourth basic assumption and its applications to clinical work was published in 2001 as 'Difficult patients in group analysis:

The personification of (ba) I:A/M' in *Group 25*, 3, 139-173, using the case of Pandoro in order to illustrate the clinical application of the theory. This special issue consisted of my article, an Introduction by the editor, Jeffrey Kleinberg, a Foreword by Jerome W. Kosseff, and invited critical commentaries from Richard M. Billow, Howard D. Kibel, Malcolm Pines, Bennett Roth, Jill Savege Scharff and David E. Scharff, Victor L. Schermer and Walter N. Stone, as well as a brief Afterword from me. My colleagues have summarised my theory, highlighted some of the strengths and weaknesses of it, and suggested alternative ways of reading the clinical material. In fact, their commentaries are contributions to theory and clinical work in their own right, and I urge the reader to consult the special issue of *Group*, and to enter into the dialogue. Excerpts from these commentaries follow:

I am I:A/M – the therapist as personification of Hopper's fourth basic assumption

Richard M. Billow

Director, Postdoctoral Program in Group Psychotherapy, and Clinical Professor, Adelphi Postdoctoral Programs in Psychoanalysis and Psychotherapy. Dermer Institute, Adelphi University Garden City, New York.

Any gain in self-understanding is accompanied by separation from objects, and by consequent feelings of annihilation, persecution, and depression that recapitulate good-breast absent/bad-breast present infantile anxieties. As Bion says 'all objects that are needed are bad objects because they tantalize ...' (Bion 1962; Billow 1998). Therefore, the persistence and redeployment of states, including those involving annihilation anxiety, fragmentation of identity and confusion between self and other, is ubiquitous and manifest in human experience, even for those who have not been severely traumatised (Hopper 1991; Sandler and Joffe 1967).

Bion (1961) coined the term, 'proto-mental' to refer to the most undifferentiated level of symbolic experience, on the border of the psychical and physical. Ogden (1991) has referred to this primitive state as the 'autistic-contiguous position'. It corresponds to Hopper's (ba) I:A/M.

In all individuals the 'painful bringing together of the primitive and the sophisticated...is the essence of the developmental conflict' (Bion 1961), that is, the intrapsychic conflict that both contributes to and interferes with the development of intersubjective thinking. Like other group members the group analyst is forever being co-opted by his or her own primitive mental processes, as well as by pressures emanating from other members, into basic assumption thinking. 'The preverbal matter the psychoanalyst must discuss is certain to be an illustration of the difficulty in communication that he himself is experiencing' (Bion 1970).

Hopper's group

Pervasive resistance to awareness is illustrated by the lack of auditory, visual, and linguistic attention to an 'increasingly intrusive and disturbing' buzzing which emanated from behind a wall dripping with yellow-brown liquid. Pandoro first put the here-and-now situation into group consciousnesses: 'This is a wasps' nest'. From my point of view, the comment appropriately metaphorised the adaptive context (Langs 1978). However, Hopper saw Pandoro's ironic trope quite oppositely, as a jokey attempt to escape from consciousness of personal and social powerlessness. Supporting my view, the group members evaluate Hopper's interpretations as communications from a preoccupied and unresponsive parent. Their comments are perceptive, for Hopper himself realised his difficulty in responding to the real danger from the 'outside'.

Hopper reminds the group that, while wasps can only follow their instincts, human beings have choices. But in the following sessions, Hopper did not display this type of consciousness. Hopper attempts to facilitate a more secure atmosphere by interpreting envy and separation anxiety. However, Pandoro forthrightly evaluates these interpretations as 'a bloody waste of time', which provokes Hopper's acknowledgement of his neglect as group guardian and his possible role in creating the group situation. But he undoes the intervention with interpretations about his forthcoming holiday and Pandoro's homosexuality and violent fantasies. The women shun these stinging interpretations as irrelevant, characterising Hopper as a combined child prodigy-senior citizen. Hopper and Pandoro are out of it, and the women choose to flee as well. But Hopper's subsequent interventions advance self and group consciousness (and unconsciousness). Group members, appreciating Hopper's 'only human' and context-relevant response, reciprocate with improved work group functioning.

After the summer's break, Pandoro again spurred work group functioning by initiating the exploration of the group leader's 'weaknesses and flaws'. Hopper concedes that he had not been 'as sensitive to the Group as I would have liked', but asserts, quite fairly, that he had played an important part in the Group's working through 'a painful experience of aggregation based on failed dependency while being in the company of people whom we trusted and knew very well'. Indeed, Hopper must trust himself, as well as his group (and our group, his readers) to self-disclose his own evolutionary process from incohesion to a linguistically articulated self-consciousness.

Further discussion and conclusion

Certainly, the incohesion concept is of no small clinical utility. The theoretical question is whether any such axis of experience and defence merits the special status of a basic assumption. Incohesion and the defences of aggregation and massification might be collapsed into the existing triad of basic assumptions. Therefore, the necessity for positing a fourth basic assumption remains controversial.

It should be remembered that the basic assumptions are not 'distinct states of mind', but 'duals' or reciprocals of each other. In any therapeutic interaction, it is possible to find elements of incohesion, dependency, pairing, and fight/flight. The three, or four (or more), variations of primitive intersubjective response may best be understood as 'myth' or metaphor – Row C of Bion's Grid. As with all metaphors, the value of the basic assumption concept is to locate experience, the goal being to stimulate and advance conscious and unconscious meaning making, without implying a single vision of reality.

Bion (1961) held that the basic assumptions represent an inevitable response to any leader who displays a 'questioning attitude'. I suggest that the dual to the group's basic assumptive mentality is the leader's counter-mentality. As group therapists, we feel intersubjective tensions that relate not only to our complementary and concordant introjective identifications (Racker 1968), but also, from our own primitive affects, thoughts, and fantasies, activated by social participation, and representing the currency and history of our own struggles with the incohesive, paranoid-schizoid, manic, and depressive parts of our personalities.

In Hopper's group the therapist displayed aggregative and massified defences, countertransferential duals of the collective basic assumptive transferences, while at times members maintained work group functions. For example, Pandoro served as Hopper's work leader 'twin' (see Bion 1967), symbolising and putting into words the reality of the here and now situation. Hopper initially seemed encapsulated in an autistic-like depression, an unarticulated mass onto himself, unable and unwilling to take constructive action. Many interventions seemed overly abstract, stereotypically Kleinian and far from his experience-near intentions. But, by bearing and acknowledging, with a courageous transparency, the limitations in his personal functioning, and consciously (and unconsciously) thinking about the group's assessment of his functioning, Hopper emerged as the true work group leader and provided a powerfully therapeutic experience. Hopper's remarkable social capacity allowed him to struggle towards self-awareness, and to share his journey with us his readers, as it evolved in, and was supported as well as challenged by his therapy group.

In thinking about my own groups, I have come to understand and apply personally Hopper's concept of a fourth basic assumption, Incohesion, and its predominant defences, contact-shunning Aggregation, and merger-hunger Massification. The group therapist often and perhaps necessarily personifies Incohesion: Aggregation and Massification. Hence, I am I:A/M.

Bridging Individual and Group Psychology

Howard Kibel

Clinical Professor of Psychiatry at New York Medical College in Valhalla, New York and in private practice in Valhalla, New York.

One of the most comprehensive attempts to apply Bion's theories (Ashbach and Schermer 1987) postulates the existence of three separate but interrelated systems in the group: the individual, the interactive, and the group-qua-group. Although acknowledging the reciprocal relationship of the individual on the group and vice versa, Ashbach and Schermer still consider these to be separate systems that are linked by the interactive one. Although they do not offer a specific therapeutic model for conducting treatment, their comprehensive examination of group psychology demonstrates that the group and the individual cannot be juxtaposed, even though they are inextricably related.

Hopper's postulate of a fourth basic assumption proposes to do what others have not been able to do. He has defined a basic assumption mentality whose leader is represented by one actual member of the group. By interpreting both that leader's role and that of the other members, he proposes that the process can be mutative, at least for the group itself. This is something that has not been successfully accomplished before.

Hopper's concept of 'personification' offers a challenge to contemporary theory, namely, that when difficult patients are in the group, individual and group psychology interface. Should Hopper prove correct, a significant advance in theory will have been made. Finding an interface between individual and group psychology could pave the way for the development of techniques that treat the group itself while benefiting the individual, something that has not proven successful previously.

The fourth basic assumption

Rioch (1970) helped us to understand the meaning of the basic assumption group by reformulating Bion's terminology using ordinary language. She noted that 'Basic assumption means exactly what it says – namely, the assumption which is basic to the behaviour. It is an 'as if' term' (p.59). Hopper's basic assumption of Incohesion occurs when a group is not cohesive, that is, when members are no longer bonded to one another in a substantive way and interdependence has dissipated. Then the members act as if they are working together, that is, that they are cohesive, when they are not.

In Hopper's Group the members have the experience of the Group as having been a psychological whole. They had become interdependent with one another and they have a history of being important to one another. However, in the face of something traumatic or disruptive the group has effectively fragmented. They then try to act 'as if' cohesiveness is present, but it is not. They form an aggregate or a mass, which are kinds of loose psychological group formations that only barely resemble what was before. The fundamental process is a regressive one. The aggregate or mass forms as a kind of illusion that serves to deny the existence of the trauma or disruption, its nature, and its effect on the Group's functioning. In short, in the face of psychological group dissolution, the members act *as if* the Group remains a psychological whole.

What Hopper describes is similar to the 'loosely organised psychological group' (Kaplan and Roman 1963), on the one hand, and Anzieu's (1984) 'group illusion', on the other. However, the former refers to a newly formed group that has not yet developed cohesion of any sort. This is the earliest phase of group development and one in which members relate to the leader as singletons. The members are not yet bonded to one another and relate as singletons to any notion of the group-as-a-group. This was never intended to refer to a basic assumption state since it describes a phase of group development that precedes the development of a psychological group, that is, a cohesive one. However, at times, something analogous can occur in an on-going group. We have all observed groups that transiently lose their psychological organisation in the face of severe stress, that is, when they are traumatised. 'Group illusion' refers to a state of pseudo-mutuality, in which members believe that a high degree of cohesion is present while denying destructive elements within. This was never claimed to have basic assumption qualities, but appears to. In the state of group illusion, a group behaves 'as if' the members are united, that they work unusually well together, that they may even be identical to one another, and that they have the best leader imaginable or don't even need one. However, this is an illusion since the group assumes this state as a hypomanic defence against internal destructiveness.

In this author's experience the dissolution of a psychological group occurs frequently in groups of patients with severe psychopathology (Kibel 1991). The therapist must work to help these patients attain the inclusion phase of development. But, for such patients, inclusion is associated with fears of merger and loss of autonomy. Once these patients develop some semblance of cohesion, or do so briefly, aggressively linked introjects are stimulated, which cause the members to emotionally pull away from one another, that is, to psychologically disperse. They are together in a physical sense, but not in a psychological one. Thus, they constitute an aggregate. The concept of aggregation can help to expand our understanding of the group treatment of patients with severe psychopathology by furthering the phenomenological description of the process.

The state of group illusion is a frequent occurrence and can disarm the therapist. Denial of significant, destructive intra-group forces can cause patients to develop defensive pseudo-mutuality. Feelings of twinship amongst the members become quasi-delusional so that universalisation dominates at the expense of true therapeutic work (Kibel 1993). The aggression is split-off, as euphoria places a moratorium on the pain of the group experience. At times, it leads to pernicious blaming of others or even scapegoating. The members' belief that they are just like one another holds them together as a mass, rather than a working group. Hopper's concept of Massification can help alert us to such group-wide resistances.

As Hopper notes, these group states are analogous to the developmentally earliest experience of unity with the mother and separation from her. Scheidlinger (1974) noted that such early experience is at the heart of the formation of the psychological group. He stated that, in the face of a multitude of stresses during the formation of the psychological group, there is a particular kind of regression that occurs which enables the group to be experienced as an entity, one that binds the members together and gives the group emotional meaning. He stated that an individual's self-involvement in the group can constitute a regression in the service of the therapeutic alliance, one that is analogous to the classic regression in the service of the ego. Specifically, it involves 'a "giving up" of an aspect of personal identity – from the *I* to the *We*' (p.420). In these terms, we can redefine the state of Incohesion as a regression from the *We* to the *I*, but in this case, the new state is adorned with the guises of a group, namely, as aggregation or massification (both of which are, according to Hopper, grotesque versions of 'I' and, according to Turquet, comprised of 'Isolates' and 'Singletons', on the one hand, and 'Membership Individuals', on the other).

Bridging psychologies

Hopper proposes that the fourth basic assumption group is embodied in the difficult patient, the one with borderline and narcissistic pathology. This member becomes its spokesman and, by default, its titular leader. In contrast to Bion's three basic assumptions wherein the leader has qualities that the others lack but seek, this leader personifies the members' current state of being. Therefore, Hopper proposes, interpretation of this member's behaviour is integral to the group working through the fourth basic assumption. Specifically, he states that 'group analysis presents opportunities for working in a contained way with the personification of the roles associated with unconscious basic assumption process'.

Although the method appears to be an 'inductive' one, in that work with one member becomes the basis for work with the group-as-a-whole, Hopper claims that interpretive work with both is done inside the domain of a basic assumption. Herein lies the attempt to merge individual and group psychology. The Tavistock method of Ezriel (1950) was an attempt to integrate the two, but failed (Kibel and Stein 1981). The reasons for that failure continue to raise doubts as to whether Hopper's attempt will prove successful.

Hopper introduces the notion of 'personification' to define the central persons of this fourth basic assumption group. He notes that it is an unconscious process in which there is an intimate, dynamic relation between the group and this central person. Because such individuals, namely, difficult patients, have particular patterns of anxiety and defence that are consonant with the group's mentality at that point in treatment, they are more than accidental central figures.

By using the term personification, Hopper deems Redl's (1963) concept of 'role suction' to be wanting. But Redl's idea seems to me to be more suited to clinical practice. Granted, some people do use groups to live out their individual pathology or personality needs. That is why Kernberg's (1991) analysis of certain group leaders whose personality fits the group, so to speak, makes sense. Redl noted that some people 'seem to reserve some role-acting for some groups only, and do not show much of it in the rest of their lives' (p.144). In other words, while the behaviour may be specific to the individual, it is not necessarily central to that person's psychopathology. This is consistent with Scheidlinger's (1982) view regarding scapegoating. Moreover, Redl also noted that there are times when the role that is seemingly imposed by the group on the individual is one that is ego-dystonic.

Personification, for Hopper, is related to the concept of 'fractal', borrowed from the computer sciences. It seems similar to the concept of 'isomorphy', which comes from general systems theory and has been applied to group psychotherapy (Durkin 1972). However, a member of a group has personal characteristics and internal psychic processes, both conscious and unconscious, whereas the group is comprised of related aspects of each member that interdigitate with others to from a dynamic whole. In short, the error of the 'argument (of isomorphy) lies in the confusion between analogy and identity' (Horwitz 1977). Although Hopper is fully aware of this problem, I would stress that although there are times when an individual will personify group-wide dynamics, more often it only seems that way. Frequently, a difficult patient only appears to personify the group's condition because his ego is malleable. The role taken by the patient does not necessarily typify his behaviour outside the group, but rather is paradigmatic of a primitive ego, one that is incoherent and seeks anchoring in relationships in order to create the illusion that he has a coherent self. The patient, in essence, accommodates his behaviour to a perceived group need. That is exactly what occurs in role suction (Redl 1963) and is substantively different from personification.

The disparity between individual and group dynamics complicates the therapist's job. It makes it difficult, if not impossible, to interpret the multiple levels of dynamics in a group in an integrated way, as Hopper proposes. In his example, interpretations were made to the group-as-a-whole about complex transferences to him as therapist and to a member of the group who personified the incohesive state of aggregation. There are two aspects of the therapist's interventions that cause the effect to be uncertain. First, there is the reaction of one or more members to the intervention itself. In the example presented by Hopper, he found that his interpretation caused the women to become rivalrous with the men. They experienced the member who personified the group dynamic as a little brother who received special attention from the father-analyst.

The second, and more relevant aspect to the discussion here, derives from a general systems perspective on the complexities of group process. An intervention that is directed at one level of the group – let us say, at group-level processes, such as aggregation – can have effects at other levels; let us say, on the transference to the leader. From a general systems perspective a group operates as a multi-level system with delineated, but non-congruous sub-systems (Kernberg 1975). This means that sub-systems of, for example, the group-as-a-whole, transference to the leader, and peer transferences operate in non-hierarchical ways, in terms of their relationship to one another. Moreover, dynamically they overlap. It follows then that interventions at one level of the group will have unpredictable and unintended effects on its other sub-systems. This is because an intervention aimed at one level also speaks to another, unloosening unintended forces.

Conclusions

Hopper has enriched the seminal contributions of Bion by proposing a fourth basic assumption. Inadvertently, he has given dynamic meaning to the often-abused term 'cohesion' by delineating its opposite, namely, 'incohesion'. The fourth basic assumption neatly describes the dynamic processes of group dissolution that one frequently sees in groups composed of patients with severe psychopathology. One moment such groups function effectively, while the next moment the group is dysfunctional. This assumption also enriches the concept of the 'group illusion', which is a state of group resistance disguised as productive work. However, Hopper has challenged us further by proposing that so-called difficult patients personify this fourth basic assumption. Certainly, it has long been recognised that such patients are sensitive to the group's dynamics and often speak to the unspoken in a group. But Hopper appears to have gone further than that. He claims that the dynamics of the difficult patient intertwine with group-level processes. This is an attempt to create an interface between individual and group psychology. To do so raises conceptual issues that still have to be worked out in our field. Until then, group psychology, for the practising clinician, remains incomplete and we must be content, as Scheidlinger (1980) has noted, with 'limited-domain' theory.

Moments of Meeting in Group Analysis

Malcolm Pines

A founding member of the Group Analytic Society and The Institute of Group Analysis, the Editor of *Group Analysis*, and in private practice in London, England.

Not many psychoanalysts remain faithful to their basic discipline after psychoanalytic training: they undergo a conversion-like change and, like true converts, have to assert the dedication and devotion to some form of psychoanalysis. One of those Earl Hopper is not. Foulkesian group analysis attracts him because its theory base arises from a dynamically informed view of the primacy of the social, laid out from 1940 onwards by S.H. Foulkes. Foulkes's close friendship and collaboration with Norbert Elias, who Hopper knew when they were both in the Department of Sociology at Leicester University, has been celebrated and reviewed by Farhad Dalal (1998). At one time Elias thought of becoming a group analyst, but did not take that step. Hopper took the step that Elias did not: having trained as a psychoanalyst and as a group analyst, but his writings are informed by the intertwining of social and psychoanalytic thought, *vide* his writings on the social unconscious and the problem of context in group analysis (Hopper 2003).

Hopper now writes of the consequences of trauma on its subjects in groups. Hopper's sociological vector is evident in his exploration of the fourth basic assumption. He finds his evidence for this in the large scale group events of conferences, in the dynamics of organisations to which he has consulted and in traumatised societies. He also argues that the fourth basic assumption is apparent in small therapeutic groups, especially those comprised of traumatised people. Whether these phenomena can in fact be recognised in small therapeutic groups will be considered in my contribution.

I propose to deal mainly with the clinical issues having to do with difficult patients, about whom I have written (Pines 1998). Hopper agrees with Kauff (1991) that the most important difference between individual and group therapy with borderline and other difficult patients is the help that the group gives to the therapist's countertransference problems. I acknowledge this difference, but do not put it in the forefront as, to my mind, this over-emphasises the role of the therapist and downplays the therapeutic factors inherent in a well-selected and conducted group. I have argued for the need to balance neurotic and borderline patients in a group and that a predominance of the latter militates against the group moving towards norms of meaningful interaction and understanding, and lessens the group's ability to present and to maintain the resources of holding and containment which are vital to therapeutic progress.

I agree with Hopper in emphasising the narrative mode of the therapeutic process. The maturation of the therapy group shows through its increased capacity for therapeutic dialogue, for grasping the meaning of the ever-present phenomena of mirroring, resonance, attunement and misattunement. This increased capacity I regard as a movement from lower forms of cohesion to higher forms, towards coherence, much as Hopper outlines (Pines 1986).

The importance of this concept of coherence is increasingly recognised in developmental psychology arising out of research into attachment theory. Attachment research demonstrates that coherent 'internal working models of attachment' are tied to participation in coherent forms in parent-child dialogue. Here dialogue is being used in its broader sense. According to the philosopher Greis, coherence in communications is achieved by adhering to maxims governing quantity, quality and manner, that is, being truthful, clear, relevant and succinct, yet complete. Thus coherent dialogue is collaborative and truthful. Research in child development shows that coherent open dialogue between parents and infants is characterised by parental 'openness' to the state of mind of the child, including the entire array of the child's communications: nothing is foreclosed, particularly the negative affects. I believe that we can extend this developmental paradigm to the therapeutic situation. In my view the therapist helps the group to become therapeutic by exemplifying these forms of coherence for the group to witness, thereby to be helped to develop coherence for themselves and for the group as a whole. Indeed, much that I have learned as a group therapist has been from being present in groups where the participants themselves have used the opportunity of being together in the space-time and have created authentic moments of dialogue.

These moments of dialogue are crucially important in all therapeutic situations. In an important paper, Stern and colleagues (1998) called these moments of dialogue 'moments of meeting'. At these moments of meeting 'something other' than the accuracy of interpretations carries the therapeutic process forward. Indeed, I have argued against emphasis on the 'exact' interpretation in my (Pines 1998) paper 'What should the psychotherapist know'. They should know how to give an inexact interpretation, one that is open to being used by the auditors in their own manner, to stimulate their own thoughts and feelings.

According to Stern, moments of meeting are therapeutically seized and mutually realised. Each partner has actively contributed something unique and authentic of his or herself as an individual in the construction of such a moment. When the therapist especially, but also the patient, grapples with the 'now' moment, explores and experiences it, it can become a 'moment of meeting'. There are several essential elements. The therapist uses a specific aspect of his or her individuality that carries a personal signature. The two, patient and therapist, meet as persons relatively unhidden by their usual therapeutic roles, for that moment. Such occasions cannot be routine, habitual or technical; they must be novel and fashioned to meet the singularity of the moment. This requires a manner of empathy, an openness to affective and cognitive reappraisal, a signalled affect attunement, a viewpoint that reflects and ratifies that what is happening is occurring in the domain of the 'shared implicit relationship', that is, a newly created dyadic state specific to the participants.

Kohut and the self-psychologists have emphasised how therapy moves forward through moments of empathic failure or misattunement by the therapist to the patient, moments which are later acknowledged and understood through exploration of how the therapist 'failed' the patient; no doubt we remember Winnicott's dictum that the prime function of the caregiver to an infant is progressively to fail, that is to withdraw from meeting the child's wish for omnipotence. Skilled caregiving involves gradually extending the infant's motivation to act meaningfully and to grasp the moment.

I believe that such a moment of meeting occurs in the session described by Hopper where he acknowledged that he had failed the group's expectations and was determined to do the best he could. 'I said that I was not asking for their forgiveness, but acknowledging their right to be disappointed and angry. However, I would not let them destroy the group'. And the group moved on to a sense of shared responsibility in the sense that they had shared a very special event from which they would learn a great deal. Hopper concludes, and I do not disagree with this, that failed dependency had led to a painful experience of aggregation, involving feelings of extreme loneliness and isolation in the company of people trusted and known well.

Hopper's noble statements conveyed empathy for the experience of the group during the period of his self-preoccupation and empathy for himself as a therapist burdened by his therapeutic task at a time of personal difficulty. This is a situation which I know well from my own experience. In subsequent sessions the conversation again flows, dialogue resumes, there is a re-establishment of the climate of inquiry that characterises a functioning group-analytic group.

I have not viewed these therapeutic impasses in the light of Hopper's fourth basic assumption. Rather, I have seen them as times of breakdown of therapeutic dialogue to be accounted for by the phasic nature of group life, of the sense that periods of pause and withdrawal into individual selves are necessary before a further move forward can take place. However, in the light of the theory of the fourth basic assumption, I shall be more aware of the consequences of failed dependency and fear of annihilation in response to traumatic experience. I fully agree that envy is not the primal emotion and it is more acceptable to me that envy develops as a defence against the anxieties associated with feelings of profound helplessness. I also agree that the concept of projective identification based upon the hypothetical death instinct is a much overused concept. It is especially important that we do not allow slow-open groups to disintegrate when faced with what Hopper describes as the phenomena of aggregation. It is incumbent upon the therapist to keep hope alive. Hope is a subject that Hopper has explored in depth and hopefulness maintained is a powerful antidote to the despair of helplessness.

Lighting Candles in the Darkness of the Group

Bennett Roth

A member of the Faculty of the Post Doctoral Program in Group Psychotherapy at Adelphi University, New York, and a psychoanalyst and psychoanalytical group psychotherapist in private practice in New York.

This author did not wish me to include excerpts from his contribution. Therefore, I have attempted to summarise it briefly:

After reviewing Bion's ideas about the container and the contained, it was argued that although Incohesion: Aggregation/Massification is both theoretically and clinically important, it should not be regarded as a basic assumption. It was asserted that Hopper has returned to a trauma theory of human development and psychic life, especially in connection with the aetiology of the psychopathology of difficult patients, and that in this connection has over-emphasised the value and relevance of the work of Tustin with respect to autistic phenomena, on the one hand, and Foulkes with respect to the sociality of human nature throughout the life trajectory, on the other. Although the author prefers the work of leading Kleinian and neo-Kleinian psychoanalysts, he connects the psychopathology of a variety of types of difficult patient to their early and even later traumatic experience. The author also prefers to think in terms of a failure to contain the group and its various members, rather than in terms of a concept of failed dependency. He believes that Hopper's interpretations were out of touch with the dynamics of the group and its members, and is especially critical of his passivity and his work with Pandoro. While appreciating the opportunity that Hopper afforded the reader to examine his work, Roth is impressed that the group survived an insult to their boundaries, and acknowledges that something positive and worthwhile must have happened both before the experience of failed dependency and after the analytic work that occurred.

An application of Hopper's concept of Incohesion: Aggregation/Massification

Jill Savege Scharff and David E. Scharff

Co-directors of the International Institute of Objects Relations Therapy in Washington, DC, and in private practice working in psychiatry, psychoanalysis and psychotherapy with adults, children, couples and families.

Our understanding of the theory and technique described in Hopper's paper

Hopper introduces his term Incohesion: Aggregation/Massification to describe a unique set of group dynamics that he has identified during group analysis with difficult patients, especially those suffering from addiction and perversion. In Hopper's experience, addicts and other difficult patients are most often traumatised people. They show the characteristic behaviours of flatness of affect, rage, and impotence – all of which intensify to a negative therapeutic reaction in the termination phase. He interprets these affective states as reactions to loss, abandonment, damage, and trauma in relation to the object. He does not see them as being due to death-instinct driven envy of the object and destructiveness against the self. In fact he thinks that envy is a defence against the anxieties associated with profound helplessness. In taking this position, he argues against predominant Kleinian views and asserts his identification with the British Independent group. Nevertheless, like others in the Independent group he values Klein's concepts of projective and introjective identification and Tustin's descriptions of autistic defences of a crustacean (contact-shunning) or an amoeboid (merger-hungry) sort.

Hopper's practical orientation toward group work is Foulkesian in terms of his willingness to commute between the individual and the group (Neri 1998) and see himself as a member of the group contributing to and affected by its dynamics. Hopper has developed a supportive and transparent stance that is sensitive to the fears of annihilation and the shame, rage, and helplessness that difficult patients experience, particularly in response to separation. However, his theoretical orientation draws heavily on Bion's basic assumption group functioning, even though he disputes Bion's idea that envy is the main thing that drives bizarre splits in large groups. Instead, Hopper thinks that these are caused mainly by rage over unmet dependency needs, although he has also said that merging occurs as a defence against separation and individuation to avoid the envy that comes with recognition of differences in endowment, and he has recognised the extent to which it can fragment the self, the leader, or the group (Hopper 1987). In an earlier communication, Hopper (1977) agreed with Springmann (1976) that fragmentation in a group occurs to protect the leader from being destroyed by member rage. From his background in sociology Hopper now adds the concepts of aggregation and massification to arrive at a new way of describing the fourth basic assumption.

Observing his difficult patients in group therapy, Hopper noted that their traumatised personalities alternated between states of fission and fragmentation and states of fusion and confusion in association with damaging, abandoning objects. When individuals get together in sub-groups based on their valencies to react to traumatic stress, Hopper finds that the potentially cohesive work group enters a state of incohesion in which the group oscillates between aggregation and massification. Hopper does not support the distinction of a fifth basic assumption of 'Me-ness', proposed as a retreat from fusion by Lawrence, Bain and Gould (1996), because it is no different than Turquet's disarroy. We note that Lawrence, Bain and Gould, like Hopper, think in terms of the group's social reaction to failed dependency rather than its response to the force of the death instinct, as Turquet does. Apart from this, we remain unsure of the distinctions between the dynamics described by Hopper, Turquet, and Lawrence, Bain and Gould, but we prefer Hopper's sociologically inspired terminology because it bridges the gap between the social and psychoanalytic routes to understanding.

AGGREGATION

Aggregation is Hopper's term for a group state of fission/fragmentation (which is like Turquet's disarroy). In this state, each member shuns contact with the other and the group engages in mocking, teasing, and dark humour, interspersed with silence. Fears of annihilation inhibit competition and differentiation, and so a bland sameness characterises each separate individual. This type of group is usually led by a crustaceous personality in retreat from an overwhelming, damaging object. The therapist feels lonely and unhelpful. The individuals may then turn the aggregate group into a massification group as if hurling themselves into the soothing body of the mother where all are equally loved and there is no intrusive male presence.

MASSIFICATION

Massification is Hopper's term for a group state of fusion and confusion devoid of rage, led by an amoeboid personality ready to merge with a confusing, damaging object. It may appear to be a group with a developed language of its own that is not understood by outsiders, but it is no more cohesive than the more obviously fragmented aggregate group. This group is led by an amoeboid personality ready to merge with a confused and confusing object. The therapist is at risk of behaving in a super-supportive way that gratifies both group and therapist. The massification group has a pseudo-morale that breaks down and readily reverts to its basic aggregate status.

Comments on Hopper's concept of the fourth basic assumption

We find Hopper's conceptualization of the fourth basic assumption of Incohesion: Aggregation/Massification interesting and convincing. We are less convinced that this group dynamic is fundamentally different from Turquet's description of fusion: disarroy. There is, however, a striking difference at the level of understanding of the origin of the dynamic, with Hopper attributing it to the trauma of failed dependency and not to envy arising from the death instinct, as Turquet does. As we have argued that the death instinct is not an instinct at all, we find ourselves in sympathy with Hopper's point of view (D.E. Scharff 1992; J. Scharff and D.E. Scharff 1998; J. Scharff and D.E. Scharff 2000).

We felt that the paper presented a convincing case for viewing group process with difficult group members in terms of Hopper's theory. We totally agree with his view of individual and group responses to trauma. We think that the traumatised person develops traumatic nuclei because of primal repression, and gaps in the psyche because of dissociation. Inside these nuclei are pointed fragments, inside which are gaps, inside which are sharp pieces of encapsulated experience (Hopper 1991; J. Scharff and D.E. Scharff 1994, 1998). Since there are traumatic nuclei scattered across the vast, empty, internal space of the traumatised individual psyche, it comes as no surprise that traumatised people in a group present as an aggregate of individuals scattered across the vast landscape of the group. And we can imagine their preference for massification as an accumulation of traumatic nuclei hiding in a longed-for maternal matrix of safety. There are generative nuclei too, and in the group there is hope that these will be augmented in association to the accumulated wisdom and solidity of the group and its leader.

Comments on Hopper's clinical example

Hopper's clinical example comes from one of his long-term analytic therapy groups that was paralysed. This group is in a state of incohesion, oscillating between states of aggregation and massification, as the members use the unmanageable buzzing of wasps and threats of extermination to replace their feelings about abandonment by their therapist over the summer. Aggregation is characterised by silence, staring, sarcasm, and teasing, and massification is characterised by the group members' smoking marijuana together during the session without objection by the therapist. At one point the men form an aggregate (contra-) group and the women form a massification (contra-) group.

When the group was in a state of aggregation, Hopper resorted to intellectually complex comments that were not worked with well. Instead, group members complained about parents who were preoccupied. We might use Hopper's theory to say that he was captured by the aggregation dynamics of the group at that moment, became intellectually crusty, and then the group had experienced him as a parent preoccupied with his own concerns. Interpretation of group transferences in terms of group and leader, past and present, the internal world and the social, cultural context enabled them to confront their aggression towards parents who had failed them. At first, the group members did less well at fully expressing their rage in the transference for not being protected by the group therapist. Then Hopper's work on his countertransference was crucial in letting him move with the group beyond the state of incohesion. His work with one group member who personified the aggregation defence enabled others to join in and be helped and the group became a cohesive work group again.

We are impressed by Hopper's ability as a group therapist to keep in mind individual and social unconscious factors, past and present. He also holds a vision of the cohesive shape of the working group toward which the group can move.

In our experience as psychoanalytic clinicians and teachers of psychoanalytic concepts, the dynamics of affective learning in small groups and family groups illustrate the value of Hopper's innovative concept of the fourth basic assumption of Incohesion:Aggregation/Massification. We find it to be a useful advance. Like all concepts, its usefulness needs to be verified in the clinical and the societal setting, but because it is drawn from experience in both those areas it seems to apply well across the human spectrum. By integrating psychoanalytic and social understanding, Hopper's fourth basic assumption has the flexibility to apply to our work as individual psychoanalysts, family therapists, and group leaders in psychoanalytic education.

From I:A/M to 'Who am I' – Aggregation/Massification and trauma-based affects and object relations in groups

Victor L. Schermer

Director of the Study Group for Contemporary Psychoanalytic Process and the Institute for the Study of Human Conflict, and psychologist in private practice and clinic settings in Philadelphia, PA.

Earl Hopper's understanding of 'amoeboid' and 'crustacean' personifications of (ba) I/AM parallels T.S. Eliot's (1980) portrayal of J. Alfred Prufrock, the quintessential symbol of middle class alienation and anomie, *viz.* 'Amoeboid' as yellow fog, and 'crustacean' as 'ragged claws'. 'Amoeboid' and 'crustacean' are archetypal representations of the most primitive, 'autistic' levels of object relations.

Through persistent evidence from my daily clinical work, as well as accumulating research (Herman 1997; Herman and van der Kolk 1987) and documentation in the psychoanalytic literature (Scharff and Scharff 1994; Shengold 1989), I have become convinced that psychological trauma plays a significant role in the pathology of many patients. Robert Klein and I co-edited a book entitled *Group Psychotherapy for Psychological Trauma* (Klein and Schermer 2000), a collection of original contributions on how trauma impacts on group treatment and vice versa. One of the chapters of that book is by Ramon Ganzarain (2000) on 'Group-as-a-whole dynamics in work with traumatized patients'. That chapter gave me an opportunity to 'tri-alogue' with Earl and Ramon about their somewhat differing views of the impact of trauma on group dynamics. Except for Earl's and Ramon's pioneering work, trauma has been almost totally ignored in the group psychotherapy literature, even in the literature on trauma groups! Whatever agreements and differences I have with respect to Earl's formulations, his sustained, disciplined, and I suppose at times lonely and painful insistence on the importance of trauma in group formation has earned him an honoured place in the history of group psychotherapy and group analysis. Judith Herman (1997) has written, 'creating a protected space where survivors can speak the truth is an act of liberation'. Earl has made such a space for his and our group therapy patients and, crucially, *has studied this forgotten space* and given it a theoretical formulation.

Earl's work has two related components. The first is his conceptualisation of the dynamics of 'difficult' borderline and narcissistic patients, sexual perversion, and substance abuse in terms of infantile experience of helplessness and abandonment involving a failure of the holding environment (Winnicott 1965). He challenges the Kleinian view of pathology as a function of instinctual drives and, like his cohorts and predecessors in the British Independent school of psychoanalysis, attributes it to maternal (or we would now say parental/caregiver) 'failures' and deficits, but knowing that the interaction between infant and caregiver is complex and reciprocal (Brazelton and Cramer 1989; Stern 1984). He also questions the existence and universality of innate malign envy, splitting and projective identification in pathogenesis, and contends that another protective mechanism, at an earlier and more basic level, is the encapsulation of traumatic experience and its attendant 'annihilation anxiety' in a type of internal container, keeping it 'quarantined' from the main body of the personality. Here his thinking is similar to, though not identical with, Fairbairn's (1952) notion of the psyche as sub-egos that contain different portions of what Hopper refers to as originally 'pristine' experience in compartmentalised, dissociated parts of the self.

The second component of Earl's thinking is about group formations. Expanding upon Turquet's (1974, 1975) formulation of a 'fourth basic assumption' of Oneness, Earl posits (a) that this configuration should be called 'Incohesion', the two poles of which are 'Aggregation' and 'Massification' (hence the acronym, I/AM); and (b) that it is not simply the result of regression, especially in connection with regression in large groups in response to over-stimulation and the overwhelming nature of large numbers of people, but is primarily a function of the presence and re-evocation of primitive psychological trauma in the members. Although these two factors may co-exist, Earl in effect is positing an 'intervening variable' (between the group situation and the resulting aggregation/massification configuration) of failed dependency and encapsulated self-experience resulting from annihilation anxiety in the membership.

What is I:A/M?

It has long been known that groups can, at times, act as an aggregate of individuals who sustain only minimal emotional contact with each other; and at other times, as a 'mass' or 'horde' who behave as if they constitute one large being lacking the capacities and differentiation of individual selves. In his seminal essay *Group Psychology and the Analysis of the Ego* Freud (1921), himself distinguished between groups with a leader and more primitive 'mass' configurations, such as 'mobs', having a 'herd mentality'. However, Hopper argues that in small therapy groups, which recapitulate the dynamics of the nuclear family, the differentiated transference to the leader, the group-as-a-whole, and the set of 'sibling relations' are so prominent that although massification and aggregation states are short-lived, they do occur transitionally. In therapy groups consisting of members with histories of severe trauma, emotional lability and contagion often alternate with distancing, dissociation, and avoidance (Klein and Schermer 2000), which is another way of describing, respectively, massification and aggregation.

In large groups, mass configurations, as Turquet (1974, 1975) pointed out, are more obvious, and actually may constitute the normative behaviour of such groups in their early stages. However, Earl argues that 'aggregation,' unlike Turquet's 'disarroy,' is not a secondary defence in response to massification, but that they constitute an oscillating and inseparable polarity. Aggregation is primary, and massification is a defence against it, and vice versa. To me this seems to be an important correction to the more common notion that the fear of annihilation is co-equivalent to the fear of merger, fusion, or 're-engulfment' (Mahler, Pine and Bergman 1975). Earl, in my opinion, is correct in asserting that both aggregation and massification are defences against a still more fundamental state of helplessness, abandonment, and terror.

The question in my mind is how Earl's aggregation/massification configuration fits into Bion's (1961) notion of the basic assumption states. To Earl's view that I:A/M is a 'fourth basic assumption', I would suggest some important qualifications and modifications.

In my opinion the 'fourth basic assumption' constitutes a primitive group formation or group culture, but it is not an 'assumption', but is a '*pre*-assumption', i.e. rather than being a configuration reflecting certain implicit beliefs of the membership (which is how Bion defined the basic assumptions of dependence, fight/flight, and pairing), massification/aggregation is a still more basic primordial configuration of establishing (or, conversely, disabling) the very primitive boundary conditions that enable basic assumptions to occur in the first place. Foulkes (1965) had importantly distinguished between a 'primordial' and a 'projective' level of group regression, the primordial being a state akin to Jung's archetypes, wherein the unconscious is, paradoxically, both collective (massification) and self-contained (autistic; aggregated). Foulkes (1965) used the term 'autocosmos' for this primordial level (what Lacan (1977) called the realm of the 'Real'); and the 'projective level' or 'microsphere' where primitive experience is represented by differentiated internal objects that are projectively identified into others, as described by Melanie Klein (Segal 1964) (Lacan's 'Imaginary' realm).

In other words, unlike the basic assumptions, aggregation/massification is a 'pre-object' quasi-autistic state in which even primitive notions of leadership, interpersonal relationships, projective 'containers,' etc. do not yet exist. Instead, as in Heraclitus' description of the universe, there are, in effect, only atoms and the void, or in biblical terms, everything is contained in God before He (or She!) has created the Word and the World.

It is no accident that Earl derives his understanding of the 'personfications' of I:A/M from Tustin's (1981) studies of infantile autism. Bick (1968) pointed out that the problem of the autistic child (and of many of our narcissistic and borderline patients) is not that of managing 'bad' internalised objects and their attendant anxieties, but a more basic one of establishing a boundary between self and other. Arguing that this boundary initially is constituted by the skin, she postulated a developmental stage prior to that of the paranoid-schizoid position, and which she called the stage of 'adhesive identification'. Here, the basic task of the infant is, by the repetitive experience of contact and non-contact with the mother's body on a physical level, to discern and internalise a self/other distinction which then allows for projections and introjections between self and object to take place.

How can such primordial boundary-making experiences be revived in the group context? The answer is two-fold, stemming from 1. normative group processes and 2. traumatic repetitions. With respect to the first of these, J. Durkin (1980, 1981) posited that 'boundary openings and closings' are characteristics of groups as living systems. Systems isomorphisms (discussed by Earl under the rubrics of 'personification', 'figurations' and 'fractals') dictate that boundarying processes have components at both the individual and the group-qua-group levels. In the archaic self, the boundary is the physical body: the eyes, the skin, various openings, breathing, etc. In development, the boundary is subsequently negotiated at the interpersonal and symbolic levels. In the group-as-a-whole, boundaries negotiate between various group systems and sub-systems (Agazarian 1997), for example, the group and its context, the group and the leader, sub-groups, members, etc. In aggregation/massification, it is as if the group regresses to a state where the boundaries are concretised and extremised, so that there are few gradations and areas of semi-permeability, just as the infant's contact with mother, especially when experiencing annihilation anxiety, would be all or nothing. We would guess that the infant feels at times totally open and exposed, or else in a state of blissful symbiosis (Mahler, Pine and Bergman 1975), and at other times, totally closed off and protected, although lacking in some external supplies, an island, an aggregate. In this respect, the group as a 'fictive body' (Fornari 1974) inherently recapitulates the earliest boundary-forming processes of infancy.

In addition, I:A/M may be evoked in groups through the transference repetition or re-enactment of psychic trauma (Buchele 2000; Ganzarain 2000; Hegeman and Wohl 2000; Ziegler and McEvoy 2000). This becomes obvious when we consider that many psychic traumata involve very specifically a violation of the 'skin frontier' (Bick 1968) by aggression, damage, or sexualised touching, exposure, and penetration. Other traumata involve psychological violations which may be as much of an impingement on the self as physical intrusiveness is on the body. Such invasions are reacted to emotionally with shame and humiliation: thus, boundaries are the guardians of self-esteem and self-cohesion. Thus, the inevitable narcissistic slights, deprivations, and misunderstandings that occur in groups, not to mention blatantly hostile or erotised re-enactments of trauma, may lead to the boundary extremes of aggregation and massification, which some trauma theorists (Klein and Schermer 2000) would call respectively, 'dissociation' and 'emotional flooding' or 'contagion'.

Who am I? Encapsulated, split, or dissociated?

Earl's article reminds me that we need a trans-oceanic and trans-theoretical dialogue about trauma. Earl thoroughly addresses an issue that has been endemic and traumatic to psychoanalysts in The British Psychoanalytical Society: the ongoing dialogue (once called the 'controversial discussions') between the Kleinians and Freudians, which ultimately led to the formation of the British Independent school. In particular, Earl discusses whether annihilation anxiety is, as the Kleinians hold, the result of the death instinct manifest in primitive envy and 'bad' persecutory internal objects which attack the budding self and must be managed with splitting, projective identification, and other defences which then become the basis of personality development (and by Bion's extrapolation, the basic assumption states); or whether, as the British Independents, especially Winnicott and Harry Guntrip might contend, it is the result of aborted dependency and feelings of helplessness resulting from failures of environmental holding. Earl, of course, is clearly on the side of Winnicott and Guntrip in this respect, and also feels that Turquet neglected actual trauma histories in his understanding of the fourth basic assumption. Earl wants to bring in the real histories and the real lives of his group members, symbolised for example, by the wasps' nest outside his office window, a potentially very threatening 'persecutory object' which required government intervention! Surely, Ganzarain (2000) would have capitalised on this occurrence as symbolic of the group's aggression and envy, and Earl does not neglect these factors, but the gentle 'sting' of his interventions are sensitively directed at the narcissistic injury (Wolf 1988) experienced by the members regarding his going on holiday (abandonment).

While my own sentiments lean more towards Earl's formulations about this matter, I do think that aggression and envy play a profound role in trauma, especially if we consider the relationship between victim and perpetrator. Ganzarain (2000) correctly points out that, if traumatised group members do not address their rage in the transference, they cannot fully individuate and overcome their 'victim' and 'victimiser' roles. And certainly the encapsulation of which Earl speaks so cogently, and which I would understand as an internalised skin boundary, is heavily cathected and maintained with aggressive energy deriving from hate for the abandoning and/or intrusive victimiser.

Regarding this matter of the role of instincts and of aggression, I have always felt that, to some extent, the polarisation between the British Independent and Kleinian schools is artificial, and it is really a matter of both instincts and caregiving, rather than either/or. I personally admire Grotstein's

(2000) particular synthesis of Kleinian and British views, which of course were anticipated in some respects by Winnicott and Fairbairn themselves, who never abandoned Kleinian thought and always held that they were adding to and modifying it, not contravening it. In this connection, all of psychoanalysis is a 'dualistic' psychology which implies some early traumatic 'rupture' in the self. In my opinion, this is true regardless of whether the orientation is Freudian, Kleinian, Winnicottian, Kohutian, Lacanian, or whatever. Actually, Earl accepts that paradoxically such duality makes psychoanalysis inherently a trauma theory even when it rejects (as Freud eventually did) the etiological role of trauma!

Another issue is, therefore, how to bring a broader understanding of traumatogenesis into the discussion both of psychopathology and group psychology. Earl does us the service of bringing the impact of trauma clearly into the arena of the group-as-a-whole. But his formulation of the impact of trauma in terms of encapsulated psychosis is, while extremely interesting and important, narrow in comparison with the variations in traumatic responses that actually occur, and their relation to phases of development and the attendant self-protective mechanisms.

Some of the phenomena which Earl describes could be understood as examples of traumatic dissociation, whether Pandoro's defensive use of marijuana to flee from his feelings, or the group's avoidance of genuine interactions; and emotional flooding and contagion, for instance the group's mass feeling of abandonment and their fear of the wasps' nest (in reality, safely behind a window). Although the use of this alternative terminology may appear to be a mere matter of semantics, in actuality dissociation and emotional flooding are part of post-traumatic stress disorder per se, and are not necessarily endemic to borderline and narcissistically 'difficult' patients, while an encapsulated psychosis suggests a very deep-seated and rigidified character pathology. Of course, many of our patients, particularly those abused by their own family members in childhood, will have features of both personality disorders *and* PTSD.

There are, thus, (at least!) three 'models' of psychological trauma implied in the above discussion: 1. Earl's notion of an encapsulated psychosis resulting from failed dependency, helplessness, and annihilation anxiety; 2. a Kleinian perspective advanced by Ganzarain in which trauma induces regression to paranoid-schizoid defences of splitting and projective identification; and 3. a dissociative PTSD model in which the core self distances from the traumatic memories and affects more along the lines of Janet's (1886) autohypnotic theory of hysteria than of borderline and psychotic mechanisms as such. Moreover, the model adopted alters how we think about aggregation/massification phenomena in groups. Ganzarain's model sees trauma potentially manifest in Bion's BA flight, dependency, *and* pairing as a function of which affects are evoked in the group transference. The dissociation model views I:A/M as a kind of group level affective 'limbic system' disorder stemming from specific re-enactments, memory constellations, and emotional triggers present in the group. And Earl's encapsulated annihilation anxiety perspective views I:A/M as ubiquitous in groups, but not necessarily, in my view, a basic assumption state, as Earl contends, but rather more as a profound disruption and/or transition of the boundaries of the group matrix occurring when the basic assumptions fail in their protective and cohesion-preserving functions.

To conclude, my differences with Earl pale by comparison to my respect for him as a colleague who is pushing the envelope of our thinking in the propitious direction of taking the impact of real lives, real time narratives, and real trauma into account as we explore not only the form, but also the vital actuality of groups. I feel honoured to have been asked to respond to his seminal article and look forward to hearing his views as they continue to develop.

A Response in terms of 'Bridging', 'Psychological', and 'Clinical' Theories

Walter D. Stone

Professor of Psychiatry, University of Cincinnati College of Medicine and Past President of the American Group Psychotherapy Association. The author wishes to thank Edward B. Klein, Ph.D and Robert L. Kunkel, MD for helpful suggestions in preparation to this manuscript.

For over four decades group therapists have struggled to understand the individual and group processes that characterise 'difficult' patients' participation in group psychotherapy. Clinicians espousing interpersonal, object relations, ego psychological, and self psychological theoretical orientations have all tried to understand the impact of such individuals on group formation. However, recent theoretical advances in self psychology and intersubjectivity have illuminated members' and therapists' contributions to the emergence of problem group patients (Agazarian 1997; Durkin 1981; Gans and Alonso 1998).

As early as 1989 Earl Hopper posited a fourth basic assumption of Incohesion: Aggregation/Massification (I:A/M). Later, he (Hopper 1997) described the characteristics of the two states of Incohesion, which he suggested are bi-polar syndromes of an incohesive group formation. Aggregation is characterised by minimal recognition of others either verbally or affectively; an image of children playing in a sandbox, each building his/her own castle (parallel play), comes to mind. Massification is characterised by verbal and emotional merger and contagion. It was described by a patient attending a religious retreat where the focus was deep experiences of God. Each participant used similar expressions. My patient felt the conversation was in metaphor, and not penetrable.

According to Hopper, patients who have been traumatised are particularly vulnerable to forming groups operating at I:A/M. Having worked extensively with 'difficult' patients and with the chronically and persistently mentally ill population (primarily represented by patients with chronic schizophrenia) the descriptions of I:A/M contain elements that seem very familiar. The present contribution further extends his work to examine the role of an individual as the 'personification' of basic assumption life, thereby forging a link between group-as-a-whole dynamics and the individual's intra-psychic life.

Some thoughts about theory

Robert Michels (1999) argues that:

1. *Bridging theories* 'attempt to explain mental phenomena by tracing them across some boundary to a domain outside of mental life... They draw on knowledge from other fields of observation and disciplines in order to speculate about mental life' (p.190). Although they provide rich metaphors and images, and can serve to inspire clinical interpretations that may be valuable, such theories are not testable, because they are drawn from outside the analytic domain of the patient's inner mental life.

2. *Psychological theories* purport to be models for a general psychology. They provide ways of describing, classifying and discussing clinical material, that is, they help organise clinical material. They are taught in theoretical courses, and can become sources of rigid adherence.

3. *Clinical theories* are concerned with what happens in the consultation room. They include notions of transference, alliance, resistance, etc. 'They are directly concerned with the analytic situation and often

> suggest general clinical strategies and hypotheses that can be tested there' (p.192). They do not give specific wording, but they may suggest formal principles for our interventions.

Michels also suggests that theories influence the analyst's role, attitudes, and manner of attending to the patient. Various theories may impact differently upon the therapist, as has been clearly illustrated by the post-modern theoretical position and current controversy over the role of the therapist (Teicholz 1999).

BRIDGING THEORY

In applying this category to Hopper's manuscript, I have been struck by his rich metaphors. The imagery of the endangered cork floating on the Sea of Basic Assumptions captures my feeling of work with difficult patients, particularly when there are more than one or two in a group. My experience of a particularly difficult group, which I overly optimistically composed almost entirely of borderline patients, was of being seasick and awash after sessions. Fortunately, a colleague worked late and had his office door open and welcomed me immediately following the sessions. He provided an anchor in a safe harbour.

I have found that the basic assumption of Incohesion describes most groups at brief periods in their development. It also describes groups of 'difficult' persons, i.e. those in the borderline and narcissistic continuum, or individuals with psychotic illness, for longer periods of time. Many metaphors are evoked. Hopper says that aggregation is like billiard balls or crustaceans, and massification like amoeba or wet sponges. We also talk about patients bouncing off one another. Some groups are likened to porcupines trying to stay warm or to children building their own individual castles in the sandbox. Similarly, we hear patients anxiously express their fear of being sucked into the gooey morass of the group. These metaphors can be very valuable in the clinical encounter. In part, our task as clinicians is to find successful ways of communicating and genuinely connecting with our patients. We need a range of options and differing expressions to communicate, since no single prescription for what to say or how to say it will fit any particular situation. We cannot predict what will click and make the in-depth, genuine affective link that seems so essential in creating an atmosphere conducive to change.

Closely linked to metaphorical communication is the notion of the model-scene (Lichtenberg, Lachman and Fosshage 1992). In groups a model-scene may not be a precise memory of an event, but serves as a metaphor for emotionally meaningful transactions relevant to in-group behaviours (Correale and Celli 1998). One such example was a group patient who commented that his experience of being with the therapist was as if he (the patient) was a stubborn mule whose attention was focused by 'a whack with a "2 by 4" across the brow'. The image captured a complex response by the patient and group to the therapist's confrontation and was useful in members' subsequent communication of their displeasure with some of his interventions.

The manuscript is rich in metaphors, and I have only touched on some. They can be of use not only for patients, but also for therapists as they try to find ways of expressing or describing clinical phenomenon and linking to their groups.

PSYCHOLOGICAL THEORIES

Several differing psychological theories are of major import in Hopper's manuscript. Bion's theory of group life, with work and basic assumption components, has been one of the primary theories taught in didactic courses in group psychotherapy (Bion 1961). The theory functions as a descriptor, but has shortcomings in its strict application to the therapeutic process (Malan *et al.* 1976). Thus, additions to this theory might be of interest in the classroom, but its applicability to everyday work would require some integration or partial use with bridging or clinical theories (the rich metaphors associated with I:A/M partly fulfil this clinically-based need). Foulkesian theory of group analysis is less familiar to American readers, in part because of an absence of a 'textbook'. Clinicians in the United States have varying degrees of affinity to the notions of the matrix, mirroring and resonance, etc. Hopper does not elaborate on this aspect of his work, but his immersion in the centre of group analytic work in London and in the Group of Independent Psychoanalysts of The British Psychoanalytic Society contributes significantly to his theoretical affinities. Moreover, implicit is Hopper's theory of group dynamics, particularly of roles and of group and individual development. The multiple theories are more than can be addressed in this commentary. I will limit my examination to BA theory.

Bionian theory focuses primarily on the group's reactions to their internal images of leadership. Basic assumptions are descriptors of responses to failure or frustration of the 'designated leader' and represent group-wide defences against members' aggressive and sexual drives. I am less certain about the source for Incohesion. Hopper has previously written, 'the behaviour of the [designated] leader is an important determinant of the degree of cohesion' (Hopper 1997). I have often wondered what was the primary source of anxiety for those entering a group: is it a response to the leader's stance, or to stranger anxiety, or to a regressive image of the group as a whole, or to activation of failed development, differentially affected by the individual's unique life experiences?

I find it difficult to be certain if the group imago represents 'bedrock' of regression. My take is that in relatively non-traumatised persons the focus on the leader is a more advanced developmental response, and such a focus protects members from more disorganising and frightening regression. Incohesion is stimulated at the deepest layer by a fear of loss of self (Turquet 1975). As such, it may be either a temporary state of defending against powerful regressive pulls or a more fixed condition based upon members' character formation. Either massification or aggregation may be relatively short-lived or may linger. Affect contagion may produce a state of massification and, in accord with Freud's (1921) initial notion of contagion, may be an 'irreducible, primitive phenomenon, a fundamental fact in the mental life of man' (p.89). This formulation would account for observations of incohesion, as either aggregation or massification in non-severely-traumatised individuals.

Alternatively, incohesion could be conceptualised within Kohut's theory of the group self. Kohut (1976) wrote: 'We are then in a position to observe the group self as it is formed, as it is held together, as it oscillates between fragmentation and reintegration, etc. – all in analogy to phenomena of individual psychology to which we have comparatively easy access in the clinical (psychoanalytic) situation' (p.206). In concert with group analytic theory, the group is experienced as primary and the personal self as secondary (Karterud 1998). Within this theoretical model, which coincides with Hopper's adherence to group analytic theory, incohesion may represent a defensive (self stabilising) solution to the meaning of engagement in the group and subsequent dissolution (fragmentation) of the group self.

CLINICAL THEORY

Clinical theories have to do with the therapeutic situation, and focus on transference, resistance, alliance, and as illustrated in the vignette, holding, containing, space, and countertransference. Therefore such theories are more related to the treatment process and the clinician's task of integrating process and content.

Personification is an aspect of role theory, which provides guidance in thinking about the processes taking place in the group setting. In proposing personification as an accurate descriptor of certain processes in which an individual represents both aspects of himself and of the group-as-a-whole, Earl has introduced the notion of figuration, taken from the sociologist Norbert Elias, and fractal, derived from information and computer sciences. The descriptions, particularly of fractal, with which I was not familiar, seem particularly apt. It may be of help to the therapist who has been familiar with the less precise term 'spokesperson', which does not convey the contribution of the individual's character in describing the more complete meaning of the behaviour. Hopper uses an additional clinical theory, that of 'location', to help determine where to intervene along the continua of time and space. This pertains both to the world of the group and to the world of each participant in the group. Using these theories of personification and location we are in a position to consider the contributions of the individual and of the group processes to the presentation of a particular clinical situation. I certainly agree that Pandoro's jokes contained both personal and group tensions. They were an expression of both the desire to communicate and the desire not to do so.

Hopper's initial intervention commenting upon the presence of the previously verbally ignored buzzing and stains included his use of Kleinian focus on envy (the particular content), Freudian developmental theory (oral, anal, oedipal) and symbols. I pondered, trying to empathise with the members' response to the intervention. His intervention was not consistent with my usual way of speaking, and it was not an easy task to be empathic. Then I realised that I did not have a full context. Was the group familiar with this way of speaking? Was this Hopper's style to cut through our tendency to sanitise our language? If so, members would not be startled at all, but more likely would experience the comment as a more direct, if not startling, expression of their feelings. Theory of clinical process allows us to 'track' responses to justify our intervention.

What followed in Hopper's group were members' associations to their parents. This process is open to several interpretations, including a traditional formulation of a BA (basic assumption) flight group. However, this could be considered to be a restrictive solution (group focal conflict) which 'moved closer' to the source of the perturbation-shifting from joking about culture to a critique of parents as presumed displacements from the therapist. The theory seems coherent and fits with the data. In addition, a clinician may consider notions of containment and holding, or of 'testing' to determine if even this effort to communicate members' conflict could be responded to with respect and without additional trauma (Stone 1996).

Hopper was able to use his clinical theory to address his own inner responses and continue 'working' despite the group's extended silences (which he apparently interpreted to himself as an aggregate). In the subsequent process, Pandoro became the BA leader (personification) as he angrily complained about the 'waste of time', and then 'lit up'. This action seemed to release tension in the group, as two others took a drag. Hopper, maintaining his analytic stance (thank goodness for experience and theory that helps ground us), was then able to proceed along the time and space axes. This eventuated in considerable therapeutic attention to the members' experience of the unfolding process and was informed by a variety of clinically useful theories.

Conclusion

This manuscript increases understanding of our work along all three axes described by Michels. Rich metaphors provide ways of communicating, additions to Bionian theory help describe and categorise phenomenon, and finally these notions can be utilised in our process oriented clinical tasks as well. Hopper has demonstrated an almost seamless integration of the variety of theories that he uses in his practice. Since it is unlikely that we will ever have a composite theory that can address the specifics of each person's life experience, we must employ multiple theories, just as we need to have multiple ways of confirming or disconfirming our hypothesis about what is helpful to our patients.

Discussion and Response

Matters of theory

1. In the context of the theory of basic assumptions in general, is Incohesion: Aggregation/Massification a basic assumption, and if so, is it a *fourth* basic assumption, or a *first* basic assumption? And whether fourth or first, what are its origins? These questions are not merely academic. They have implications for both theory building and clinical work.

   The notion of a 'basic assumption' implies that the members of a group *assume* that matters are the opposite of what they actually are. In other words, although a group has regressed into either an aggregate or a mass, the members of it assume that they are a group. The notion also implies that specific patterns of interaction, normation, communication, styles of thinking and feeling, and styles of leadership and followership constitute an 'inter-personal defence' or 'inter-personal protection' against *basic*, fundamental and, therefore, universal 'psychotic' anxieties.

The model of human development that derives from the work of independent psychoanalysts, such as Fairbairn, Winnicott, Balint and Bowlby and others, implies that the fear of annihilation and the fear of separation rooted within the traumatogenic process is at the heart of the human condition and, therefore, that envy arises as a defence against these horrific anxieties. It follows from this model that there are at least four fundamental, psychotic anxieties, and at least four defensive or protective basic assumptions. It also follows that Incohesion should be called the first basic assumption, and Dependency, Fight/Flight, and Pairing should be called the second, third and fourth, in this order. This numbering is consistent with the order in which the underlying psychotic anxieties are thought to arise.

Klein dropped her early idea of a 'manic position' as a counterpart to the 'depressive position', because the notion of manic defences against the anxieties associated with the depressive position offered a more parsimonious way to conceptualise these processes. However, the development of crustacean and amoeboid defences against the fear of annihilation are 'pre-schizoid' and, therefore, it might indeed be useful to conceptualise a 'pre-schizoid' position. Ogden (1991), citing the same literature to which I have traced my own work, has conceptualised the 'autistic-contiguous' position. It is possible to think about incohesion as originating within the vicissitudes of the autistic-contiguous phase of development and position. Nonetheless, this phase and position should be conceptualised in the context of the infant-mother relationship within the family, neighbourhood, class and society as a whole. I would emphasise the importance of a 'relational' and 'attachment' perspective from the moment of conception, and similarly the importance of traumatic experience. This not to suggest that envy and aggression are not central in the experience of trauma and even in later attempts to make creative use of it.

2. The concept of 'aggregation' and 'massification', as opposed to those of 'dissaroy', and 'oneness', are not merely a matter of semantics. The former are technical terms in sociology and anthropology, and used for the denotation of specific group states, and are intended to be theoretically neutral. There is no reason for psychoanalysts and group analysts not to use such terms. These group states can be explained by many factors and processes, and social, cultural and political factors are as important as personal ones. Obviously, I have focused on only a few of the relevant factors from the point of view of psychoanalysis and group analysis.

3. Is it essential to consider unconscious fantasies, especially those associated with the Oedipus complex, in assessing whether the experience of loss, abandonment and damage is traumatic? Is it necessary to supplement an emphasis on encapsulation as a defence against the fears of annihilation and separation with a consideration of disassociation as a defence against these anxieties? These two questions should be considered together. The intensity of a traumatic experience and the capacity to symbolise and to think about the experience very much depends on the history of the person involved, especially with regard to such factors as the intensity of previous traumatic experience (either *ad infinitum* or *reductio ad absurdum*), the ways in which other people helped the survivor to stay connected and become re-connected to a community, the relationship between the survivor and the other people involved, etc. The extent to which a new traumatic experience gets attached to the previous traumatic experience is a very important determinant of the extent to which the new experience is actually traumatic. This is a function of the strength of encapsulation and disassociation with regard to previous traumatic experience. These factors regulate the likelihood that a traumatised person can exercise his transcendent imagination, be resilient, and make creative use of his experience (Hopper 2001b).

   Encapsulation and disassociation are always associated clinically, and are bound to be interdependent. However, it is possible that one kind of disassociation is typical of aggregation, and another kind of massification. For example, aggregation is personified by Pandoro, whose various addictions evince processes of schizoid disassociation, virtually by definition; and massification is personified by Pandora, whose hysterical sexualisation of her need for safety initiates the development of an illusionary group envelope.

The effects of constraints of external reality cannot be reduced to the constraints of unconscious fantasy, which are nevertheless an important mediating factor in the aetiology of trauma. I have emphasised the importance of loss, abandonment and damage, ruptures to the safety shield, and the introjection of aspects of pristine reality. I do not believe that a person is responsible for his own traumatic experience, and that he should be regarded in the same way that typically police regard victims of rape: she should not have been walking on the waterfront after midnight. A trauma in the present cannot be explained only in terms of a trauma in the past. I do not explain trauma in terms of traumatophilia, but rather the other way around. I do not reduce the explanation of all psychic conflict to envy and the so-called death instinct.

This is why I write as much as I do about the 'social unconscious' (Hopper 2003), and associate myself with Foulkesian group analysis, in which traumatic experience has been given more attention than it has in psychoanalytical group psychotherapy in general and in psychoanalysis specifically. However, I draw on the work of all authors who have been at the forefront of our attempts to understand how people continue 'to go on being' despite their experience of extreme psychic conflict.

The diversity of types of 'difficult patient' and their life trajectories pales into insignificance when compared with what they have in common: early psychic experiences that have threatened their psychic survival, and very often later psychic experiences that have done the same. Furthermore, no matter how resilient traumatised people may be, no matter what creative use they are able to make of their experience, and no matter how successful they are in sublimating their impulses and fantasies, they are vulnerable to sudden and unexpected regressions. Thus, they are likely to experience and re-experience intra-psychic oscillations between fission and fragmentation, and confusion and confusion, and their vicissitudes. This leads them to participate unconsciously in the creation of fourth basic assumption processes, and, in turn, to be especially vulnerable to the suction of roles associated with these processes, that is, to become the central persons in groups that are characterised by Incohesion.

This is why the opportunities for the treatment of difficult patients in group analysis are unique.

Matters of clinical theory

1. The containment functions of the group and of its conductor/leader are crucial. Moreover, I would stress that containers are always engendered. The containers of mother's mind and body, perhaps especially her breasts and her womb, are primary. Father's mind and body are also important, perhaps especially his penis and testicles. These objects are projected into and onto all groups, their leaders, and various elements in their environments.

   When the boundaries of the container are ruptured, traumatic experience is likely to occur. However, traumatic experience is not only a matter of failed containment. 'Failed dependency' involves failed containment, failed holding, failed nurturing and failed empathic attunement.

   In this connection, psychoanalysis and group analysis are indeed 'dualistic' or relational psychologies. They are in essence 'socio-bio-psychologies'. This perspective facilitates the conceptualisation of traumatic experience, because in essence traumatic experience is relational.

2. Group analysis helps protect both the members of the group and the group conductor from difficulties in understanding the group's communications that can be traced to countertransference problems, which are ubiquitous in the treatment of difficult patients. However, the more intense the basic assumption processes, the more likely it is that the conductor will be sucked into roles for which he has an unconscious valence. His tendency to personify these roles stems from his own difficulties and blind spots.

   Generally, my approach to the decision to address a particular member of the group at a particular time is 'inductive', that is, it is impossible for me to deduce theoretically who I will address and when I will address him. One guideline for making this decision might well be a sensitivity to the possibility that one is being mirrored by a clinical twin. However, when I become aware that the group is under the sway of a particular basic assumption, I become sensitive to the roles that might be associated with it, and to who might have tendencies to personify these roles. For example, when the group is under the sway of Incohesion, I anticipate that someone like Pandoro (or Pandora) will become a central person.

3. The failed dependency of the conductor would not be so important to the life of a group and to its individual participants if the group were not conductor-centred. If a group had a sense that the group belonged more to them and less to the conductor, his failure to meet their dependency needs and expectations of him would be less important. Of course, group analysts vary in how active they are. This is partly a matter of the personality and taste of the group analyst, but it should also be a matter of the personalities and needs of the members of the group at a particular point in time. Nonetheless, it is indeed important for a group analyst to allow himself 'progressively to fail', and to survive his patients' hatred of him for having done so. It is extremely important not to deny a failure, but to explore with patients how they feel about a failure when it happens, as inevitably it will.

4. It is necessary to explore the nature of the specific trauma. I did not protect the members of the group from the rupture that occurred to the boundaries of the group and, therefore, to their having been exposed to an intruder or a set of intruders who could be dangerous and destructive. Nor was I sufficiently containing of their appropriate anxieties and projections to allow them to explore the meanings that this had for them. Was I a mother who failed to protect her children from a stinging and intrusive and abusive father? After all, not only the breast can be turned into sharp fragments or even into a swarm of dangerous stinging objects, a breast filled with teeth. Or was I a father who failed to help a fragile and weeping mother contain her children's projections? Or a father who failed to protect his children from an intrusive mother? In other words, I should have explored the unconscious dynamics of the experience of a nest of wasps who had penetrated the boundaries of the group (Ettin 1995; Hopper 1996c), especially the unconscious Oedipal and pre-Oedipal dynamics of this.

   On the other hand, the nest of wasps occurred within the context of the group's history. Pandoro's joke was completely appropriate and meaningful within this context. We had worked with anti-Semitism for many months. The question is whether an unconscious 'reversal' took place in that the WASPs were experienced as feared and hated Jews/fathers who were intruding into the mother group and into the relationships of the participants in the group to 'her'. Whereas WASPs often regard Jews as parts of the Father and his chosen younger siblings, in this instance it was not clear whether the wasps were WASPs or the father and his chosen siblings. Or were they parts of the mother? Did they represent the return of the repressed? Certainly the nest of wasps can be understood as a projection of encapsulations of traumatic experience of which the group had much experience.

I should have explored all of this more quickly and comprehensively, and with more sensitivity to the many strands of experience that were involved. For example, I should have interpreted the group's fears that stopped them from associating to the wasps' nest, and from reflecting upon the meanings that it had for them. My passivity was a function of the meaning that the nest had for me both personally and in the context of the group. It is intriguing that the wasps' nest occurred in the context of the group's preoccupation with WASPs. Is this what Jung would call synchronicity?

5. In general terms my colleagues think that my initial interpretations were (a) either too intellectualised and complex or too direct and blunt; (b) either too oriented towards myself or too 'transferential'; (c) either too 'stereotypically Kleinian' (which means, I think, too primitive and pre-Oedipal) or too 'classical'; and (d) various combinations of all of these contradictory criticisms. These criticisms are important and relevant, but I am not convinced that they are all entirely apposite. It is possible to confuse 'intellectualised' with 'intelligent'. The patients were intelligent, and it was important to give them something to chew on. Also, I demonstrated that even if I had not sorted out the wasps' nest, I was still thinking, and trying to preserve a culture in which it was possible and desirable to reflect on unconscious processes. It is important not to withdraw from the obligation to offer interpretations of the process, especially with respect to the transference. Although in this regard the unconscious conduct of a relationship is vital, it is important to try to understand the unconscious content of the verbal and non-verbal communications. This requires a basic appreciation of symbolism and unconscious processes. I am inclined to say that if by now my colleagues do not see the connection between windows, eyes, tears, breasts, milk, urine and faeces and their functions, they never will, and in any case I will not be able to convince them by rational argument. In fact, I would argue

that in some respects my interventions were both appropriate and experience-near, and even demonstrated how to work with 'developmentally – early material' which was alive in the transference. I still believe that unconscious fantasies about mothers, fathers, siblings and their bodies and parts of them are troublesome and a source of anxiety, and that this should be interpreted. I am concerned that the fashionable emphasis on a 'relational perspective', which I very much appreciate and endorse, may itself be used defensively.

I sometimes wonder whether the accusations of 'intellectualised' and 'experience-far' are not sometimes used competitively, especially when the ideas that have been expressed by the analyst are interesting and clearly derived from classical psychoanalytical thinking, against which resistances continue to be strong. 'Breasts' and the 'penis' and other body parts are fine, as long as they are not actually put in writing. Colleagues may even have to deal with their own anxieties about the primal scene which are awakened when they are asked to think about the turmoil of a clinical feed.

Matters of clinical technique in the case of Pandoro

I would argue that the material that I used in order to illustrate the personification of aggregation by Pandoro also illustrates a failure of dependency, as I intended this material to do. The group responded to failed dependency by regressing suddenly and precipitously into a state of aggregation. I was caught in these dynamics, as seen in my intellectual and emotional isolation and self-protection, and excessive passivity. In other words, to a degree I was sucked into a role associated with aggregation, and became more of a central person of the basic assumption group and less of a leader of the work group. I then began unconsciously to 'twin' with Pandoro, who was the kind of person who was frequently caught up in the dynamics of aggregation and was highly vulnerable to the personification of aggregation roles. I began to give to Pandoro what I wished others would give to me, which is actually what he wanted me to do, rather than analyse the processes involved. In fact, I evinced a kind of narcissistic homosexual countertransference in which I related to Pandoro as someone who represented part of me, and I did this not only in terms of the relationship between a father and his son, but also in terms of a mother and her son. Thus, although I focused on Pandoro as the person who personified aggregation, I did so excessively, and at the expense of other members in the group, who were unable to maintain their identification with

Pandoro in such a way that they could benefit from this interaction. Other members of the group began to get caught in their own bystander dynamics, perhaps in connection with sibling rivalry with 'chosen' little brothers who urinated and defecated and cried at the wrong time and at the wrong places, and who were symbolised by the intrusive, stinging insects. Actually, my interaction with Pandoro was slightly punitive and not just confrontational.

I should have responded with sensitivity and empathy to the anxieties of the group when faced with a sudden attack on its boundaries, a turbulent and dangerous event, which was all the more frightening because it was invisible. (I remember that Margaret Mead once said that the earliest primal scene is an aural one, and not a visual one.) Having acknowledged my failure to prevent this event, I should have proceeded to deal with it promptly by calling in the vermin exterminators. I should then have explored the boundary violations with the members of the group, inviting their associations to it, and explored the group's experience of similar failures on the part of parents and other caretakers with regard to previous experience of boundary violations of various kinds. This should have lead to an interpretation of the unconscious Oedipal dynamics of the intrusion and failure to prevent it. An understanding of such dynamics would have contributed to our understanding of why the entire experience was traumatic. It would then have been possible to explore various levels of pre-Oedipal dynamics. In other words, starting from mother, father and siblings we would eventually have reached the boundaries of mother's mind and body. Basically, the process should have been from surface to depth, requiring attention to safety and security first. Eventually we might have explored the meanings of yellow and brown and their connotations of the colours of Nazi Germany during World War II, and the connection between this and the history of the group's preoccupations with anti-semitism both within the group and within Britain today. Certainly, I should have interpreted the existence of the fourth basic assumption of Incohesion much more assiduously than I did, and connected Incohesion in the 'Here and Now' with Incohesion at other times and social psychological spaces, especially in their respective families.

Still, my colleagues are impressed, as I am myself, with the hardiness and resilience of the Group, as seen in their ability to function without me and even to help me while I recovered my composure and equanimity. They agree that we benefited from our being able to work with my failure and survival. We agree that what transpired was not all 'bad', as seen, for example, in the fact that the entire group stayed together and continued to do some work before the holiday break. When they returned after the holiday break, they seemed able to communicate in greater depth and to re-establish and deepen their intimacy with one another and with me. My colleagues appreciate my ability to acknowledge my failed dependency and to have been able to recover my containing, holding and nurturing functions as well as my capacity to think and make interpretations of the transference. We agree that I failed, but equally that we survived, and were able to explore some of the dynamics of the traumatic experience. We even made some creative use of it, which is often the best we can do.

This clinical work took place approximately twenty years ago. I like to think that I would be able to function under such pressure better today than I did then, partly because I have learned from this experience. In any case, I have not presented this material as an example of my best clinical work, but as an illustration of fourth basic assumption processes, and as an example of how a group can help the conductor with countertransference phenomena that are particularly acute in the treatment of difficult patients in groups.

Suggestions for further research and applications

In this monograph I have concentrated on data from small groups whose members meet for the explicit purpose of psychotherapy. However, we still know very little about how best to utilise the dynamics of small groups in the service of psychotherapy, although this is at the very core of the project of group analysis and psychoanalytical group psychotherapy in general. It is important to learn more about how personifications of Incohesion are enacted in the transference/countertransference and, thus, how they involve a repetition of experience in all cells of the time/space matrix.

Incohesion in large groups has received more attention than it has in small groups who meet for the purpose of psychotherapy and in small groups in general, perhaps because Incohesion is more readily apparent in large groups. However, large groups rarely occur in natural and indigenous forms and settings. They occur mainly in training conferences for the study of groups. Of course, we need to learn more about such events, primarily because they are used as 'laboratories' for the study of large groups in other settings. However, we should direct our attention to the study of other kinds of large groups, no matter how unusual they really are. For example, social systems such as 'centres' and 'camps' for refugees, asylum seekers and displaced persons of various kinds should be considered as large groups. Their transitory nature may be particularly important. Although such social systems can and do become 'permanent' settlements, they can hardly be called 'societies', or even 'villages' and 'towns'. These large groups can be described in terms of aggregation and massification in their most extreme forms. It is hardly surprising that they are breeding grounds for terrorism. Terrorists are the 'spokespersons' of traumatised large groups, and they personify the roles that are typical of aggregation and massification. They perpetuate the dynamics of Incohesion, not only across the generations, but also across social and geographical boundaries (Volkan 2001, 2002b).

The further study of traumatised organisations is urgent.[1] Although organisations are likely to evince basic assumption processes in general and the fourth basic assumption in particular, only when they have been traumatised and therefore have regressed and become like large groups, it is disturbing to witness the speed and totality with which aggregation and massification can overwhelm the rules and regulations of effective and efficient work groups in organisations. Such regression is also ubiquitous in organisations whose membership contains a large number of traumatised people, or whose clients have been traumatised. For example, clinics and agencies for the provision of psychotherapy for Shoah survivors and refugees are especially vulnerable to Incohesion. Of special interest is the study of 'terrorist organisations'. They tend to develop encapsulated social cells, which may reflect both the encapsulation of traumatic experience and the social encapsulations of the traumatised societies within which such organisations emerge.

Many psychoanalysts and group analysts assume that societies are large groups, or at any rate that they can be considered as such. However, this perspective is helpful only when, following traumatic experience, societies regress. It is noteworthy that Kernberg (2003) has begun to refer to the study of societies *as* large groups, and has stopped using 'large group' to denote all large and complex social systems. For example, Incohesion is pronounced in chronically traumatised societies, such as Northern Ireland, Israel (Weinberg and Nuttman-Shwartz 2002), Argentina and Croatia, and in acutely traumatised societies, such as parts of Australia following extensive bushfires, and New York, Washington, DC and possibly the United States as a whole following the terrorist attacks of 11 September 2001. In addition to his work in specific societies characterised by tragic social conflict and turmoil, Volkan (2002a, b) has begun to delineate the features of traumatised and, therefore, regressed societies in general. Some have begun to refer to the social narcissism of such societies (Biran 2002), the Incohesion of which is recapitulated by their organisations and public affairs, which is appropriate for *traumatised* societies, but not necessarily for societies in general.

In every domain and level of reality within all kinds of social system, we remain largely unconscious of the destructive and self-protective processes through which we undermine our efforts to build effective and efficient work groups characterised by optimal cohesion. We must learn more about the ability of work groups to resist the attacks made by basic assumption groups in general, and by Incohesion groups in particular, and about the ability of work groups to recover from these attacks.

Are there grounds for mature optimism and hope? If we focus on the extent of chronic social violence throughout the world, the answer must be 'No'. However, if we focus on the many small but significant gains that we have made in our attempts to understand the forces of Incohesion, the answer must be 'Yes' (Hopper 2001b).

Note

1 With this in mind, I have started a study group of colleagues from various European countries and the United States who share a special interest in traumatised organisations and in organisations who have many traumatised people in them. The current members of this study group are Ann Allen, Alan Corbett, Tamsin Cottis, John Hook, Elizabeth Lloyd, Louis Reed, Melvyn Rose, Bent Rosenbaum, Christopher Scanlon, Gerhard Wilke and Gerda Winther. Discussions with them have helped me to clarify my general theory. We are preparing a collection of papers on the fourth basic assumption in organisations ranging from, for example, industrial firms whose number of personnel has been drastically reduced by redundancies to clinics and agencies for the provision of psychotherapeutic services for survivors of the Holocaust to institutes and societies for training people in the provision of psychoanalysis and psychoanalytical psychotherapy. The data suggest that many of these institutes and societies are traumatised organisations, both in connection with their loss of hegemony in the mental health profession, and in having large numbers of their members who have experienced social trauma and even a surfeit of more idiosyncratic personal trauma. The massification of training institutes and societies is similar to that which occurs in various kinds of political and religious movements in traumatised societies (Gellner 1985).

APPENDIX I

Some Conceptual Distinctions about Social Formations from Sociology and Social Psychology

Group analysts tend to conflate all social formations, and to use the word 'group' to denote all social formations as opposed to 'individuals'. However, several conceptual distinctions are commonplace in sociology and social psychology. I have reviewed these distinctions in previous publications (Hopper 1975, 1981).

1. 'Social categories' differ from 'social formations' in general. For example, 'all people who earn more than £50,000 per year' is a social category. However, social categories can be the basis for a social formation. For example, under certain conditions people who earn more than £50,000 a year can become a 'social class'. Similarly, not all social formations are 'groups'. For example, 'audiences' and 'focused' and 'unfocused crowds' are not groups. 'Aggregates' and 'masses' are barely groups. 'Families' differ from groups of people who are not related to one another. 'Schools' and 'commercial firms' are 'organisations'. There are many kinds of organisations, some of which are 'bureaucracies'. England is a 'society'. Not all societies are 'states'. 'Ethnic groups' differ from 'status groups'. And so on.
2. Social formations vary in terms of numerous properties, for example: size, range of interests, duration of interests, consciousness of kind, territory, and connection with functional problems. Social formations

can also be analysed in terms of patterns of interaction, normation and communication: interaction refers to relationship and affiliation; normation refers to beliefs, norms and values; and communication refers to imparting and exchanging information. Social formations should be described in terms of both their distinctive properties and their patterns of interaction, normation and communication. They may also be analysed in terms of their styles of thinking and feeling, and of leadership and followership. In an attempt to conceptualise some aspects of these phenomena, de Maré (1972) referred to the 'structure', 'process', and 'content' of groups: 'structure' was used to refer to all persistent patterns; 'content', to normation, communication and styles of thinking and feeling; and 'process', to change and its sources within all realms of enquiry.

3. All social formations, ranging from primitive social aggregates to complex societal nation states, can be understood as social systems. Very briefly, a system is a set of variables whose relationship is such that changes in any one of them can be explained almost entirely in terms of changes in the other variables in the set. In so far as a variable does not contribute to changes in the other variables in the set, that variable is in the environment of the system. The 'environment' of the system refers to its 'context', which is in keeping with the fundamental connections between language and the psychic life of human beings. Different kinds of system are studied through different disciplines, which are apposite for their subject matter. For example, living social systems possess the capabilities for adaptation and innovation, based on culture, communication, and active imagination which create complexity, variability and idiosyncrasy. Some mechanical systems possess adaptive capacities that exceed those of some living systems, and it is too soon to know whether the random modifications that are built into robots make them more adaptive and even innovative than some animals and some human beings; of course, animals are less durable than machines, which suggests new perspectives on the phenomenon of extinction.

4. Social formations may be defined or classified in terms of properties of social systems. For example, a social system constitutes a group to the extent that its organisational structure is relatively 'simple' rather than 'complex': the roles in a group are small in number, barely interdependent, and ambiguous and unstable in their boundaries; the

quality of interaction afforded is 'diffuse' rather than 'specific', like an intimate friendship rather than a business relationship in modern society. Groups are relatively 'open' to their contexts, including their psychological context, that is, the personalities of their members. This is why the study of people and their internal worlds is so important when it comes to the study of groups as opposed to other kinds of social system.

5. In the study of the disorder and order of social systems, many terms and concepts are used synonymously. For example, 'disorder', 'disintegration', 'insolidarity' and 'incoherence' are often used as synonyms and 'order', 'integration', 'solidarity' and 'coherence', as their antonyms. However, over the years, this usage has become more specific. With respect to 'interaction', 'disintegration' is usually juxtaposed with 'integration'; with respect to 'normation', 'solidarity' is usually juxtaposed with 'insolidarity'; and with respect to 'communication', 'coherence' is usually juxtaposed with 'incoherence'. These words refer to the disintegration and integration of particular dimensions or realms or domains of social systems, and they should really not be used interchangeably, because they are not always correlated, and because dis-junctures among them are particularly noteworthy in their personal and social consequences.

In the physical sciences 'cohesion' refers to a bonding together of particles of the same substance or of different substances in such a way that the particles do not lose their individual identity and, therefore, when they are unbound do not suffer damage to their individual boundaries, as in the formation and dissolution of a droplet of liquid on the surface of another matter. In contrast, 'adhesion' refers to a bonding together of particles in such a way that they lose their individual identities and, therefore, when unbound are severely damaged, as in the adhesion and tearing apart of the membrane of two or more organs of the body. In other words, a cohesive bonding implies that the resultant body is not unified, or only temporarily unified, and an adhesive bonding implies that the resulting body has become a new entity. In traditional individual psychology, which has always been positioned between philosophy and biology, 'coherence' was, and occasionally still is, used to refer to the association of feelings and sensations in the perception of an object, or to the association of the outcomes of several sensory perceptions, such as seeing, smelling and touching a rose. However, by the end of the eighteenth century, 'coherence' was used in a more general way, mainly to refer to how logical were the connections of the parts of a composition or piece of writing, or to the hanging or holding together of the parts of a statement, or to the consistency of an argument or disputation, or even to the correspondence of a disputation with evidence external to it. In ordinary discourse today, 'coherence' refers almost exclusively to verbal communication.

In the field of group relations, group psychotherapy and group analysis, the topic of disorder and order, or disintegration and integration, is called 'incohesion' and 'cohesion'. In general, the cohesion of groups refers to the experience of the unity of feelings and purpose that enables at least three people to work in harmony within similar roles towards a common goal (Hartmann 1981). However, Pines (1983, 1986) has argued that the cohesion of groups is always a matter of their coherence, because the essence of affiliation in groups is one of verbal and non-verbal communication. Nonetheless, I would suggest that the cohesion of social systems is not based only or even primarily on patterns of communication, and that 'coherence' should only be used to refer to cohesion based on patterns of communication. 'Coherence' is apposite for groups and group-like social systems whose cohesion stems mainly from their patterns of communication, for example, groups who meet for the purpose of psychotherapy.

APPENDIX II

Encapsulation as a Defence against the Fear of Annihilation[1]

Definition of the concept of encapsulation

According to the OED 'encapsulation' means 'to enclose in a capsule, to summarise or isolate as if in a capsule'. 'Capsule' refers to: generally, a little case or receptacle; physiologically, a membranous envelope; botanically, a dry seed case that opens when ripe by the parting of its valves; medically, a small case of gelatine enclosing a dose of something potent but unpalatable; and from modern space science, the detachable nose-cone of a rocket or the cabin of a spacecraft containing instruments or crew. On the basis of such connotations, 'encapsulation' and its synonyms, such as 'encasement', have begun to appear with increasing frequency in both the popular and professional literature, for example: schizoid inaccessibility, split-off parts of the ego, a general sense of being contained, existing within the 'unconscious' mind, the defence of isolation and the primary process of condensation.

Consistent with these connotations but in contrast to their generality, 'encapsulation' is defined here as a defence against annihilation anxiety through which a person attempts to enclose, encase and to seal-off the sensations, affects and representations associated with it. The formation of a scab is an apposite metaphor, but this implies that healing will begin beneath it, which is not consistent with the clinical data. The formation of a cyst seems more precise, but the sense of 'inner-centrality' should be augmented by 'split-off'. This definition of encapsulation is intended to convey a sense of 'having enclosed' and 'of being enclosed', of the construction of internal 'worlds' that are not empty but filled with animate and inanimate objects who are in relationships with one another involving very intense feelings.[2]

Theoretical orientation: a brief outline

The definition of 'encapsulation' can be extended through a brief outline of a theoretical orientation for the explanation of annihilation anxiety and of the inter-personal and intra-personal responses to it.

Annihilation anxiety

Primitive sensations of annihilation anxiety have been described in various terms, for example: ontological insecurity, i.e. fear of explosion, implosion and engulfment, primitive agony, nameless dreads and the great awe, aphanisis, nothingness, abjectness, and ambiguity. Nonetheless, there is consensus that annihilation anxiety is more basic than the 'paranoid-schizoid' anxiety associated with initial splitting. The fear of annihilation is a function of fission and fragmentation, which is a schizoid phenomenon rather than a paranoid one. The essence of the matter is that both feelings of persecution and feelings of primal depression are completely intertwined and undifferentiated. This is the realm of sensations that are not quite feelings, although 'affective meaning' is implicit in them, as suggested by the concept 'fantasies in the body'.

Traumatic experience

The explanation of annihilation anxiety does not require the assumptions that it arises from the initial workings in the mind of the so-called 'death instinct', and/or that on the basis of the failed containment of innate malign envy as the first psychic representation of the work of the death instinct, the infant fragments projectively the primal object and then introjects an array of annihilating objects. It is difficult to accept the hypothesis that even 'in the beginning' a sense of loss that follows an actual deprivation is based upon the prior wish to reject the object and, therefore, that the fear of annihilation is based on the prior desire to annihilate. Annihilation anxiety is likely to be caused by an experience of absolute helplessness and failed dependency following from catastrophic loss, impingement, inadequate containment, and breaks in holding and attachment relationships. The importance of trauma in the aetiology of annihilation anxiety as a central feature in borderline personality organisation is stressed by many psychoanalysts. Specific traumata are often involved, such as intrusive penetrations, physical pain and interference with bodily rhythms. Also relevant are more indirect factors that threaten the safety and security of parents in such a way that they are unable to respond to the basic needs of an infant, such as rampant inflation and high rates of unemployment, and divorce and precipitous birth of a sibling.

Primitive sensations of annihilation anxiety are especially likely to follow a traumatic break in the relationship between an infant and mother before the infant develops an ego of agency, and while he lives in a state of 'unintegration', 'undifferentiated' from his mother, a phase of life that is distinguished by the existence of two organisms but one person, two brains but one mind. During this phase of development an infant is likely to experience a traumatic break in his relationship with mother in terms of a loss of parts of his self-representation. For example, if the infant is not yet able to distinguish his mouth from a breast, he is likely to experience a loss of a breast as a loss of his mouth.

A loss of this kind and at this stage of development is likely to be associated with the sense of a 'black hole', an infinitely powerful cauldron of pain that annihilates all that enters it. It is difficult to heal because it is unclear whether it exists within the self or within the other or within both. The phenomenology of a psychic black hole involves the paradox of infinite contraction and infinite expansion, infinitely 'white' and infinitely 'black', the epitome of chaos, nothingness and absolute meaninglessness, based on the loss of all that seemed meaningful prior to knowledge that 'meaningfulness' is not absolute. Paradoxically, the experience of a loss of part of the self is likely to involve a kind of negative hallucination, a 'blank'. Actually, 'negative hallucination' is not quite right because it implies a loss of an object that has already been 'registered', whereas the experience of a loss of part of the self undifferentiated from part of the other is likely to occur so early in life that it is virtually without representation. It is as though what Kant would call 'the-thing-in-itself' were lost, a point recognised by Bion and Lacan.

To a degree, traumatic experience is ubiquitous during the earliest phases of life and, therefore, it is likely that all people will have experienced fear of annihilation or at least intimations of it. It may be assumed that the primal fear of annihilation is the prototype of all subsequent experience of this type of anxiety, and of the extremely primitive fantasies, wishes, impulses and sensations associated with it, and that the working through of such fears will inform the subsequent experience of all other types of anxiety. Of course, people are likely to vary in the intensity of such experience and in their ability to make constructive use of it, depending on the usual, proverbial mixture of social and constitutional factors.

Processes of defence: the encapsulation process

PHASE 1: INTROJECTION

An overwhelming sense of fission and fragmentation is the essential characteristic of annihilation anxiety, and the first defence against it is an attempt to fuse and confuse the nascent, incipient representation of self with the nascent, incipient representation of the lost and abandoning object. This introjective process is based on feelings of primary envy towards the lost and abandoning object. Feelings of primary envy are a primitive form of 'love' or 'greedy possessiveness', and originate in an attempt to mitigate the hatred caused by the prior experience of helplessness and loss. In other words, fusion is based on the sexualisation of aggressive feelings that have arisen as a result of specific experience. It may be useful to distinguish processes of pathological fusion and confusion, as they are discussed here, from processes of benign fusion, e.g. 'oceanic bliss', 'true mutuality' and 'affective attunement'. Introjective fusion is more akin to 'incorporation' than to 'introjection' and 'identification'.

One aspect of the wish to fuse is the hatred of all that is perceived to be an obstacle to it. Sometimes, this is expressed as the denial of the very existence of anything perceived to be an obstacle or an intrusive impurity. If the hallucinated wish to fuse is experienced as a yearning for and participation in absolute whiteness or complete colourlessness (or infinite blackness, which is in essence the same thing as infinite whiteness) any sign of colour is likely to be denied. Similarly, the combination of smoothness and any sign of roughness. The breast and the nipple are the bodily prototype for such experience, but the combination of silence and noise may be equally 'primitive', in the same sense that the earliest primal scene may be an aural one with respect to parents talking. The point is that any real external object will be a complex mix of properties, and the wish to fuse with the object as a whole will inevitably and invariably involve the desire to attack and obliterate, and to deny the existence of, some part of it. At later stages of development, the wish to fuse with the 'maternal' object may be combined with the wish to attack and to deny the existence of the 'paternal' object, but this is likely to be an aspect of an early Oedipus complex rather than of the primal fear of annihilation.

PHASE 2: THE INTROJECTED OBJECT

The 'contents' of an encapsulation are likely to consist of the psychic representations of the lost and abandoning object and of various aspects of the traumatic situation, including those elements of the self that have been lost as a result of it. Although these representations will always be based upon an admixture of the 'real' properties of the external object and fantasised perceptions of it, emphasis must always be given, at least in the first instance, to the properties of the 'real' external object. The introjected object functions as a foreign body in the psyche. The notion of the 'parasite' is relevant, as is that of the 'identificate'. The image of an identificate within a hollow husk is especially compelling, and is consistent with my statement that the 'feel' of an encapsulation is like a knot in a plank of wood or a fault in a piece of silk.

PHASE 3: CONFUSIONAL ANXIETIES

Fusion and confusion are likely to produce the further anxieties of fears of engulfment, suffocation, mastication and dissolution. These anxieties are related in a polar way to those that gave rise to the fusional and confusional process in the first place. These confusional anxieties are based on the fears of being trapped and controlled by and within an object who, in turn, has been and is being trapped and controlled. They are also based on envious attacks towards the introjected object, experienced in terms of a combination of mouth, nipple and breast, and perhaps in terms of parents combined in luscious and creative intercourse. However, these envious attacks are secondary to those through which the object was incorporated.

PHASE 4: SECONDARY FISSION AND FRAGMENTATION

As a consequence of processes of secondary envy and internal projections, the fusional and confusional introjected object is likely to be perceived as dangerous. As a defence against the anxieties associated with fusion and confusion with an object who is perceived to be dangerous, there is likely to occur a regressive shift back towards processes of fission and fragmentation. These are processes of 'secondary' fission and fragmentation, and are akin to 'secondary splitting'.

PHASE 5: NON-DIALECTICAL OSCILLATION

A process of non-dialectical oscillation is likely to occur between fission and fragmentation, on the one hand, and fusion and confusion, on the other, as well as between the two sets of anxieties associated with them. The term 'non-dialectical' is used in order to indicate a state of structural stasis: although a process is evident, growth and development within the encapsulation are foreclosed. 'Merger-hungry' and 'contact-shunning' personalities are manifestations of the non-dialectical oscillation between these two polarities. Both types of personality may occur in the same person but one type is likely to predominate, especially during a particular period of time. A similar distinction can be made between the 'amoeboid' and the 'crustacean' forms of self-protection.

The parallel development of the encapsulated

In early infancy an encapsulation is likely to be devoid of imagery, like a molecular soup or molecules of gas in which space seems more dominant than particles, without form and co-ordination, certainly without coherence, and possibly highly explosive. For the most severely traumatised, an encapsulation may remain devoid of imagery, intact but stunted. However, for the less severely traumatised these sensations of initial anguish may become associated with words, images, thoughts, people and their parts, feelings and fantasies. Although such transformations and transmutations are likely to be 'meaningful', they are also likely to be grotesque and mutant. In other words, this innermost Russian doll of encapsulation may develop in parallel with the rest of the self, and the development of the rest of the self may depend on the integrity of the encapsulation, used as a protected psychic space within which the initial trauma, pain and defence are re-enacted repeatedly, partly in an attempt to make sense of early loss, and to repair the damage that is felt to have resulted from it.

It is possible to sublimate the impulses and defences associated with encapsulated traumatic experience. However, as defences, such sublimations are precarious, because they are in essence manic attempts at reparation; although they may function to help a person avoid psychotic anxiety, resolution remains impossible, and creative work requires a compulsive and insatiable quality. In our attempts to understand these patients in the context of what are usually very long analyses, it is difficult to know whether to emphasise the creative aspects of acting out, or to emphasise the functions for creativity of acting out, but it is important to realise that creativity might be important if not essential for psychic survival. This applies to creative productions from a conventional point of view, as well as through the use of the body in psychosomatic disorders and in deviant sexuality. My clinical uses have in common the experience of severe, early and cumulative trauma, involving relationships or attempts to make relationships with mothers who were 'absent', either literally or by way of their own depression and withdrawal from mothering. Note must be taken of the frequency of early miscarriages and hasty subsequent pregnancies. Studies of the early origins of the Oedipus complex suggest that, typically, such patients were traumatised by mother's pregnancy during the 'polymorphous perverse' phase of development around fifteen months of age. Note must also be taken of the prevalence of divorce, being sent away to boarding school, and of the absence of fathers.

Special attention should be given to trauma at birth. An infant who is subjected to major medical interventions in connection with premature birth will experience a psychic trauma (which is not to argue that post-traumatic experiences cannot be therapeutic or even curative). More specifically, one may wonder about the nature of an infant's experience inside an incubator, the first container outside the womb. Does the infant form a mental representation of space beneath the skin, of layers of skin, of laminated layers of plastic alternating with layers of skin, of plastic skin, etc.? Actually, with the benefit of judicious hindsight, early discussions of birth trauma might now be read with benefit. What could be more difficult than the transformation from the status of the unique object of the foetus within the womb to the transitional status of one mind but two organisms, even when all goes well? In so far as they exist, *primary* mental representations of the vagina as a birth canal, the cervix and the womb may be even more relevant to the fear of annihilation than those of the empty mouth, stomach and breast, and may be the representational prototypes for them. Perhaps encapsulation can be used to deny the experience of birth.

I would also draw attention to the prevalence of phenomena suggesting that these patients suffered severe impingements to their egos of adaptation. The patients refer to: dark spaces of damage; the lack of air and of room to breathe; latex, rubber and leather (the anal smells of which allow them to be introjected through the nose); hard surfaces of tiles, glass and mirrors (producing echoes and split-off reflections); crustacean fish and reptiles, crabs, tortoises, armadillos, encased insects such as beetles; rigid boxes of wood and metal, including safe deposit boxes, coffins and caskets; laminated surfaces; suits of armour; holes in the ground for rabbits, foxes, moles, etc.; clearings within jungles and forests. These images may be understood in terms of attempts to avoid the experience of the 'black hole'. They offer contrasts with 'nothingness', and they reflect the earliest wishful attempts to establish and to maintain a sense of containment and holding, the boundaries between self and others, and the boundaries of internal encapsulations. It is as though such people seek to replace their skin and internal membranes, or to establish skin and membranes that did not develop. Relevant here are discussions of 'thin skin' and certain types of narcissistic disorders; the conceptualisation of 'principal configurations' of 'sound', 'olfactory', 'thermal' and 'muscular' egos, and of the 'envelope' in general; 'second skin' and the boundaries of self; skin disorders, and skin phenomena, and dermatitis in infants. The 'autistic-contiguous position' is based on bodily contiguity.

Similarly, it is understandable that such patients refer to the contents of their dark spaces of damage both in terms of sharp pointed fragments (ranging from pins to slithers of broken glass to splinters of wood, pieces of metal, insects that are not only encased but which can also fly and sting, such as bees, hornets, wasps and termites, etc.) and in terms of explosive pressure (gas, turning into smoke, etc.). They are also preoccupied with sensations of falling into space, falling to bits, and leaking out. These phenomena are the mental representations of encapsulated objects that have been subjected to processes of fusion and confusion and of secondary fission and fragmentation. This is the stuff of 'autistic shapes' and of 'bizarre objects' created through the re-introjection of explosive projections into external objects (especially, I would add, into those external objects who/which 'fitted' the projections, who/which were the source of failed dependency in the first place).

Some applications of the concept of encapsulation to particular issues in clinical work

In general, encapsulation is likely to be prevalent in people with borderline disorders and to be a distinguishing feature of those with narcissistic disorders. However, our understanding of encapsulation processes might be applied to several specific issues in clinical work:[3]

1. The syndrome of addiction, somatisation, perversion, criminality and risk taking: many clinical illustrations of over-determination, masking, localisation, disavowal, foreclosure and resourceless dependence have been based on work with patients who evinced elements of this syndrome. One may recall the patients discussed by Anna Freud, Bion, Freud himself, Ferenczi, Deutsch, Lacan, Green, Balint and Khan. Nonetheless, data from the analyses of these very disturbed patients are rare, and the literature remains sparse and repetitive.

It would be worth exploring the relationship between addictions and trauma at birth, especially the effects of adrenaline and of artificial stimulants on the perceptual apparatus and skins. The experience of new born babies of major medical investigations and of care in neo-natal units is associated with adolescent suicide and with some types of drug abuse.

The dynamic, kaleidoscopic relationship among the elements of encapsulation and the 'addiction' syndrome can be seen in data from the long analysis of an alcoholic and drug addict who was an incubator baby. I suggested that on the basis of the search for excitement as a manic defence against psychotic depressive anxieties, the addict was prone to gamble, in particular, to take dangerous risks, and in general, to engage in delinquent and criminal activities; on the basis of his search for soothing tranquillity as a defence against psychotic persecutory anxieties, he was prone to the eroticisation of hatred in the form of perverse sexuality; also, somatisation seemed to be based on a projection into the body of anxieties that would be experienced as sensations rather than as feelings, for example, as a rodent ulcer and as various forms of 'alimentary orgasm'. In other words, the addict seemed to be ensnared between various sets of psychotic anxieties characterised by a 'tense depression', or what was later termed an 'agitated depression'.

People who are in a state of mind characterised by foreclosure are likely to oscillate between an intensive search for contact with an external object (merger-hungry) and an intensive withdrawal from and rejection of it (contact-shunning). The fear of annihilation alternating with the fear of alienation is the central element of the 'core complex', an essential feature of perversions. It has been argued that perversion is based on the desire to subvert all 'natural' differences between the sexes and the generations, and on the compulsion to confuse all that would 'ordinarily' be regarded as 'appropriately' separate, or in other words, on regression to the universe of confusion typical of the anal phase of psychosexual development. In fact, during analysis the dissolution of encapsulation is presaged by the somewhat sudden appearance of obsessional phenomena. However, perversion functions as a defence against feelings of fission and fragmentation oscillating with feelings of fusion and confusion, and the anal universe of chaos is based on the vicissitudes of the oral universe of mastication and swallowing. In other words, perversions reflect a desperate search for escape from the foreclosed oscillations of annihilation anxiety. In the same sense that perversion is said to be the negative of neurosis, encapsulated psychotic anxiety is the negative of perversion.

In retrospect, the case of the Wolfman offers an excellent illustration of virtually every feature of the encapsulation process, including its aetiology and even the long, interminable analyses that occur when it is overlooked or misunderstood. For example, in the Wolfman homosexuality and potential addiction (perhaps to analysis itself) were 'sealed-off' and somatised (specifically the pimple on his nose). He had more than merely a sadistic interest in wasps, which can now be understood not only in terms of castration and the 'pre-Oedipal mother', but also in terms of 'bits of nipple', the poisonous colouration of black faeces and yellow urine and damage to the breast. I would also stress the nature of a wasp society in its nest, essentially a society without a culture, a social aggregation which may appear to be a swarm of fragments. Similarly, the Wolfman's interest in the butterfly may be seen not only in terms of a frightened invitation into the open legs of a female, but also in terms of a beautiful, evocative object that had been lost. I would not be surprised to learn that he had wanted to 'mammock' the butterfly, as the child Coriolanus was said to have done, because for the Wolfman and Coriolanus the butterfly was not a butterfly but concretely a part of the mother – certainly neither a symbol nor a sign of her and her parts. The rubber enema bulb offers a condensation of the whole story, which is not only a matter of anality with special reference to an anal vagina, anal intercourse and faecal children, but also one of orality, specifically an anal mouth and a faecalised, rubberised breast (a representation the origins of which may include the experience of a real rubber teat).

More recently, it has been suggested that disavowal was based on encapsulation, and that encapsulation would be prevalent among patients who evinced elements of the syndrome of addiction, somatisation, perversion, criminality and risk taking. I would suggest that the essential element of disavowal, the representations of the 'blind eye' and of the vagina, are based on the previously established representations of an empty breast and of an open mouth, representations that derive from the traumatic experience of helpless hunger and from the sense of being 'empty of oneself'. Several psychoanalysts have discussed annihilation anxiety and fusion as the central elements in the aetiology of transsexualism, and implied that the female identity of male transsexuals is based on early, encapsulated traumatic experience.

The syndrome of addiction, somatisation, perversion, criminality and risk taking and its connection with encapsulation is rarely illustrated with data from the analyses of females.

This may reflect our limited understanding of heterosexual perversion in females. I would suggest that an adult female is likely to use her whole body and specifically her womb in order to maintain prior encapsulations, as though she projects prior encapsulations into the womb and then regards the products of her womb, i.e. menstrual blood and unborn children, as the contents of her encapsulations or as screen phenomena for them. The intensity with which some females experience menstruation may be based on the fantasy that it is the dissolution of the encapsulation of traumatic loss and separation. This may also be the basis of the confusion of menstrual blood with faeces, and of the confusion of rituals associated with defences against the anxieties of mourning with those associated with defences against aggressive feelings and chaos. An adult female may transform early encapsulations into perverse attacks upon her own reproductive organs and functions, as well as upon her children. These processes may be the basis for some cases of infertility, and for some cases of 'compulsion to be pregnant', i.e. in order to feel full and to have extensions who are available for manipulation and abuse.

Is the 'internal saboteur' an amalgam of encapsulated hard and grotesque objects? Is the internal saboteur of a female an amalgam of the contents of an encapsulation, i.e. a distorted female figure? Are encapsulations the habitat of witches? Or do they live in Nineveh (Jonah: 3, 4)?

2. The development and functions of the central masturbation fantasy: the central masturbation fantasy warrants more attention, both in connection with pathology associated with adolescence, and as a normal phenomenon. Again, analytical data are rare, and the literature is sparse. Although such fantasies may be organised into more permanent form during adolescence, their analysis may disclose a series of screen-like fantasies and memories that occurred prior to the

'classical' Oedipal phase. Like traumatic dreams and dreams within dreams, central masturbation fantasies are coded statements about the nature of fundamental conflicts, in the same way that plays within plays provide the basic insights that are essential for understanding the 'parent' play. It is as though the central masturbation fantasy is a recent version of the original contents of an encapsulation.

Are the seductive, exciting and tantalising figures of central masturbation fantasies the same as the internal saboteurs who are so prominent in perversion? Careful attention to every detail of these fantasies is of value in the analysis of patients who evince the syndrome outlined above, both because their conscious fantasy life in general is so often impoverished and repetitive, and because the analysis of the central masturbation fantasies of such patients invariably leads back towards encapsulated traumatic experience. This is consistent with the view that the central sexual fantasies and scenarios of perverts and of perversions are symbolic recreations of early traumatic experience in which the roles of perpetrator and victim are reversed.

3. The personal consequences of trauma that occur 'later' in life: no matter how early in life the prototype occurs, annihilation anxiety can erupt and encapsulation may be used as a defence against it at any time, provided the trauma is sufficiently great. It is necessary to think further about the possibility of phase specific forms of this anxiety and defence, and about the revival of archaic forms of them. Although the nature of traumatic experience is dependent on ego development and the content of fantasy, each experience must be considered in its own terms. The events that can be traumatic are infinite in number and variety, but some sources of trauma may be structured socially.

   The fear of annihilation and encapsulation as a defence against it are prevalent among those who have suffered various kinds of massive social and collective trauma, for example, among survivors of accidental collective disasters such as the King's Cross fire and the Clapham train crash, and 'natural' disasters such as the Armenian earthquake. 'Encapsulation' has been used in studies of the post-traumatic stress disorders of Vietnam veterans, and to refer to a kind of atomisation and collective repudiation among a generation of Germans of their experience of anti-Semitism and Nazi phenomena in general. In studies of survivors of the Shoah and their children, it has been suggested that following the loss of significant others, they perceived that 'holes' developed in the ego, which is reminiscent of Freud's discussion of fetishism. Several analysts refer to a perception that the social fabric has been 'torn' or 'rent', and suggest that special attention be given to separation anxiety and skin phenomena.

Patterns of 'unauthorised' and 'illegitimate' social mobility are pathogenic, as are certain patterns of migration. Mental health workers in Stockholm have begun to discuss the prevalence of annihilation anxiety and encapsulation phenomena among immigrants from less developed countries, especially the Middle East. Encapsulation processes may be prevalent among long stay prisoners, not only because they are likely to have suffered early traumatisation, but also because imprisonment is itself likely to be traumatic, and to provide an external concrete form of encapsulation.

Notes

1 This Appendix has been excerpted from 'L'incapsulamento come difesa contro il timore di annientamento', *Plexus... Lo Spazio del Gruppo*, September 1994, 103–128. A previous version of this article was published in 1991 as 'Encapsulation as a defence against the fear of annihilation', *The International Journal of Psychoanalysis 72*, 4, 607–624, based on a paper presented at the 37th International Psychoanalytical Congress, July 1991, Buenos Aires. These two articles have extensive bibliography concerning the fear of annihilation and encapsulation. For their encouragement and helpful comments on previous drafts, I am indebted to Jeremy Christie-Brown, Barbara Elliot, Juliet Hopkins, Lionel Kreeger, Joyce McDougall, Jonathan Pedder, Joan Raphael-Leff, Hans Reijzer, Saul Scheidlinger and Riccardo Steiner.

2 Pandoro, described in Chapter 6, and Pandora, described in Chapter 7, are patients who are characterised by the encapsulated fears of annihilation and its vicissitudes.

3 I have discussed and illustrated the addiction syndrome in Hopper 1995, which is a development of the two articles from which this Appendix has been excerpted.

References

Abraham, K. (1907) [1927] 'The Experiencing of Sexual Traumas as a Form of Sexual Activity'. In E. Jones (ed) *Selected Papers on Psycho-Analysis.* London: The Hogarth Press (Original work published 1907).

Agazarian, Y.M. (1997) *Systems Centered Therapy for Groups.* New York: Guilford.

Agazarian, Y. and Carter, F. (1993) 'Discussions of the large group'. *Group 17,* 4, 210–234.

Alexander, F. (1942) *Our Age of Unreason.* Philadelphia: Lippincott.

Anzieu, D. (1981) *Le Groupe et l'Inconscient: L'Imaginaire Groupal.* Paris: Dunod.

Anzieu, D. (1984) *The Group and the Unconscious.* London: Routledge and Kegan Paul.

Ashbach, C. and Schermer, V.L. (1987) *Objects Relations, the Self, and the Group: A Conceptual Paradigm.* New York: Routledge and Kegan Paul.

Balint, M. (1968) *The Basic Fault.* London: Tavistock Publications.

Balint, M. (1969) 'Trauma and object relationship'. *International Journal of Psychoanalysis 50,* 429–436.

Barker, E., Beckford, J.A. and Dobbelaere, K. (eds) (1993) *Secularization, Rationalism and Sectarianism: Essays in Honour of Bryan R. Wilson.* Oxford: Clarendon Press.

Barrows, P. (2001) 'The use of stories as autistic objects'. *Journal of Child Psychotherapy 27,* 1, 69–82.

Baschwitz, K. (1938) [1951] *Du und die Masse: Studien zu einer exakten Massenpsychologie.* Leiden: Brill (Original work published 1938).

Battegay, R. (1973) 'Defective Developments of Therapeutic Groups'. In A. Uchtenhagen, R. Battegay and A. Friedmann (eds) *Group Therapy and Social Environment.* Berne/Stuttgart/Vienna: Hans Huber.

Battegay, R. (1987) 'Narcissism as an essential of group psychotherapy in a fast changing world'. *Rivista Italiana di Gruppoanalisi 11,* 1, 7–28.

Battegay, R., Hubermann, I., Schlosser, C., and Visoiu, C. (1992) 'Trends in group psychotherapy with borderline patients'. *Group Analysis 25,* 66–73.

Battegay, R. (1994) 'Cohesive and disintegrative dynamics in group psychotherapy and their moderation by the leader'. *Chinese Psychiatry 8,* 2, 69–82.

Bednar, R.L. and Kaul, T. (1994) 'Experiential Group Research: Can the Canon Fire?' In A. Bergin and A. Garfield (eds) *Handbook of Psychotherapy and Behavior Change, IV.* New York: Riley.

Behr, H.L. (1979) 'Cohesiveness in families and therapy groups'. *Group Analysis 12,* 1, 9–12.

Bendix, R. (1966) 'A memoir of my father'. *Canadian Review of Sociology and Anthropology 2,* 1.

Ben Yakar, M. (1987) 'The multi-dimensionality of group psychotherapy'. Unpublished paper.

Bernfeld, S. (1929) 'Der soziale Ort und seine Bedeutung für Neurose, Verwahrlosung und Pädagogik'. *Imago XV.*

Bettelheim, B. (1979) *Surviving and Other Essays.* London: Thames and Hudson.

Bick, E. (1968) 'The experience of the skin in early object relations'. *International Journal of Psychoanalysis 49,* 484–486.

Billow, R.M. (1998) 'Entitlement and the presence of absence'. *Journal of Melanie Klein and Object Relations 16,* 537–554.

Bion, W.R. (1948–51) 'Experiences in groups: I–VII'. *Human Relations Vols 1–4.*

Bion, W.R. (1956) 'Development of schizophrenic thought'. *International Journal of Psychoanalysis 37,* 344–346. Reprinted in 1967 in W.R. Bion *Second Thoughts.* London: Heinemann.

Bion, W.R. (1958) 'On hallucination'. *International Journal of Psychoanalysis 39,* 144–146. Reprinted in 1962 in *Learning from Experience.* London: Heinemann.

Bion, W.R. (1961) *Experiences in Groups and Other Papers.* London: Tavistock Publications.

Bion, W.R. (1962) *Learning from Experience.* London: Heinemann.

Bion, W.R. (1963) *Elements of Psychoanalysis.* London: Heineman.

Bion, W.R. (1965) *Transformations.* London: Heinemann.

Bion, W.R. (1967) *Second Thoughts.* London: Heinemann.

Bion, W.R. (1970) *Attention and Interpretation.* London: Tavistock Publications.

Biran, H. (1995) Personal communication.

Biran, H. (2002) Personal communication.

Blatner, A. (2000) *Foundations of Psychodrama: History, Theory and Practice.* New York: Springer.

Blau, P. (1977) *Inequality and Heterogeneity: A Primitive Theory of Social Structure.* New York and London: The Free Press.

Bleger, J. (1966) 'Psychoanalysis of the psychoanalytic frame'. *International Journal of Psychoanalysis 48,* 511–519.

Bloch, S. and Crouch, E. (1985) *Therapeutic Factors in Group Psychotherapy.* London: Oxford University Press.

Bollas, C. (1989) *Forces of Destiny: Psychoanalysis and the Human Idiom.* London: Free Association Books.

Braaten, L. (1991) 'Group cohesion: A new multi-dimensional model'. *Group 15*, 39–55.

Brazelton, T.B. and Cramer, B.G. (1989) *The Earliest Relationship: Parents, Infants, and the Drama of Early Attachment.* Reading: Addison-Wesley.

Brenner, C. (1985) 'Discussion'. In A. Rothstein (ed) *The Reconstruction of Trauma: Its Significance in Clinical Work.* Madison, CT: International Universities Press.

Britton, R. (1994) 'The blindness of the seeing eye: Inverse symmetry as a defence against reality'. *Psychoanalytical Inquiry 14*, 3, 365–378.

Brown, D.G. (1985) 'Bion and Foulkes: Basic Assumptions and Beyond'. In M. Pines (ed) *Bion and Group Psychotherapy.* London: Routledge and Kegan Paul.

Brown, D.G. (2003) 'Pairing Bion and Foulkes: Towards a Metapsychosociology'. In R. Lipgar and M. Pines (eds) *Building on Bion: Roots.* London: Jessica Kingsley Publishers.

Buchele, B. (2000) 'Survivors of Sexual and Physical abuse'. In R.H. Klein and V.L. Schermer (eds) *Group Psychotherapy for Psychological Trauma.* New York: Guilford.

Budman, S., Demby, A., Feldstein, M., Redondo, J., Scherz, B., Bennett, M., Kopernaol, G., Sabin, D., Huster, M. and Ellis, J. (1987) 'Preliminary findings on a new instrument to measure cohesion in group psychotherapy'. *International Journal of Group Psychotherapy 37*, 75–94.

Bychowski, G. (1948) *Dictators and Disciples from Caesar to Stalin.* New York: International Universities Press.

Camus, M. (1983) *The Outsider.* London: Penguin (Original work published in French as *L'Etranger* (1942).

Canetti, E. (1935) [2000] *Auto-da-Fé.* London: Vintage (Original work published in German).

Canetti, E. (1960) [1972] *Crowds and Power [Masse und Macht].* New York: Continuum.

Canetti, E. (1980) [1989] *The Torch in my Ear.* London: Deutsch (Original work published 1980).

Cartwright, D. and Zander, A. (eds) (1953) *Group Dynamics: Research and Theory.* Evanston, Ill: Row.

Celan, P. (1971) *Speech Grille and Selected Poems.* New York: E.P. Dutton.

Chadwick, M. (1929) 'Notes upon the fear of death'. *International Journal of Psychoanalysis 10*, 321–334.

Chasseguet-Smirgel, J. (1975) *L'Idéal du Moi.* Paris: Claude Tchou.

Chasseguet-Smirgel, J. (1985) *Creativity and the Perversions.* London: Free Association Books.

Cohen, B.D. and Schermer, V.L. (2002) 'On scapegoating in therapy groups: A social constructivist and intersubjective outlook'. *International Journal of Group Psychotherapy 52*, 1, 89–110.

Cohn, N. (1957) *The Pursuit of the Millennium.* London: Secker & Warburg.

Cohn, N. (1967) *Warrant for Genocide. The Myth of the Jewish World-Conspiracy and the Protocols of the Elders of Zion.* London: Secker & Warburg.

Coleridge, S.T. (1798) [1999] *The Rime of the Ancient Mariner.* London: Palgrave Macmillan (first published 1798).

Coltart, N. (1989) 'Personal Communication'. In J. Berke (ed) *The Tyranny of Malice: Exploring the Dark Side of Character.* London: Simon and Schuster.

Cooley, C.H. (1909) *Social Organization.* New York: Charles Scribner.

Correale, A. and Celli, A.M. (1998) 'The model-scene in group psychotherapy with chronic psychotic patients'. *International Journal of Group Psychotherapy 48,* 55–68.

Dalal, F. (1998) *Taking the Group Seriously.* London: Jessica Kingsley Publishers.

Danieli, Y. (1980) 'Countertransference in the treatment and study of Nazi Holocaust survivors and their children.' *Victimology: An International Journal 5,* 2–4, 355–367.

Danieli, Y. (1981) 'The ageing survivor of the Holocaust: On the achievement of integration in ageing survivors of the Nazi Holocaust'. *Journal of Geriatric Psychiatry 14,* 2, 191–210.

Danieli, Y. (1982) Group project for Holocaust survivors and their children. Prepared for National Institute of Mental Health, Health Service Branch. Contract #092424762. Washington, DC.

de Maré, P. (1972) *Perspectives in Group Psychotherapy.* London: Allen and Unwin.

de Maré, P. (1991) *Koinonia.* London: Karnac Books.

de Mendelssohn, F. (2000) 'The aesthetics of the political in group analytic process – the wider scope of group analysis'. *Group Analysis 33,* 4, 438–458.

de Swaan, A. (1999) 'Dyscivilisatie, massavernietiging en de staat'. *Amsterdams Sociologisch Tijdschrift 26,* 289–301.

Drescher, S., Burlingame, G. and Fuhriman, A. (1985) 'Cohesion: An odyssey in empirical understanding'. *Small Group Behavior 16,* 3–30.

Dunning, E. and Hopper, E. (1966) 'Industrialisation and the problem of convergence: A critical note'. *The Sociological Review 14,* 2, 163–186.

Durkheim, E. (1893) [1933] *The Division of Labor in Society* (trans George Simpson). New York: Macmillan (Original work published 1893).

Durkin, J. (1972) 'Analytic Group Therapy and General Systems Theory'. In C.J. Sager and H.S. Kaplan (eds) *Progress in Group and Family Therapy.* New York: Brunner/Mazel.

Durkin, J. (1980) 'Boundarying: The structure of autonomy in living groups'. Seventh Annual Ludwig von Bertalanffy Memorial Lecture. San Francisco: Society for General Systems Research Annual Convention.

Durkin, J. (1981) *Living Groups: Group Psychotherapy and General System Theory.* New York: Brunner/Mazel.

Elias, N. (1938) [1995] *The Civilising Process.* Oxford: Blackwell (Original work published 1938).

Eliot, T.S. (1980) *The Complete Poems and Plays: 1909–1950.* New York: Harcourt Brace.

Elliott, P. (1999) *Assassin!* London: Blandford.

Elster, J. (1989) *The Cement of Society.* Cambridge: Cambridge University Press.

Emery, F.E. and Trist, E.L. (1960) 'Sociotechnical Systems'. In C.W. Churchman and M. Verhulst (eds) *Management Science Models and Techniques, II.* Oxford: Permagon Press.

Erikson, E. (1948) 'Hitler's Imagery and German Youth'. In C. Kluckhorn and H. Murray (eds) *Personality in Nature, Society and Culture.* New York: Knopf.

Erikson, E. (1956) [1959] 'The problem of ego identity'. In *Identity and the Life Cycle.* New York: International Universities Press (Original work published 1959).

Erikson, E. (1968) *Identity, Youth and Crisis.* New York: Norton.

Ettin, M. (1995) 'The spirit of Jungian group psychotherapy: From taboo to totem'. *International Journal of Group Psychotherapy 45*, 4, 449–470.

Ezriel, H. (1950) 'A psychoanalytical approach to group therapy'. *British Journal of Medical Psychology 23*, 59–74.

Fairbairn, W.R. (1952) *Psycho-Analytic Studies of the Personality.* London: Tavistock Publications.

Fairbairn, W.R. (1954) *An Object-Relations Theory of the Personality.* New York: Basic Books.

Ferenczi, S. (1922) [1980] 'Freud's "Group Psychology and the Analysis of the Ego" – its Contribution to the Psychology of the Individual'. In M. Balint (ed) *Final Contributions to the Problems and Methods of Psycho-Analysis.* London: Karnac Books (Original work published 1922).

Finkelstein, N. (2000) *The Holocaust Industry.* London: Verso.

Fogelman, E. (1989) 'Group Treatment as a Therapeutic Modality for Generations of the Holocaust'. In P. Marcus and A. Rosenberg (eds) *Healing their Wounds.* New York: Praeger.

Fornari, F. (1974) *The Psychoanalysis of War.* New York: Anchor Books.

Forsyth, F. (1971) *The Day of the Jackal.* London: Hutchinson.

Foulkes, S.H. (1937) 'On introjection'. *International Journal of Psychoanalysis 18*, 269–293.

Foulkes, S.H. and Anthony, E.J. (1964) *Group Psychotherapy: The Psychoanalytic Approach.* London: Penguin.

Foulkes, S.H. (1965) *Therapeutic Group Analysis.* New York: International Universities Press.

Foulkes, S.H. (1968) 'On interpretation in group analysis'. *International Journal of Group Psychotherapy 18*, 4, 432–44.

Freud, A. (1946) [1966] *The Ego and the Mechanisms of Defense.* New York: International Universities Press (first published 1946).

Freud, S. (1913) [1975] *Totem and Taboo.* Standard Edition, Vol. XIII. London: The Hogarth Press (Original work published 1913).

Freud, S. (1920) *Beyond the Pleasure Principle.* Standard Edition, Vol. XVIII. London: The Hogarth Press.

Freud, S. (1921) *Group Psychology and the Analysis of the Ego.* Standard Edition, Vol. XVIII. London: The Hogarth Press.

Freud, S. (1923) *The Ego and the Id.* Standard Edition, Vol XIX. London: The Hogarth Press.

Freud, S. (1931) *Libidinal Types.* Standard Edition, Vol. XXI. London: The Hogarth Press.

Gaddini, E. (1992) *A Psychoanalytic Theory of Infantile Experience.* A Limentani (ed). London: Routledge.

Gampel, Y. (1996) 'The Interminable Uncanny'. In L. Rangell and R. Moses-Hrushovki (eds) *Psychoanalysis at the Political Border.* Madison, CT: International Universities Press.

Gans, J. and Alonso, A. (1998) 'Difficult patients: Their construction in group therapy'. *International Journal of Group Psychotherapy 48,* 311–326.

Ganzarain, R. (1989) *Object Relations Group Psychotherapy: The Group as an Object, a Tool and a Training Base.* Madison, CT: International Universities Press.

Ganzarain, R. (2000) 'Group-as-a-Whole Dynamics in Work with Traumatized Patients: Technical Strategies, their Rationales, and Limitations'. In R.H. Klein and V.L. Schermer (eds) *Group Psychotherapy for Psychological Trauma.* New York and London: Guilford.

Garland, C. and Hopper, E. (1980) 'Overview'. In C. Garland (ed) 'Proceedings of the Survivor Syndrome Workshop' 1979. *Group Analysis,* Special Edition, November, 93–97.

Garwood, A. (1996) 'The Holocaust and the power of powerlessness: Survivor guilt, an unhealed wound'. *British Journal of Psychotherapy 13,* 2, 243–258.

Geiger, T. (1969) *On Social Order and Mass Society.* Chicago and London: The University of Chicago Press.

Gellner, E. (1985) *The Psychoanalytic Movement.* London: Granada.

Gfaller, G.R. (1996) 'Diskussion: Zum aufsatz von Earl Hopper'. *Gruppenanalyse 6,* 1, 114–117.

Gibbard, G., Hartman, J. and Mann, R. (eds) (1974) *Analysis in Groups.* Maryland: Jossey-Bass.

Giddings, F.H. (1924) *The Scientific Study of Human Society.* Chapel Hill, NC: University of North Carolina Press.

Giddens, A. (1991) *Modernity and Self-Identity: Self and Society in the Late Modern Age.* Cambridge: Polity Press.

Glasser, M. (1979) 'Some Aspects of the Role of Aggression in the Perversions'. In I. Rosen (ed) *Sexual Deviation.* Oxford: Oxford University Press.

Gouldner, A.W. (1955) *Wildcat Strike: A Study of an Unofficial Strike.* London: Routledge and Kegan Paul.

Grotstein, J. (2000) *Who is the Dreamer who Understands the Dream?* Hillsdale, NJ: Analytic Press.

Guntrip, H. (1971) *Psychoanalytic Theory, Therapy, and the Self.* New York: Basic Books.

Gutmann, D. (1989) 'The Decline of Traditional Defences against Anxiety'. In F. Gabelnick and W. Carr (eds) *Proceedings of the First International Symposium on Group Relations.* Keble College Oxford: A.K. Rice Institute.

Hartman, J. (1981) 'Group Cohesion and the Regulation of Self-esteem'. In H. Kellermann (ed) *Group Cohesion: Theoretical and Clinical Perspectives.* London: Grune and Stratton.

Hegeman, E. and Wohl, A. (2000) 'Management of Trauma-related Affect, Defenses, and Dissociative States'. In R.H. Klein and V.L. Schermer (eds) *Group Psychotherapy for Psychological Trauma.* New York: Guilford.

Herman, J. (1997) *Trauma and Recovery.* New York: Basic Books.

Herman, J. and van der Kolk, B. (1987) 'Traumatic Antecedents of Borderline Personality Disorder'. In B. Van der Kolk (ed) *Psychological Trauma.* Washington, DC: American Psychiatric Press.

Hillenbrand, F.K. (1995) *Underground Humour in Nazi Germany 1933–1945.* London and New York: Routledge.

Hirsch, F. (1977) *Social Limits to Growth.* London: Routledge and Kegan Paul.

Holmes, R. (1995) *Foot Steps.* London: HarperCollins.

Homans, P. (1989) *The Ability to Mourn.* Chicago: The University of Chicago Press.

Hopper, E. (1965) 'Some effects of supervisory style: A sociological analysis'. *British Journal of Sociology 16,* 3, 189–205. Reprinted in Hopper, E. (2003) *The Social Unconscious: Selected Papers.* London: Jessica Kingsley Publishers.

Hopper, E. (1975) [2003] 'A Sociological View of Large Groups'. In L. Kreeger (ed) *The Large Group: Dynamics and Therapy.* London: Constable. Reprinted in 1994 in London by Karnac Books and in Hopper, E. (2003) *The Social Unconscious: Selected Papers.* London: Jessica Kingsley Publishers.

Hopper, E. (1977) 'Correspondence'. *Group Analysis 10,* 3, 24.

Hopper, E. (1981) [2003] *Social Mobility: A Study of Social Control and Insatiability.* Oxford: Blackwell. Excerpts reprinted in Hopper, E. (2003) *The Social Unconscious: Selected Papers.* London: Jessica Kingsley Publishers.

Hopper, E. (1982a) 'A Comment on Professor M. Jahoda's "Individual and the Group"'. In M. Pines and L. Rafaelsen (eds) *The Individual and the Group: Boundaries and Interrelations.* New York: Plenum.

Hopper, E. (1982b) 'Group analysis: The problem of context'. *Group Analysis XV,* 2.

Hopper, E. (1985) 'The Problem of Context in Group Analytic Psychotherapy: A Clinical Illustration and Brief Theoretical Discussion'. In M. Pines (ed) *W.R. Bion and Group Psychotherapy: A Critical Reappraisal.* London: Routledge and Kegan Paul. Reprinted in Hopper, E. (2003) *The Social Unconscious: Selected Papers.* London: Jessica Kingsley Publishers.

Hopper, E. (1987) 'Anti-Semitic sentiment in the transference and countertransference'. Unpublished paper prepared for the Association of Child Psychotherapists.

Hopper, E. (1989a) 'Notes on Psychotic Anxieties and Society: Fission (Fragmentation)/Fusion and Aggregation/Massification'. Paper for the Conference of The Royal College of Psychiatry. Cambridge, UK.

Hopper, E. (1989b) 'Notes on Aggregation/Massification and Fission (Fragmentation)/Fusion: A Fourth Basic Assumption?' Paper for the VIII Conference of the International Association of Group Psychotherapy. Amsterdam, Holland.

Hopper, E. (1991) 'Encapsulation as a defence against the fear of annihilation'. *The International Journal of Psychoanalysis 72,* 4, 607–624.

Hopper, E. (1992) 'Two ways of experiencing envy'. Comment on the paper by E. Spillius. *The British Psychoanalytical Society Bulletin 28,* 11, 15–16.

Hopper, E. (1994) 'L'incapsulamento come difesa contro II timore di annientamento'. *Plexus... Lo Spazio del Gruppo.* September, 103–127.

Hopper, E. (1995) 'A psychoanalytical theory of drug addiction: Unconscious fantasies of homosexuality, compulsions and masturbation within the context of traumatogenic processes'. *International Journal of Psychoanalysis 76,* 6, 1121–1142.

Hopper, E. (1996a) 'Incohesion (Aggregation/Massification): A Fourth Basic Assumption of Unconscious Life in Social Systems'. Public Lecture, London Centre for Psychotherapy. Summarised by Sally Baldwin in *Reflections 14.*

Hopper, E. (1996b) 'The social unconscious in clinical work'. *Group 20,* 1, 7–43. Reprinted in Hopper, E. (2003) *The Social Unconscious: Selected Papers.* London: Jessica Kingsley Publishers.

Hopper, E. (1996c) 'Response to the spirit of Jungian group psychotherapy'. *International Journal of Group Psychotherapy 46,* 4, 553–557.

Hopper, E. (1997) 21st S.H. Foulkes Annual Lecture: 'Traumatic Experience in the Unconscious Life of Groups: A Fourth Basic Assumption'. *Group Analysis 30,* 4, 439–470.

Hopper, E. (2000) 'From objects and subjects to citizens: Group analysis and the study of maturity'. *Group Analysis 33,* 1, 29–34.

Hopper, E. (2001a) 'Difficult patients in group analysis: The personification of (ba) I:A/M'. *Group 25,* 3, 139–171.

Hopper, E. (2001b) 'On the nature of hope in psychoanalysis and group analysis'. *British Journal of Psychotherapy 18,* 2, 205–226. Reprinted in Hopper, E. (2003) *The Social Unconscious: Selected Papers.* London: Jessica Kingsley Publishers.

Hopper, E. (2003) *The Social Unconscious: Selected Papers.* London: Jessica Kingsley Publishers.

Horwitz, L. (1977) 'A group-centered approach to group psychotherapy'. *International Journal of Group Psychotherapy 27,* 423–439.

Hudson, M. (2001) *Assassination.* Phoenix Mill: Sutton.

Isherwood, C. (1954) *The Berlin Novels.* New York: New Directions.

Issroff, J. (1979) 'The phenomenon of affect contagion as an ongoing effect following massive traumatisation'. Unpublished paper presented at the First International Congress of Children of Survivors of the Holocaust, New York.

Jacobson, E. (1964) *The Self and the Object World.* New York: International Universities Press.

Jaques, E. (1955) 'Social Systems as a Defense against Persecutory and Depressive anxiety'. In M. Klein, P. Heimann and R.E. Money-Kyrle (eds) *New Directions in Psycho-Analysis.* New York: Basic Books.

Janet, P. (1886) 'Les actes inconscients et le dédoublement de la personalité pendant le somnambulisme provoqué'. *Revue Philosophique 22,* II, 577–792.

Joffe, W. (1969) 'A critical review of the envy concept'. *International Journal of Psychoanalysis 50,* 533–545.

Jucovy, M.E. (1992) 'Psychoanalytic contributions to Holocaust studies'. *International Journal of Psychoanalysis 73,* 267–282.

Kaplan, S.R. and Roman, M. (1963) 'Phases of development in an adult therapy group'. *International Journal of Group Psychotherapy 13,* 10–26.

Karterud, S.W. (1998) 'The Group Self, Empathy, Intersubjectivity and Hermeneutics: A Group Analytic Perspective'. In I.N.H. Harwood and M. Pines (eds) *Self Experience in Group: Intersubjective and Self-Psychological Pathways to Human Understanding.* London: Jessica Kingsley Publishers.

Kauff, P. (1991) 'The Unique Contributions of Analytic Group Therapy to the Treatment of Preoedipal Character Pathology'. In S. Tuttman (ed) *Psychoanalytic Group Theory and Therapy.* Madison, CT: International Universities Press.

Kellermann, H. (ed) (1981) *Group Cohesion: Theoretical and Clinical Perspectives.* London: Grune and Stratton.

Kernberg, O. (1975) *Borderline Conditions and Pathological Narcissism.* New York: Jason Aronson.

Kernberg, O. (1978) 'Leadership and organizational functioning: Organisational regression'. *International Journal of Group Psychotherapy 28,* 1, 3–25.

Kernberg, O. (1984) 'The couch at sea: The psychoanalysis of organisations'. *International Journal of Group Psychotherapy 34,* 1, 5–23.

Kernberg, O. (1991) 'The Moral Dimension of Leadership'. In S. Tuttman (ed) *Psychoanalytic Group Theory and Therapy.* Madison, CT: International Universities Press.

Kernberg, O. (1993) 'Paranoiagenesis in Organisations'. In H. Kaplan and B.J. Sadock (eds) *Comprehensive Textbook of Group Psychotherapy.* Baltimore: Williams and Witkins.

Kernberg, O. (1994a) 'Mass Psychology through the Analytic Lens'. In A.K. Richards and A.D. Richards (eds) *The Spectrum of Psychoanalysis: Essays in Honor of Martin Bergmann.* Madison, CT: International Universities Press.

Kernberg, O. (1994b) 'Leadership Styles and Organizational Paranoiagenesis'. In J. Oldham and S. Bone (eds) *Paranoia: New Psychoanalytic Perspectives.* Madison, CT: International Universities Press.

Kernberg, O. (1998) *Ideology, Conflict, and Leadership in Groups and Organizations.* New Haven: Yale University Press.

Kernberg, O. (2003) 'Socially Sanctioned Violence: The Large Group as Society'. In S. Schneider and H. Weinberg (eds) *The Large Group Re-visited: The Herd, Primal Horde, and Masses.* London: Jessica Kingsley Publishers.

Kestenberg, J. (1989) 'Coping with Losses and Survival'. In *The Problem of Loss and Mourning.* Madison, CT: International Universities Press.

Khaleelee, O. and Miller, E. (1985) 'Beyond the Small Group'. In M. Pines (ed) *Bion and Group Psychotherapy.* London: Routledge and Kegan Paul.

Khan, M. (1988) *When Spring Comes.* London: Chatto and Windus.

Kibel, H.D. (1991) 'The Therapeutic Use of Splitting: The Role of the "Mother-group" in Therapeutic Differentiation and Practicing'. In S. Tuttman (ed) *Psychoanalytic Group Theory and Therapy: Essays in Honor of Saul Scheidlinger.* Madison, CT: International Universities Press.

Kibel, H.D. (1993) 'Object Relation Theory and Group Psychotherapy'. In H.I. Kaplan and B.J. Sadock (eds) *Comprehensive Group Psychotherapy* (3rd edn). Baltimore: Williams & Wilkins.

Kibel, H.D. and Stein, A. (1981) 'The group-as-a-whole approach: An appraisal'. *International Journal of Group Psychotherapy 31*, 409–427.

King, P. (1969) 'The concept of regression to more primitive forms of social behaviour as applied to institutions, societies and communities'. Unpublished paper.

King, P. (1997) Personal communication.

King, P., and Steiner, R. (eds) (1991) *The Freud-Klein Controversies 1941–45.* London: Routledge.

Klein, M. (1935) [1975]'A contribution to the psychogenesis of manic-depressive states'. *International Journal of Psychoanalysis 16*, 145–174. Reprinted in 1975 in *The Writings of Melanie Klein, Vol. I.* London: The Hogarth Press (Original work published 1935).

Klein, M. (1940) [1975] 'Mourning and its relation to manic-depressive states'. *International Journal of Psychoanalysis 21*, 25–153. Reprinted in 1975 in *The Writings of Melanie Klein, Vol. I.* London: The Hogarth Press (Original work published 1940).

Klein, M. (1946) [1952] 'Notes on Some Schizoid Mechanisms'. In J. Riviere (ed) *Developments in Psychoanalysis.* London: The Hogarth Press (Original work published 1946).

Klein, M. (1957) [1975] *Envy and Gratitude.* London: Tavistock Publications. Reprinted in 1975 in *The Writings of Melanie Klein, Vol. I.* London: The Hogarth Press (Original work published 1957).

Klein, R.H., Bernard, H. and Singer, D. (eds) (1992) *Handbook of Contemporary Group Psychotherapy.* Madison, CT: International Universities Press.

Klein, R.H. and Schermer, V.L. (eds) (2000) *Group Psychotherapy for Psychological Trauma.* New York and London: Guilford.

Kohut, H. (1976) 'Creativeness, Charisma, Group Psychology'. In J.E. Gedo and G.H. Pollock (eds) *Freud: The Fusion of Science and Humanism.* New York: International Universities Press.

Kohut, H. and Wolf, E. (1978) 'The disorders of the self and their treatment'. *International Journal of Psychoanalysis 59,* 414–425.

Kornhauser, W. (1960) *The Politics of Mass Society.* London: Routledge and Kegan Paul.

Kreeger, L. (ed) (1975) [1994] *The Large Group: Dynamics and Therapy.* London: Constable. Reprinted in 1994 in London by Karnac Books (original work published 1975).

Kreeger, L. (1992) 'Envy pre-emption in small and large groups'. *Group Analysis 25,* 4, 391–408.

Kreeger, L. (1997) 'Response to lecture by Earl Hopper'. *Group Analysis 30,* 4, 471–474.

Kris, E. (1956) 'The personal myth: A problem in psychoanalytical technique'. *The Journal of the American Psychoanalytical Association 4,* 653–681.

Krystal, H. (1968) *Massive Psychic Trauma.* New York: International Universities Press.

Lacan, J. (1977) *Ecrits: A Selection.* (trans A. Sheridan) New York: Norton.

Laing, R.D. (1960) *The Divided Self.* London: Tavistock Publications.

Langs, R. (1978) *The Listening Process.* New York: Jason Aronson.

Lasch, C. (1978) *The Culture of Narcissism.* New York: Norton.

Lawrence, W.G. (1993) 'Signals of transcendence in large groups as systems'. *Group 17,* 4, 254–266.

Lawrence, W.G., Bain, A., and Gould, L.J. (1996) [2000] 'The fifth basic assumption'. *Free Associations 6,* 37, 28–55. Reprinted in 2000 in *Tongued with Fire: Groups in Experience.* London: Karnac Books (Original work published 1996).

Lawrence, W.G. (2000) *Tongued with Fire: Groups in Experience.* London: Karnac Books.

Levinson, H. (1968) *The Exceptional Executive: A Psychological Conception.* Cambridge: Harvard University Press.

Lévi-Strauss, C. (1961) *World on the Wane.* London: Hutchinson.

Lewin, K. (1948) *Resolving Social Conflicts.* New York: Harper and Row.

Lichtenberg, J.D., Lachman, F.M. and Fosshage, J.L. (1992) *Self and Motivational Systems: Toward a Theory of Psychoanalytic Technique.* Hillsdale, NJ: Analytic Press.

Liff, Z. (1981) 'The Role of the Group Therapist in the Treatment of Character Disorder Patients'. In H. Kellermann (ed) *Group Cohesion.* London: Grune and Stratton.

Lifton, R.J. (1986) *The Nazi Doctors: A Study of the Psychology of Evil.* London: Macmillan.

Limentani, A. (1969) 'Symposium on Envy' Society. Special Issue of *The British Psychoanalytical Society Bulletin.*

Lipgar, R. and Pines, M. (eds) (2003) *Building on Bion: Roots.* London: Jessica Kingsley Publishers.

Lockwood, D. (1964) 'Social Integration and System Integration'. In G.K. Zollschan and W. Hirsch (eds) *Explorations in Social Change.* London: Houghton Mifflin.

Lockwood, D. (1992) *Solidarity and Schism.* Oxford: Clarendon Press.

Macauley, T. (1880) *History of England.* London: Appleton.

Maccoby, H. (1982) *The Sacred Executioner.* London: Thames and Hudson.

MacIver, R.M. (1937) *Society: A Textbook of Sociology.* New York: Farrar and Rinehart.

Mackenzie, R. and Tschuschke, V. (1993) 'Relatedness, group work, and outcome in long term inpatient group psychotherapy'. *Journal of Psychotherapy Practice and Research 2,* 147–156.

Mahler, M.S. and Furer, M. (1968) *On Human Symbiosis and the Vicissitudes of Individuation.* New York International Universities Press.

Mahler, M., Pine, F., and Bergman, A. (1975) *The Psychological Birth of the Human Infant.* New York: Basic Books.

Main, T. (1975) [1994] 'Some Psychodynamics of Large Groups'. In L. Kreeger (ed) *The Large Group: Dynamics and Therapy.* London: Constable. Reprinted in 1994 in London by Karnac Books (Original work published 1975).

Malan, D.H., Balfour, F.H.G., Hood, V.G. and Shooter, A.M.N. (1976) 'Group psychotherapy: A long term-term follow-up study'. *Archives of General Psychiatry 33,* 1303–1315.

Mann, T. (1933) [1996] *Mario and the Magician and other Stories.* London: Minerva (first published 1933).

Marrone, M. (1998) *Attachment and Interaction.* London: Jessica Kingsley Publishers.

Marziali, E., Munroe-Blum, H., and McCleary, L. (1997) 'The contribution of group cohesion and group alliance to the outcome of group psychotherapy'. *International Journal of Group Psychotherapy 47,* 4, 475–498.

McDougal, W. (1920) *The Group Mind.* New York: Putnam.

Menzies-Lyth, I.E.P. (1981) 'Bion's Contribution to Thinking about Groups'. In J. Grotstein (ed) *Do I Dare Disturb the Universe?* Beverley Hills: Caesura Press.

Michels, R. (1999) 'Psychoanalysts' Theories'. In P. Fonagy, A.M. Cooker and R.S. Wallerstein (eds) *Psychoanalysis on the Move: The Work of Joseph Sandler.* London: Routledge.

Mitscherlich, A. (1963) *Auf dem Weg Zur waterlosen Gesellschaft: Ideen Zur Sozial-Psychologie.* Munich: R. Piper.

Mitscherlich, A. and Mitscherlich, M. (1975) *The Inability to Mourn.* New York: Grove Press.

Money-Kyrle, R. (1929) *The Meaning of Sacrifice.* London: The Hogarth Press and The Institute of Psychoanalysis.

Money-Kyrle, R. (1978) *The Collected Papers of Roger Money-Kyrle.* Perthshire: Clunie Press.

Moscovici, S. (1981) *L'Age des Foules.* Paris: Librairie Arthème Fayard.

Mosley, N. (1972) *The Assassination of Trotsky.* London: Joseph.

Mudrack, P. (1989) 'Defining group cohesiveness'. *Small Group Behavior 20,* 37–49.

Munich, R. (1993) 'Varieties of learning in an experiential group'. *International Journal of Group Psychotherapy 43,* 3, 345–362.

Neri, C. (1998) *Group.* London: Jessica Kingsley Publishers.

Ogden, T.H. (1991) 'Analysing the matrix of transference'. *International Journal of Psychoanalysis 72,* 593–605.

Ortega y Gasset, J. (1929) [1976] *La Rebelión de las Masas.* Madrid: Expasa-Calpe (Original work published 1929).

Orwell, G. (1949) *Nineteen Eighty Four.* London: Penguin.

Pines, M. (1983) 'Psychic development and the group analytic situation'. Keynote Address to the Canadian Association of Group Psychotherapy, Banff, *Group (1985) 9,* 1, 24–37.

Pines, M. (1984) [1998] 'Group-analytic psychotherapy and the borderline patient'. *Analytic Psychotherapy and Psychopathology 1,* 1, 57–70. Reprinted in *Circular Reflections.* London: Jessica Kingsley Publishers.

Pines, M. (1986) [1998] 'Coherency and disruption in the sense of the self'. *British Journal of Psychotherapy 2,* 3,180–185. Reprinted in M. Pines (1998) (ed) *Circular Reflections.* London: Jessica Kingsley Publishers.

Pines, M. (1987) 'Shame – What psychoanalysis does and does not say'. *Group Analysis 20,* 1, 16–31.

Pines, M. (1998) 'What should a Psychotherapist Know?' In M. Pines (ed) *Circular Reflections.* London: Jessica Kingsley Publishers.

Piper, W.E. (1995) 'Discussions of group as a whole'. *International Journal of Group Psychotherapy 45,* 2, 157–162.

Piper, W.E., Marrache, M., Lacroix, R., Richardsen, A. and Jones, B. (1983) 'Cohesion as a basic bond in groups'. *Human Relations 36,* 93–108.

Post, J. (1991) 'Saddam Hussein of Iraq: A political profile'. *Political Psychology 12,* 279.

Racker, H. (1968) *Transference and Countertransference.* New York: International Universities Press.

Rangell, L. (1974) 'A psychoanalytic perspective leading currently to the syndrome of the compromise of integrity'. *International Journal of Psychoanalysis 55,* 3–12.

Redl, F. (1942) 'Group emotion and leadership'. *Psychiatry 5,* 573–596.

Redl, F. (1963) 'Psychoanalysis and group therapy: A developmental point of view'. *American Journal of Orthopsychiatry 33,* 135–147.

Reeves, P. (2001) 'Imad was a devout and single teenager – the perfect candidate for a suicide bomber'. *The Independent,* 28 April, 15.

Reich, W. (1933) [1970] *The Mass Psychology of Fascism.* New York: Farrar, Strauss and Giroux (original work published 1933).

Reijzer, H.M. (1996) 'On Having Been in Hiding'. In H. Groen-Prakken, A. Ladan and A. Stufkens (eds) *The Dutch Annual of Psychoanalysis: Traumatisation and War.* Lisse: Swets & Zeitlinger BV.

Rickman, J. (1938) 'Uniformity and diversity in groups'. Unpublished paper.

Rioch, M. (1970) 'The work of Wilfred Bion on groups'. *Psychiatry 33,* 56–66.

Rioch, M. (1971) '"All we like sheep" (Isaiah 53:6): Followers and leaders'. *Psychiatry 34,* 3, 258–273.

Roberts, J. and Pines, M. (eds) (1991) *The Practice of Group Analysis.* London: Tavistock/Routledge.

Roller, B. and Nelson, V. (1999) 'Group psychotherapy treatment of borderline personalities'. *International Journal of Group Psychotherapy 49,* 3, 369–386.

Rosenfeld, D. (1988) *Psycho-Analysis and Groups.* London: Karnac Books.

Rosenfeld, H. (1971) 'A clinical approach to the psychoanalytic theory of the life and death instincts: An investigation into the aggressive aspects of narcissism'. *International Journal of Psychoanalysis 52,* 169–178.

Ross, C. (1994) *The Osiris Complex: Case Studies in Multiple Personality Disorder.* Toronto: University of Toronto Press.

Roth, B.E. (1980) 'Understanding the development of a homogenous identity impaired group through countertransference phenomena'. *International Journal of Group Psychotherapy 30,* 4, 405–426.

Roth, B.E., Stone, W.N. and Kibel, H.D. (1990) *The Difficult Patient in Group.* Madison, CT: International Universities Press.

Ruiz, J. (1972) 'On the perception of the "mother group" in T-groups'. *International Journal of Group Psychotherapy 22,* 488–491.

Rutan, S. and Stone, W. (2000) *Psychodynamic Group Psychotherapy* (3rd edn). New York: Guilford.

Sandler, J. and Joffe, W.G. (1967) 'The tendency to persistence in psychological function and development with special reference to fixation and regression'. *Bulletin of the Menninger Clinic 31,* 257–271.

Scharff, D. and Scharff, J. (1987) *Object Relations Family Therapy.* Northvale, NJ: Jason Aronson.

Scharff, D.E. (1992) *Refinding the Object and Reclaiming the Self.* Northvale, NJ: Jason Aronson.

Scharff, J. and Scharff, D.E. (1994) *Object Relations Therapy of Physical and Sexual Trauma.* Northvale, NJ: Jason Aronson.

Scharff, J. and Scharff, D.E. (1998) *Object Relations Individual Therapy.* Northvale, NJ: Jason Aronson.

Scharff, J. and Scharff, D.E. (2000) *Tuning the Therapeutic Instrument: Affective Learning of Psychotherapy.* Northvale, NJ: Jason Aronson.

Scheidlinger, S. (1952) *Psychoanalysis and Group Behavior.* New York: Norton.

Scheidlinger, S. (1968) 'The concept of regression in group psychotherapy'. *International Journal of Group Psychotherapy 18,* 3–20.

Scheidlinger, S. (1974) 'On the concept of the Mother group'. *International Journal of Group Psychotherapy 24,* 417–428.

Scheidlinger, S. (1980) *Psychoanalytic Group Dynamics.* Madison, CT: International Universities Press.

Scheidlinger, S. (1982) 'On scapegoating in group psychotherapy'. *International Journal of Group Psychotherapy 32,* 131–143.

Scheidlinger, S. (1997) 'Group dynamics and group psychotherapy revisited: Four decades later'. *International Journal of Group Psychotherapy 47,* 2, 141–160.

Schermer, V.L. and Pines, M. (1994) *Rings of Fire: Primitive Affects and Object Relations in Group Psychotherapy.* London and New York: Routledge.

Schindler, W. (1966) 'The role of the mother in group psychotherapy'. *International Journal of Group Psychotherapy 16,* 198–200.

Schlachet, P. (1992) 'The capacity to join in the formation of shared group-dispositional space'. Unpublished paper presented at the 11th International Congress of Group Psychotherapy, Montreal, Canada.

Segal, H. (1957) 'Notes on symbol formation'. *International Journal of Psychoanalysis 38,* 391–7.

Segal, H. (1964) [1974] *Introduction to the Work of Melanie Klein.* New York: Basic Books (Original work published 1964).

Shapiro, R. and Zinner, N. (1979) 'The Adolescent, the Family and the Group: Boundary Considerations'. In G. Lawrence (ed) *Exploring Individual and Organizational Boundaries.* London: Wiley.

Shengold, L. (1989) *Soul Murder: The Effects of Childhood Abuse and Deprivation.* New Haven: Yale University Press.

Socarides, C. (1979) 'Why Sirhan killed Kennedy: Psychoanalytical speculations on an assassination'. *Journal of Psycho-history 6,* 447–460.

Sonne, J.C. (1994a) 'The relevance of the dread of being aborted to models of therapy and models of the mind. Part I: Case examples'. *The International Journal of Prenatal and Perinatal Psychology and Medicine 6*, 1, 670–686.

Sonne, J.C. (1994b) 'The relevance of the dread of being aborted to models of therapy and models of the mind. Part II: Mentation and communication in the unborn'. *The International Journal of Prenatal and Perinatal Psychology and Medicine 6*, 2, 247–275.

Spillius, E. (1992) 'Two ways of experiencing envy'. *The British Psychoanalytical Society Bulletin 28*, 9, 2–11.

Springmann, R. (1970) 'A large group'. *The International Journal of Group Psychotherapy 20*, 210–218.

Springmann, R. (1975) 'Psychotherapy in the Large Group'. In L. Kreeger (ed) *The Large Group: Dynamics and Therapy.* London: Constable. Reprinted in 1994 in London by Karnac Books (Original work published 1975).

Springmann, R. (1976) 'Fragmentation in large groups'. *Group Analysis 9*, 3, 185–188.

Steinberg, J. (ed) (1990) 'Two Types of Charisma'. In *The Axis and the Holocaust 1941–43.* London: Routledge.

Steiner, J. (1990) 'Pathological organisations as obstacles to mourning: The role of unbearable guilt'. *International Journal of Psychoanalysis 71*, 87–94.

Steiner, R. (1999) 'Some notes on the heroic self and the meaning and importance of its reparation for the creative process and the creative personality'. *International Journal of Psychoanalysis 80*, 4, 685–718.

Stern, D. (1984) *The Interpersonal World of the Infant.* New York: Basic Books.

Stern, D.N *et al.* (1998) 'Non-interpretative mechanisms in psychoanalytic therapy: The "something more" than interpretation'. *International Journal of Psychoanalysis 79*, 5, 903–921.

Stone, W.N. (1996) 'Self psychology and the higher mental functioning hypothesis: Complementary theories'. *Group Analysis 29*, 169–181.

Sumner, W.G. and Keller, A.G. (1927) *The Science of Society.* New Haven: Yale University Press.

Sutherland, J.D. (1985) 'Bion Re-visited: Group Dynamics and Group Psychotherapy'. In M. Pines (ed) *Bion and Group Psychotherapy.* London: Routledge and Kegan Paul.

Teicholz, J.G. (1999) *Kohut, Loewald & the Postmoderns: A Comparative Study of Self and Relationship.* Hillsdale, NJ: Analytic Press.

Thucydides (1954) *History of the Peloponnesian War.* London: Penguin Classics.

Tucker, R. (1992) *Stalin in Power: The Revolution from Above 1928–1941.* New York: Norton.

Turquet, P. (1973) Personal communication.

Turquet, P. (1974) 'Leadership: The Individual in the Group'. In G.S. Gibbard, J.J. Hartman and R.D. Mann (eds) *Analysis of Groups.* San Francisco, CA: Jossey-Bass.

Turquet, P. (1975) 'Threats to identity in the large group'. In L. Kreeger (ed) *The Large Group: Dynamics and Therapy.* London: Constable. Reprinted in 1994 in London by Karnac Books (Original work published 1975).

Tustin, F. (1981) *Autistic States in Children.* London: Routledge and Kegan Paul.

Tuttman, S. (1990) 'Principles of Psychoanalytic Group Therapy Applied to the Treatment of Borderline and Narcissistic Disorders'. In B. Roth (ed) *The Difficult Patient in Group.* Madison, CT: International Universities Press.

Van der Hal, E., Tauber, Y. and Gottesfeld, J. (1996) 'Open groups for children of Holocaust survivors'. *International Journal of Group Psychotherapy 46,* 2, 193–208.

Volkan, V. (1972) 'The linking objects of pathological mourners.' *Archives of General Psychiatry 27,* 215–221.

Volkan, V. (1980) 'Narcissistic personality organisation and "reparative" leadership'. *International Journal of Group Psychotherapy 30,* 31, 131–152.

Volkan, V. (1981) 'Immortal Ataturk: Narcissism and Creativity in a Revolutionary Leader'. In W. Muensterberger, L.B. Boyer and S.Grolnick (eds) *The Psychoanalytic Study of Society.* New Haven: Yale University Press.

Volkan, V. (1991) 'On chosen traumas'. *Mind and Human Interaction 3,* 13.

Volkan, V. (2001) 'Transgenerational transmissions and chosen traumas: An aspect of large group identity'. *Group Analysis 34,* 1, 79–98.

Volkan, V. (2002a) 'Violence, forced immigration and politics'. Plenary Lecture at the 12th European Symposium in Group Analysis 'The Economy of the Group', Bologna, Italy.

Volkan, V. (2002b) 'September 11 and societal regression'. *Group Analysis 35,* 4.

Volkan V. and Itzkowitz, N. (1984) *The Immortal Ataturk: A Psycho Biography.* Chicago: University of Chicago Press.

Von Bertalanffy, L. (1966) 'General Systems Theory and Psychiatry'. In S. Arieti (ed) *American Handbook of Psychiatry III.* New York: Basic Books.

Weber, M. (1947) *The Theory of Social and Economic Organization.* T. Parsons (ed). New York: Oxford University Press.

Weinberg, H. and Nuttman-Shwartz. (2002) 'Group therapy in Israel'. *Group 26,* 1, 5–16.

Welldon, E. (2000) Personal communication.

Wexler, B., Johnson, D., Geller, J. and Gordon, J. (1984) 'Group psychotherapy with schizophrenic patients – an example of the oneness group'. *International Journal of Psychotherapy 34,* 3, 451–473.

Whitaker, D.S. (1985) *Using Groups to Help People.* London: Routledge and Kegan Paul.

Wilson, B.R. (1975) *The Noble Savages: The Primitive Origins of Charisma and its Contemporary Survival.* Berkeley: University of California Press.

Wilson, E.O. (1975) *Sociobiology: The New Synthesis.* Cambridge: Harvard University Press.

Winnicott, D.W. (1953) [1971] 'Transitional objects and transitional phenomena'. *International Journal of Psychoanalysis 34,* 2. Reprinted in 1971 in *Playing and Reality.* London: Tavistock Publications.

Winnicott, D.W. (1965) [1985] *The Maturational Process and the Facilitating Environment.* London: The Hogarth Press (Original work published 1965).

Winnicott, D.W. (1967) [1971] 'The location of cultural experience'. *International Journal of Psychoanalysis 48,* 3, 368–372. Reprinted in 1971 in *Playing and Reality.* London: Tavistock Publications.

Winnicott, D.W. (1971) 'Mirror-role of Mother and Family in Child Development'. In *Playing and Reality.* London: Tavistock Publications.

Winnicott, D.W. (1971) *Playing and Reality.* London: Tavistock Publications.

Winnicott, D.W. (1980) *Human Nature.* New York: Schocken Books.

Wolf, E.S. (1988) *Treating the Self: Elements of Clinical Self Psychology.* New York: Guilford.

Wright, R. (1953) *The Outsider.* New York: Harper Collins.

Wrong, D. (1961) 'The over-socialized conception of man in modern sociology'. *American Sociological Review 26,* 81–193.

Yalom, I. (1975) [1995] *The Theory and Practice of Group Psychotherapy.* New York: Basic Books (Original work published 1975).

Yalom, I. (1989) *Love's Executioner.* London: Penguin.

Zelaskowski, P. (1998) 'The suboptimal group'. *Group Analysis 31,* 4, 491–504.

Zaleznik, A. (1979) 'Psychoanalytic knowledge of group processes'. Panel Report, *Journal of the American Psychoanalytical Association 27,* 146–150.

Zetzel, E.R. (1958) [1970] 'Therapeutic Alliance in the Analysis of Hysteria'. In *The Capacity for Emotional Growth.* London: The Hogarth Press and The Institute of Psycho-Analysis (Original work published 1958).

Ziegler, M. and McEvoy, M. (2000) 'Hazardous Terrain: Countertransference Reactions in Trauma Groups'. In R.H. Klein and V.L. Schermer (eds) *Group Psychotherapy for Psychological Trauma.* New York: Guilford.

Subject Index

Author Index

Printed in Dunstable, United Kingdom

91343452R00138